STEAK with FRIENDS

Other books by Rick Tramonto

OSTERIA: Hearty Italian Fare from Rick Tramonto's Kitchen

FANTASTICO: Little Italian Plates and Antipasti from Rick Tramonto's Kitchen

TRU: A Cookbook from the Legendary Chicago Restaurant

AMUSE-BOUCHE: Little Bites That Delight Before the Meal Begins

AMERICAN BRASSERIE: 180 Simple, Robust Recipes Inspired by the Rustic Foods of France, Italy, and America

BUTTER SUGAR FLOUR EGGS: Whimsical Irresistible Desserts

STEAK with FRIENDS

AT HOME, WITH RICK TRAMONTO

RICK TRAMONTO

WITH MARY GOODBODY

PHOTOGRAPHY BY BEN FINK

Andrews McMeel
Publishing, LLC

Kansas City · Sydney · London

10 11 12 13 14 SDB 10 9 8 7 6 5 4 3 2 1

ISBN-13: 978-0-7407-9257-1

ISBN-10: 0-7407-9257-1

Library of Congress Control Number: 2009938774

Photography: Ben Fink

Design: Vertigo Design, NYC

Prop Stylist: Joe Maer

www.andrewsmcmeel.com

www.tramontocuisine.com

I dedicate this book to my Heavenly Father, with whom I have a great covenant, and my Lord and Savior Jesus Christ, who always leads me down the right road and who brings me through every storm every time. One verse in particular guides me through my life: "I can do all things through Christ who strengthens me." Philippians 4:13.

To the love of my life and my best friend, my wife, Eileen Tramonto, who kept me on track throughout the process of organizing and writing, and stepped in wherever needed and did whatever it took—with true grace and unconditional love. Thank you very much.

To my sons Gio, Sean, and Brian, who keep me cooking and eating all the time. I love you guys.

And finally to my mom and dad, Frank and Gloria Tramonto, who have both gone home to be with the Lord. I love you and miss you and wish you could have enjoyed this book because you gave me the spirit of hospitality and truly taught me Joshua 24:15: "But as for me and my house, we will serve the Lord."

CONTENTS

ACKNOWLEDGMENTS

Thanks to my friend and cowriter, Mary Goodbody, who for the fifth time has helped me put all of my thoughts and recipes into this book. Thanks for your attention to detail and for making me sound so good and all of the kumbaya.

Thanks to my supportive and loving family, Eileen Tramonto; Gio Tramonto; Sean and Brian Pschirrer; Luke, the star German Shepherd, who holds a special place in our family's hearts; Paul and Dorothy Tramonto; Ed and Mary Carroll; Kathleen (Carroll), Lenny, Jesse, and Hannah Williams; and Joe and Bridget Carroll. You all continue to show me how to live and breathe outside the culinary world. Thanks for the breath of fresh air.

Thanks to my spiritual family, my pastor Gregory Dickow and his wife Grace Dickow of Life Changers International Church, for their love, blessings, teachings, prayers, and feeding me the Word of God. I can't thank you enough. Thanks also to Bishop T. D. Jakes; Joel and Victoria Osteen; Pastor James McDonald at Walk in the Word; Pastor Greg Laurie at New Beginning; Joyce Meyer for her teachings and wisdom of the Word of God; and Sarah Kelly for her music ministry.

Thanks to my loyal and longtime agent and friend, Jane Dystel; my editor, Jean Lucas; publisher Kirsty Melville; and the great team at Andrews McMeel for their trust and faith in this book and me. Thanks to my friend and photographer, Ben Fink, and his team for the incredible photographs and the brilliance of using natural light. Thanks for sharing my passion for this style of cooking at home with friends and family.

A big thanks to Allison Lew and Vertigo Design for bringing the book to life, and to Joe Maer for propping the photos so brilliantly.

Special thanks to the culinary team: Chef Jared Van Camp, Chef Ray Stainis, Chef Tim Graham, and Pastry Chef Erin Swanson. Thanks to Kendall College Executive Chef Chris Keacki and the impressive students, Allie Seeberg, Ben Beroin, and Philip Goldbroch, for being my at-home culinary team on this book. And very special thanks to Allen Brothers, who supplied the steaks for this book so that we could showcase how beautiful steaks can be.

I would like to thank my chefs and staffs at Tru and at Tramonto Steak and Seafood.

Thanks to sommelier Chad Ellegood for his wine and other beverage notes and for staying true to his passion for good service.

I would also like to thank Reggie Anderson who kept me healthy and strong during the writing of this book and who kept me "Regi-fied"! I usually gain weight when I write a book but with Reggie's diligence, I actually lost a little.

I would also like to thank the City of Chicago, Mayor Richard Daley, and the food press for supporting me and allowing me to hone my craft in this great city.

Thanks to those who inspire me on a daily basis and who support my culinary efforts. You know who you are.

Thanks to my supportive friends who I rarely get to see but who I love to cook for at home and who inspired me to write this. I love you guys. Thanks to Ron, Jill, Zeke, and Olivia Losoya; Jim and Linda Murdough; Wendy Payton; and Paul, Carley, and Emily Lagerquist. Last but not least, thanks to my culinary partner and pastry chef extraordinaire Gale Gand, who continues to travel this journey with me and provides daily inspiration—both in and out of the kitchen.

A very special thanks to the vendors and the farmers I work with every day across the country. This book would not be possible without you. You work so hard to find and grow the best-of-the-best ingredients and products for me to use in my restaurants and recipes, and especially at home for my friends and family. And a special shout-out to Chicago's Green City Market, which is more awe-inspiring with every visit. Thank you. God bless you all and may the grace of God be with you. **—RICK TRAMONTO**

A tremendous thanks to Rick for yet again entrusting me with his words and his amazing food. This is a book to cook out of, day in and day out, and I can hardly wait to get started. Thanks, too, to Eileen Tramonto for being there whenever I had a question or needed something extra, and to Chad Ellegood for his good humor and timely information about wine and cocktails. This book would not have been possible without the help, guidance, and support of our agent, Jane Dystel. Thank you, Jane. Thanks, too, to Lisa Thornton for her help with the manuscript and keeping track of the original recipes. And again, thanks to Laura, who is a pretty cool daughter and who has always supported her mom. **—MARY GOODBODY**

INTRODUCTION

The title of this book says it all: This is about eating steak dinners with good friends and enjoying all that implies. To me, this means delicious yet casual dinners at home. It means cooking with the season, making note of what is best in the gardens and orchards at any given time, and cooking up a storm with those ingredients. It means gathering around the grill to cook a big, juicy steak or another mouthwatering, finger-lickin', great-tasting meat, fish, or vegetable. It means sitting down at the kitchen table to sample food laid out on big platters. It means encouraging everyone who wants to help to chop this, stir that, set the table, or open the wine.

Most of all it means sharing relaxed time, good stories, great music, home-cooked food, and laughter with our friends and our families. It means living life as it should be celebrated.

But there is more. The name also means getting to know and cooking those foods that are, for lack of a better word, "friends" with steak. Steak and potatoes, steak and salad, steak and squash, steak and green beans, steak and oysters. I have scores of recipes that work beautifully for every steak or beef dinner you might want to cook. You might be more in the mood for burgers than prime rib, but take my word for it: The creamed spinach on page 239, the shell bean ragout on page 249, or the battered onion rings on page 236 will taste amazing with both—or any of the other beef dishes on these pages.

I view this book somewhat similarly to how I understand an à la carte menu. The recipes here are best if they are mixed and matched according to your tastes and prejudices. You may prefer chicken to steak; I have recipes for chicken. You may be hankering for a big, juicy porterhouse; look no further than page 137. You may want to make a soup as the first course for a steak dinner but don't know what would work best. Turn to Chapter 4 on page 69 for soup recipes. You may be cooking dinner for folks who claim they are "steak and potato eaters, through and through." You're in the right place!

As I say in the introduction to Chapter 11, which is where you find a glorious array of side dishes, I am very happy making entire meals from sides. If you feel like doing so, go for it. Nothing would make me happier than hearing from you about how much you and yours liked the roasted beets on page 242 or the macaroni and cheese on page 234. Prefer salads? Try the garbage salad (yes, you read that right!) on page 51, the Lyonnaise salad on page 60, or the peanut noodle salad on page 66.

ENTERTAINING, TRAMONTO STYLE

My wife Eileen and I entertain at least once a month and more often in the summertime at home near the city of Chicago. We are fortunate to live in a quiet, pretty setting, with a large patio that looks over a small pond. We like to liven the place up with a group of friends from church on Sundays or our three sons and their friends from the neighborhood. We play

music as we cook, we swap ideas and stories. In short, we have fun. We anticipate the meal but we love the process just as much. In our family, when it's time to start cooking someone invariably will say that it's time "to put the water on." Even my kids know that when you cook, there's nearly always something that requires boiled water and so it's an apt turn of phrase. And one we all "get."

I like to grill when I entertain and think nothing of firing up a grill all year long, despite the fact that I live outside Chicago where the weather is far from balmy in January and February. I find that a hot grill is a cool place for a party to catch fire. People just naturally gravitate to the grill as I cook, and I am more than happy for the company. I am also happy to hand the tongs and a spatula to a friend or my wife who can help me watch closely as the meat sizzles and browns.

The party usually starts in our kitchen and no doubt you have experienced what I have: The best parties begin and end in the kitchen. Eileen and I have a kitchen island lined with stools and it is here that our guests enjoy a glass of wine along with cold or hot appetizers. These, described in Chapters 1 and 2, set the mood for the evening's festivities. They should be tempting enough to get everyone excited and keep them happy until the main event, but should never overshadow it. And yet again, as I said about sides, you could easily make a meal of these. If that's what you want to do, far be it from me to dissuade you!

Most of the cold appetizers and a few of the hot ones can be served family style, on platters and in bowls. This is how I like to serve when I entertain at home. Everyone can sample as much as they want, when they want.

Once the party gets underway, I fire up the grill. When the fire is hot, I head outside with the food to cook, and without fail, nearly everyone follows. I have three grills: a large gas grill with two tanks that is big enough for whole pigs, whole fish, large cuts of meat, and multiple steaks; a smaller gas grill that I use for simple grilling tasks; and a charcoal grill that I light when I want the unmistakable and irreplaceable flavor that charcoal imparts to food. I usually use one of the three when I entertain at home, although some dishes are cooked entirely in the oven or on the stovetop.

Once the food is cooked, we might eat outside on the patio or we might head back inside the house to eat around the kitchen table or island. Dessert is often eaten while some helpful souls put the food away and clean up.

As Eileen and I prepare for the dinner party or cookout, we listen to music. When the guests arrive, I keep the music going, although I might tone down the volume. I have speakers all over the house and on the patio. As you will see when you read the "Music Box" at the beginning of most chapters, my tastes are eclectic. I love just about any kind of music and have found it keeps a dinner party alive, moving, and festive. The music boxes suggest music from artists as varied as Bach, Sarah Kelly, Led Zeppelin, and Frank Sinatra. And I would like to assure you here and now that Pink Floyd is always appropriate—regardless of what you are cooking or who your guests are!

WHY STEAK?

I am well aware that you may want to cook something other than steak when you entertain or have dinner with your family. I often do, too. But I chose steak as the centerpiece of this book not only because it's one of my favorites, but for many Americans it represents the ultimate luxury. Great steaks also are hallmarks of Chicago, the city I call home and that figures predominantly in many of the photographs on these pages. Steak is expensive, no doubt about it, and therefore is an indulgence we never enjoy lightly. Knowing how to cook a steak perfectly is important. If you overcook it, there is no going back. You are stuck with gray, dry meat. And so, on these pages, you will learn how to be a confident cook when you decide to splurge on steak.

Steak also is a metaphor for great American food. In her eminently entertaining and well-researched book, *Raising Steaks*, Betty Fussell writes about America's love affair and history with beef. "The beefsteak is American," wrote William Allen White in 1923 in *The Nation*, says Fussell. "It's not regional," he wrote, but is "the same on every American table" from Seattle to Palm Beach.

This is true today. And literally so, as beef suppliers prefer cattle that is raised under uniform conditions and fed a diet rich in corn that gives the meat its flavor and texture. Good beef is marbled with creamy fat and, as I explain in more detail in Chapter 6, Steak on a Plate, must be for the juiciness and lush flavor we associate with steak.

Beef has a powerful history in my adopted hometown of Chicago, where the Union Stock Yards opened shortly after the Civil War as part of a plan to build a centralized stock-yard on more than three hundred acres of swampland on the outskirts of the city. Fussell discusses how this move coincided with the invention of refrigerated rail cars and thus fed the public's desire for a beloved commodity that now could be delivered anywhere in the nation with relative speed and without spoiling. Before long the stockyard was run by the Beef Trust made up of five slaughterhouses, says Fussell: Armour, Hammond, Swift, Morris, and Cudahy. This meant that by 1900, Chicago controlled 90 percent of the cattle market in America. The stockyards are no longer part of our city's landscape, but the memory lingers and so we, here in the Second City, think of our steaks as something special.

As Fussell also points out, beef is the one meat Americans eat nearly raw. We love our steaks charred on the outside and pink and juicy—dare I say bloody?—on the inside. This gives it an almost primal character that is very American and hearkens back to the time when the West was settled by people who had to shoot their dinner and cook it over open fires. It takes us back to the days of cattle drives when hungry cowboys chowed down at the end of the day on char-cooked meat.

We Americans like big things: big cars, big houses, tall buildings, wide open spaces, never-ending skies, broad grins, and hearty belly laughs. We also like our steaks gigantic and thick. Today's steakhouses boast that they serve steaks that barely fit on the plate, they are so enormous. The professional cooks who grill steaks at restaurants over searingly hot fires, often raging at 900°F, are considered "macho." It's not a job for sissies. Grilling steak is for men, we joke—although there are plenty of women who do the job as well.

In reality, very few of us can eat a whole steakhouse steak and thankfully today we can carry it home to eat later. When I cook at home, I serve large steaks but usually I slice and serve them on platters so that my guests can take what they want.

I don't expect you to serve only steak. The book has recipes for beef classics such as beef Wellington on page 144 and meat loaf on page 158. I have recipes for fish and others for lamb and pork and poultry.

There's something for everyone here. While I hope you like the food as much as I do—and as much as my family and friends do—mostly I hope that these recipes will inspire you to invite your loved ones to your kitchen to enjoy steak, friends, and family.

There's nothing better! God bless and *bon appétit!*

What I like most about the recipes in

this chapter is that they all are about relaxed celebrations. Most can be shared, served on a big platter so that everyone can graze, pick, and choose what and how much they want to eat. Many are made from the best produce of the season, available from farmers' markets or your own backyard garden. These appetizers are perfect for accompanying a cold beer, glass of wine, iced tea, or one of those stylish cocktails everyone is so crazy about.

When I have people over, after an hour or so of appetizers, I fire up the grill or head to the kitchen to make the steaks or whatever food I am cooking that evening, and most people drift toward the action of the grill or stove. This is the second phase of any party, followed soon after with the main meal, when we sit down, give thanks to God, and enjoy what's on our plates and discuss what's on our minds. But without the very first part of the evening—when we casually and happily share cold appetizers—the rest of the meal would never be as festive or successful. It's a natural progression, a train of good eats and conversation that first leaves the station with these delights, gaining speed as it moves through the party.

I thought long and hard about what recipes to include here—just as I did for every chapter in the book—and kept coming back to the sharing characteristics of the dishes. I also relied on my own affection for "surf and turf." Ever since I first discovered the marriage of seafood and beef as an eighteen-year-old line cook at the Scotch 'n Sirloin steakhouse in Rochester, New York—where I learned how to broil steaks—I have been an enthusiastic fan of pairing seafood and good beef. I have even been known to stop at a sushi restaurant for a few bites before going on to a steak house and often serve homemade sushi at home before a steak dinner. This explains why I have included tuna rolls, spicy shrimp in lettuce, and the hamachi sashimi. All are perfect before a steak meal.

I also like to start off a steak dinner with another meat, as evidenced by the charcuterie plate and the steak tartare. If you prefer appetizers with no seafood or meat, try the beets. I have never put out platters of these and had a single leftover!

For cold appetizers, I like cool, easy music and so turn on:
BILLY JOEL | ELTON JOHN | THE DOORS | BRUCE SPRINGSTEEN |
STING | THE GOO GOO DOLLS | THE ALLMAN BROTHERS

COLD APPETIZERS

Steak tartare, a full-flavored dish made from raw beef, is very often associated with stylish Parisian bistros of the last century, but it goes well beyond nostalgia. It's a spectacular starter and one that your most carnivorous friends will love. But before you make it, make sure your relationship with your butcher is good. Since you will be serving raw meat, you must be certain that you buy the freshest, highest quality prime meat possible.

Steak tartare got its name from the Tatars—sometimes erroneously called Tartars—who, legend has it, ate their meat raw because it took too long to dismount their horses and build a fire when they were racing across the steppes. The name applies to many groups of both Turkic and Mongolian descent who migrated to Europe from Asia centuries ago. **SERVES 4**

STEAK TARTARE WITH VIOLET MUSTARD

1 tablespoon violet mustard (see Note) or Dijon mustard

3 oil-packed anchovy fillets, minced

2 teaspoons brined capers, drained, rinsed, and chopped

3 large egg yolks

¾ pound prime beef tenderloin, finely diced, covered, and refrigerated

2 tablespoons finely chopped red onion

2 tablespoons finely chopped fresh flat-leaf parsley

1 tablespoon extra-virgin olive oil

1 teaspoon finely minced jalapeño pepper

4 dashes of Worcestershire sauce

Kosher salt and freshly ground black pepper

12 to 18 thin slices toasted French baguette or brioche

In a chilled mixing bowl, mix the mustard, anchovies, and capers. With a fork or the back of a spoon, mash until evenly combined. Mix in the egg yolks. With a rubber spatula, fold in the beef, onion, parsley, olive oil, jalapeño, and Worcestershire. When thoroughly mixed, season well with salt and pepper.

Serve the tartare spread on the toasted bread or alongside the bread. For a more impressive presentation, use a scoop to form small quenelles of the tartare. Put one quenelle on each of 6 small, chilled plates and serve with the toasts.

Note *Violet mustard, or* moutarde violette*, has been enjoyed in French grape-growing regions for centuries. It is made each autumn by blending freshly pressed red grape juice with just ground mustard seed. The name refers to the color, not the flavor.*

Must-Haves for the Bar

BELOW ARE TWO LISTS OF THE ESSENTIALS needed for any great home bar. There are a number of stylish kits of bar equipment available so that you can select a combination that most appeals to you. Or you can pick and chose the equipment as you like.

When it comes to the liquor that are must-haves, you need a sense of adventure. Liquor almost never goes bad, so it is great to take the occasional risk on some never-before-tried spirit—especially if the bottle is cool looking or the liquor is an exotic color.

EQUIPMENT

SHAKER: Purists like the clear pint glass combined with the large metal tumbler, but the shakers that have a lid with a built-in strainer negate the need for a Hawthorn strainer.

HAWTHORN STRAINER: A handled strainer with a coiled wire spring around its circumference that allows the strainer to fit neatly on top of a cocktail shaker.

JIGGER: This is a bar measuring cup, usually with both 1-ounce and 1½-ounce measurements.

LONG-HANDLED BAR SPOON

CHANNEL KNIFE: This citrus reamer is critical for making long twists of lemon or orange peel.

CORKSCREW: Your choice. Keep more than one on hand and make sure you are comfortable using them.

HANDHELD CITRUS JUICER: This looks something like a large, round garlic press, or a bowl with a fluted bulge in the middle.

MUDDLER: This tool allows you to crush mint leaves and other ingredients in the bottom of a glass. It is usually made of wood and looks like a small club.

LIQUOR AND MIXERS

Whiskey (both Scotch and bourbon)

Brandy

Gin

Light and dark rum

Triple sec

Sweet and dry vermouth

Vodka

Tequila

New Zealand Sauvignon Blanc

Bual Madeira (This dark, sweet Madeira lasts forever when opened, tastes great with dessert, and is useful for cooking.)

Angostura bitters (experiment with other flavors of bitters)

Fresh lemons, limes, and oranges

Olives (lots of large olives filled with all sort of fancy things such as onions, cheese, and cherry peppers)

Sparkling mineral water and tonic

Ice (You can never have too much.)

Oysters on the half shell are very often served with a traditional mignonette of red wine and shallots; I've tweaked it by using pomegranate juice instead of red wine. It is acidic enough to work, with the same flavor profile—just a little bit cooler! Nowadays, it's not hard to find pomegranate juice and so this twist on convention should be easy to do at home. **SERVES 4**

OYSTERS ON THE HALF SHELL WITH POMEGRANATE MIGNONETTE

POMEGRANATE MIGNONETTE

1 cup rice wine vinegar

1 cup fresh or store-bought pomegranate juice

1 large shallot, minced

1 tablespoon cracked black peppercorns

1½ teaspoons sugar

1½ teaspoons freshly squeezed lime juice

1 teaspoon freshly grated ginger

OYSTERS

24 fresh, shucked oysters

Oyster liquor reserved

1 large lemon, cut into 6 wedges, for garnish

To make the mignonette: In a small bowl, mix together all of the ingredients. Stir in enough of the liquor from the oysters to flavor it nicely. Discard any remaining liquor. Cover and chill for at least 1 hour or up to 24 hours to allow the flavors to come together.

To serve the oysters: Fill 4 shallow serving bowls with crushed ice. Arrange the shucked oysters on their half shells on the ice. Garnish each serving with lemon wedges and serve a spoonful of the mignonette on the side.

So Many Oysters to Choose From!

I LIKE ALL OYSTERS and suggest you try as many different kinds as you can. The most important thing when selecting them is that they be fresh. If you're on or near the East Coast, look for Blue Point, Chesapeake, Kent Island, or Wellfleet oysters. If you are on the other side of the country, try Hama Hama, Tomales Bay, Hog Island, or 30 Olympia oysters. The last are very small and are found almost exclusively on the West Coast.

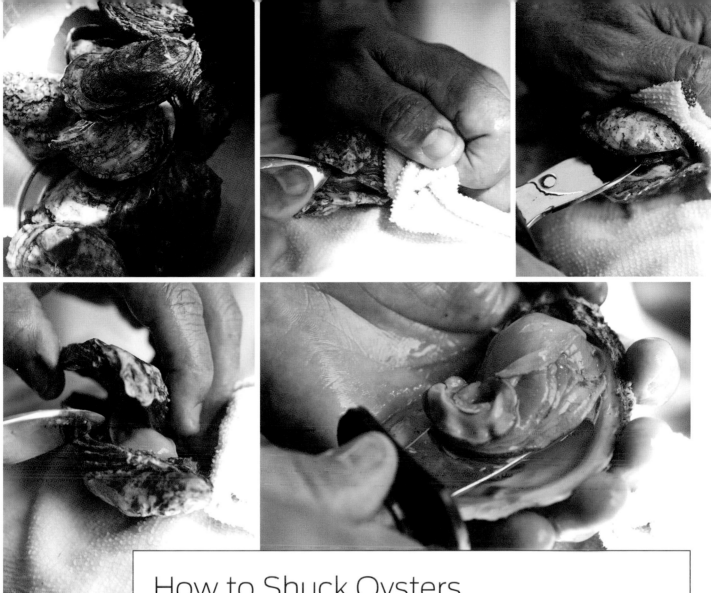

How to Shuck Oysters

RINSE the oysters under cool, running water. Use a stiff brush to clean the shells.

HOLD the oysters over a bowl while opening them to catch the liquor that will spill from the shells. Grasp an oyster in a kitchen towel or clean thick glove with the flatter side facing up. Locate the seam near the hinge and use the oyster knife like a key to "unlock" the shells with a twist. Separate the top and bottom shells by working along the seam with the flat of the knife. Take care to hold the knife as level as you can.

RUN the sharpest part of the blade between the muscle and upper shell to sever the cord that binds them. Unhinge and discard the top shell. Sever the cord on the lower shell so that the oyster meat is completely detached from the shell. Using care, set the shucked oyster on a bed of ice to serve. When all the oysters are shucked, discard the liquor, add it to fish stock, or set aside for another use.

For more on oysters, turn to page 36.

I am totally enthralled by beets. Lately, I have cooked more of them at home than ever before, and don't think I will ever stop doing so, especially when they are young, fresh, sweet, and very recently dug. Look for them in farmers' markets and when you see 'em, buy 'em! Now that I have mastered an easy technique for oven roasting beets, I have them on hand in the refrigerator most of the time and use them in salads, sandwiches, and even heat them up to serve warm with a little butter. I love them with any kind of soft, white cheese: feta, goat cheese, burrata. If you have never tried burrata, this is a good place to start. It is one of the best fresh cheeses you will ever taste, made from the creamy remnants of mozzarella and lusciously smooth and rich. But if you can't find it, substitute handmade bufala mozzarella or another high-quality mozzarella. **SERVES 4**

ROASTED BEETS WITH BURRATA CHEESE AND WALNUTS

BEETS

About 3 cups kosher salt, for baking

8 baby red beets, washed and trimmed but not peeled

8 baby yellow beets, washed and trimmed but not peeled

8 baby candy-striped beets, washed and trimmed but not peeled

4 tablespoons olive oil

1 teaspoon freshly ground black pepper

2 bunches watercress, gently torn

½ cup toasted chopped walnut pieces

WALNUT VINAIGRETTE

¼ cup walnut oil

2 tablespoons sherry vinegar

1 teaspoon finely grated orange zest

1 tablespoon freshly squeezed orange juice

1½ teaspoons honey

1 tablespoon minced shallot

1 teaspoon chopped fresh thyme

Kosher salt and cracked black pepper

2 (4-ounce) balls burrata cheese, quartered

Sea salt

Extra-virgin olive oil, for drizzling

To roast the beets: Preheat the oven to 350°F. Spread all but 1 tablespoon of the salt over the bottom of a shallow roasting pan or jelly roll pan.

In a large bowl, toss the red, yellow, and candy-striped beets with the reserved 1 tablespoon salt, 3 tablespoons of the olive oil, and the pepper until coated.

Spread a large sheet of aluminum foil on a work surface and place the beets in the center. Fold the foil around the beets to make a neat package and then place the package on top of the salt. You might find it easier to make two packets rather than one. Roast the beets for about 45 minutes, or until tender. Let the beets cool in the foil; this will make them easier to peel.

When cool enough to handle, peel the beets (the skins should slip right off). Cut into halves, quarters, or slices so that they are all about the same size. Combine the beets, watercress, and ¼ cup of the walnuts in a mixing bowl and toss to mix.

To make the vinaigrette: In a small bowl, whisk together the walnut oil, vinegar, orange zest and juice, honey, shallot, and thyme. Season to taste with salt and pepper.

Drizzle the dressing over the beets and toss gently. Season to taste with salt and pepper.

Arrange 2 pieces of burrata near the outside of each chilled plate and spoon the beets and watercress over and around the cheese. Sprinkle the remaining ¼ cup walnuts on top, finish with sea salt and a little olive oil, and serve.

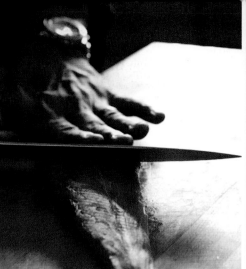

When you start with really great fish, you will be as crazy about this appetizer as I am. The fatty hamachi is amazing with the fresh, mildly acidic pineapple. Once you have these two ingredients in tow, you are halfway there. I also use shiro miso, which is white miso and found in most Asian markets. Hamachi is far easier to find nowadays than it used to be, but if you must, substitute any good, fresh tuna or salmon. Hamachi is young yellowtail, also called amberjack, and is not tuna. **SERVES 4**

HAMACHI SASHIMI WITH PINEAPPLE BUBBLES

1 skinned hamachi fillet,
12 to 14 ounces

1 (12-ounce) can sweetened pineapple juice

1 cup chopped fresh pineapple

¼ cup shiro (white) miso

2 teaspoons rice wine vinegar

1 teaspoon soy lecithin granules (see Note)

1 teaspoon fleur de sel or other good-quality sea salt

Freshly ground black pepper

1 tablespoon extra-virgin olive oil

2 whole shiso leaves

1 tablespoon chopped fresh chives

1 tablespoon chopped fresh mint

1 tablespoon chopped fresh basil

Grated zest of 1 lemon

Red Chili Oil (page 182), for garnish

With a very sharp knife, slice the hamachi on the diagonal into 12 thin pieces (about 1 ounce each). Refrigerate until needed, or for up to 3 hours.

In a saucepan, bring the pineapple juice and chopped pineapple to a simmer over medium heat. Simmer, stirring constantly, for about 10 minutes, or until the pineapple begins to break down. With an immersion blender, puree the pineapple mixture until smooth. Alternatively, puree in a blender or food processor.

Whisk in the miso, puree again, and add the vinegar and lecithin. Bring the mixture back to a simmer, cover to keep warm, and set aside.

Lay 3 hamachi slices each on 4 serving plates or arrange on a platter. Season with salt and pepper and drizzle with the olive oil.

With the immersion blender, buzz the pineapple-miso until very frothy. Spoon the frothy, bubbly pineapple mixture over the hamachi and garnish with the whole shiso leaves. Sprinkle with the chives, mint, basil, and lemon zest, drizzle with chili oil, and garnish with shiso leaves. Serve immediately.

Note
Soy lecithin helps stabilize the pineapple emulsion. Granules are easy to find in natural food stores and some supermarkets and are perfectly natural.

A Party Pitcher

THE MOJITO HAS BECOME THE DRINK OF CHOICE for many summer parties. Not only does it taste great, it can be made in a pitcher and is so easy to serve. Like most classic cocktails, its beauty and popularity come from its very simplicity. The gentle kick of white rum balanced with the sweet-and-sour combo of sugar and fresh lime and the fresh flavor of mint makes it a drink that is hard to "stop at just one."

I suggest you mix up a batch in a pitcher. When you get a request for a mojito, squeeze a lime wedge over ice in a stylish rocks glass, drop the wedge in the glass along with a few fresh mint leaves, and then fill it two-thirds of the way with the mojito. Top it off with club soda. Party on!

PITCHER OF MOJITOS
MAKES 10 SERVINGS

15 ounces (2 cups minus 2 tablespoons) white rum

10 ounces (1¼ cups) freshly squeezed lime juice (from 5 to 7 limes)

10 ounces (1¼ cups) Mint Simple Syrup (recipe follows)

In a large pitcher, stir together the rum, lime juice, and syrup. Serve at once or refrigerate until needed. Do not add ice to the pitcher.

MINT SIMPLE SYRUP
MAKES ABOUT 1 CUP

2 cups sugar

2 cups water

About 25 fresh mint leaves

In a saucepan, mix together the sugar and water and heat over medium-high heat. Let the syrup cook for a few minutes or until the sugar dissolves and the syrup looks clear. This will be about the time it takes for the syrup to begin to bubble.

Remove from the heat and add the mint leaves. Cover and set aside for about 10 minutes so that the mint can infuse the syrup. Strain the syrup and use immediately or refrigerate in a lidded container for up to 1 week.

Salmon pastrami? Why not! Typically, pastrami is made from corned and smoked beef, cured with peppercorns, coriander, and other seasonings—and I love it, especially when I buy it from a great Jewish deli. I cure salmon using the same spices, although I don't smoke it. If you have a home smoker, you might want to smoke the fish. But if not, make it as I describe here and you will love every mouthful. I cure a fairly large salmon fillet because it's inefficient to cure a smaller piece. You may not use it all but it will keep in the refrigerator for about five days and you will no doubt find many uses for it, as an addition to salads, in sandwiches, and for midnight snacks! I have also cured salmon with bourbon, sugar, and orange juice. The salmon pastrami and the cucumber salad are very friendly with each other and with steak. Enjoy a feast! **SERVES 4**

SALMON PASTRAMI WITH CUCUMBER-DILL SALAD

SALMON

¾ cup kosher salt

½ cup sugar

1 skinless salmon fillet, about 3 pounds

1 bunch cilantro, chopped

1 bunch fresh flat-leaf parsley, chopped

3 shallots, chopped

1 tablespoon grated orange zest

¼ cup coriander seeds, toasted and roughly cracked

¼ cup black peppercorns, toasted and roughly cracked

½ cup blackstrap molasses

CUCUMBER-DILL SALAD

1 cucumber, peeled, seeded, and cut into ½-inch dice

½ cup sour cream

1 tablespoon chopped fresh dill

1 tablespoon chopped fresh flat-leaf parsley

1 teaspoon freshly squeezed lemon juice

Kosher salt and cracked black pepper

To prepare the salmon: Mix together the salt and sugar. Lay a piece of plastic wrap large enough to easily wrap around the salmon on a work surface. Lay the fillet in the center and pack the salt and sugar evenly on the top, bottom, and sides.

In a small bowl, toss together the cilantro, parsley, shallots, and orange zest and then spread over the salt and sugar, pressing to pack securely.

Wrap the salmon in the plastic wrap and put in a shallow baking dish. Refrigerate for 2 days.

Unwrap the salmon and scrape off the cure. Rinse the fish briefly under cold water and then pat dry.

In a small bowl, mix together the coriander seeds and peppercorns. Lay a clean piece of plastic wrap on the work surface and position the salmon in the center. Brush the fillet with the molasses and then sprinkle with the coriander and peppercorns, pressing them into the salmon. Wrap the fillet in the plastic wrap and return to the shallow dish. Refrigerate for at least 8 hours or up to 1 week.

When ready to serve the salmon, make the cucumber salad: In a small bowl, mix the cucumber with the sour cream, dill, parsley, and lemon juice. Season to taste with salt and pepper.

Unwrap the salmon and, holding a sharp knife at a 30-degree angle, cut into thin slices.

Serve the slices on separate plates or arrange, shingled on top of each other, on a large serving platter. Spoon the cucumber salad alongside the salmon and serve.

Rémoulade and seafood form a happy union, sure to last until the last bit has been scraped from the plates. The sauce originated in France, although several cuisines have adapted it and claim it as their own, most notably Louisiana Creole cooking. It's nothing more fancy than a mayonnaise to which you add mustard, pickles, parsley, and other flavorings. Traditional French rémoulade includes gherkins; I prefer cornichons. It often includes a hard-cooked egg; I do not use egg (although you can toss in a chopped, hard-cooked egg if you like). I dress the sauce up with horseradish, lemon juice, and Worcestershire sauce and then serve it with simply cooked shrimp. Doesn't get any better. **SERVES 4**

SHRIMP RÉMOULADE

RÉMOULADE FOR THE SHRIMP

2 cups mayonnaise

3 cornichons, chopped

1 rib celery, minced

1 shallot, minced

2 tablespoons freshly squeezed lemon juice

1 tablespoon whole-grain mustard

1 tablespoon prepared or grated fresh horseradish

1 tablespoon Worcestershire sauce

1 tablespoon chopped fresh flat-leaf parsley

1 tablespoon thinly sliced scallion

1 tablespoon paprika

1½ teaspoons finely grated orange zest

1 teaspoon sugar

Kosher salt and freshly ground black pepper

¼ cup red wine vinegar

¼ cup extra-virgin olive oil

SHRIMP

6 cups water

6 tablespoons Old Bay seasoning

3 tablespoons kosher salt

1 lemon, halved; plus 1 lemon, quartered, for garnish

16 fresh medium shrimp, unpeeled

1 head butter lettuce (such as Bibb or Boston)

1 bunch scallions, white parts only, sliced thinly on the bias

To make the rémoulade: In the bowl of an electric mixer fitted with the paddle attachment, stir together the mayonnaise, cornichons, celery, and shallot. Add the lemon juice, mustard, horseradish, Worcestershire, parsley, scallion, paprika, orange zest, sugar, salt, and pepper. With the mixer on medium speed, mix until well blended.

Add the vinegar, a little at a time, and mix well after each addition. With the mixer on low speed, add the oil in a steady stream until emulsified into the mayonnaise. Transfer to a plastic or glass container with a tight-fitting lid and refrigerate for at least 2 hours or up to 1 week.

To cook the shrimp: In a large saucepan, combine the water, Old Bay, salt, and lemon halves. Bring to a boil over high heat, reduce the heat, and simmer for about 20 minutes to infuse the broth with flavor.

Meanwhile, fill a large bowl with ice cubes and cold water and set near the stove.

Add the shrimp to the pan and when the broth returns to a simmer, cook for about 5 minutes. Remove from the heat and let the shrimp sit in the liquid until it cools slightly and the shrimp are cooked through and opaque.

Lift the shrimp from the cooking liquid and plunge them in the water bath. When cool enough to handle, peel the shells from the shrimp, but leave the tails intact. With a small, sharp knife and your fingers, pull the dark vein from the curled outside of the shrimp.

Put the peeled shrimp in a bowl, add about ½ cup of the rémoulade, and toss to coat.

Arrange lettuce leaves on each of 4 chilled plates and cup the shrimp in them. Sprinkle with the scallions and serve with the quartered lemons for garnish. Pass the remaining rémoulade for dipping.

Manhattan on the "Rocks"

THE MANHATTAN IS ABOUT AS CLASSIC AS A COCKTAIL GETS. There are subtle variations, but the drink consists of whiskey, sweet vermouth, and a maraschino cherry garnish. Variations include additions of Angostura bitters, lime peel, or orange peel and it is served straight up or on the rocks, depending on preference. The rocks version here gives the drink a dynamic twist by using flavored ice cubes. Get a set of silicone ice-cube trays and give this a shot.

THE MANHATTAN
SERVES 1

½ ounce (1 tablespoon) sweet vermouth

3 Flavored Ice Cubes (recipe follows), 1 of each flavor

2 ounces (¼ cup) bourbon

1 maraschino cherry

Choose a glass that holds 3 ice cubes snugly. Pour in the sweet vermouth and swirl to coat the glass. Fill the glass with the ice cubes and then pour in the bourbon. Garnish with the maraschino cherry and a cocktail stirrer. Encourage your guests to use a bit of patience to allow the ice to melt and flavor the drink.

FLAVORED ICE CUBES
MAKES ABOUT 25 ICE CUBES

2 cinnamon sticks

1 vanilla bean

¼ cup dried cherries

3 cups hot water

In three separate bowls, combine each ingredient with 1 cup of hot water. Cover the bowls and let them steep for at least 30 minutes. It's difficult to say exactly how long each should steep because it's essentially a matter of taste. The cinnamon should be ready first, while the cherries will take the longest. Strain each bowl and discard the solids. Let the water cool and then pour each one into its own ice-cube tray. Freeze.

My grandfather Vincenzo made cured salumi at home and hung them in his basement to cure. To this day, I have fond memories of accompanying him down into the pungent-smelling cellar and sampling the slices of cured meat he cut with his pocketknife. Making your own sausages is a great endeavor. It is a dying art that is enjoying something of a revival. If it interests you, experiment with various meats and different seasonings.

I consider this the ultimate "sharing plate" to set in front of guests so that they can nibble a little of this, a little of that, one bite better than the next. I like to make the pâté with rabbit livers, but you may not be able to find them, in which case you can use chicken livers. And if you don't feel like smoking your own duck breasts, go ahead and buy smoked duck. When I make the pâté at the restaurant, I use quail, pheasant, and squab, but at home I rely on chicken. Please don't skimp on the foie gras—it makes the terrine rich and sublime. I like to make the pâté in a cast-iron terrine mold, such as those made by Le Creuset. **SERVES 8 TO 10**

CHARCUTERIE PLATE WITH COUNTRY PÂTÉ, SMOKED DUCK, SALUMI, PICKLED RED ONIONS, AND PRETZEL BREAD

COUNTRY PÂTÉ

1 pound boneless chicken (a combination of legs, thighs, and breast meat is best)

4½ ounces foie gras

4½ ounces chicken or rabbit livers

18 ounces pancetta

2 tablespoons brandy

1 shallot, minced

1 teaspoon fresh thyme leaves

3 juniper berries, crushed

About 16 slices good-quality smoked bacon

SMOKED DUCK

2 quarts water

¾ cup kosher salt

½ cup light brown sugar

½ cup honey

2 tablespoons mixed fresh herbs (such as rosemary, thyme, and sage)

1 tablespoon whole black peppercorns

1½ tablespoons pink salt (see Note)

1 clove garlic, smashed

4 boneless pekin or magret duck breasts with skin, trimmed of excess fat

To make the pâté: Cut the chicken, foie gras, livers, and pancetta into 1-inch squares and transfer to a chilled mixing bowl. Add the brandy, shallot, thyme leaves, and juniper berries and stir well. Cover and refrigerate for at least 8 hours or overnight.

Line an 11-by-3-inch terrine mold (or one of similar size) with the bacon strips, laying them widthwise (not along the length of the mold) and hanging over the edges. Overlap them slightly so that there are no gaps. Refrigerate the mold for at least 30 minutes, until chilled.

Preheat the oven to 325°F.

Fit a meat grinder with the medium-sized blade. Push the meat mixture through the grinder and when uniformly ground, pack into the chilled terrine. Fold the bacon over onto the top of the meat. Give the terrine a couple of good whacks on the countertop to rid it of air bubbles.

Cover the terrine with foil and set in a roasting pan. Set the roasting pan on the center rack of the oven and pour enough hot water into the pan to come about 1 inch up the sides of the terrine. Bake for about 1½ hours, or until an instant-read thermometer inserted in the center registers 165°F.

Just before the terrine is finished baking, fill an appropriately shaped pan with enough ice cubes and water to reach a depth of 2 inches. The pan must be large and deep enough to hold the terrine.

Put the hot terrine in the ice water bath and then weight down the terrine. The best way to do this is to cut out a piece of cardboard that is the same size as the terrine mold. Set the cardboard on top of the terrine and then set 2 boxes of Morton's kosher salt—the size is perfect—on the cardboard.

½ pound high-quality salumi (such as finocchiona, mortadella, coppa, guanciale, prosciutto, or sopressata), thinly sliced

1 cup Pickled Red Onions (recipe follows)

1 cup cornichons

1 cup mixed olives

1 cup pepperoncini

½ cup Dijon mustard

1 loaf pretzel or crusty bread

Refrigerate the weighted terrine, still in the water bath, for at least 8 hours or overnight.

Now is the moment of truth. Remove the weights and gently set the terrine in warm water for about 2 minutes. (I suggest you use the same pan as for the ice bath, but this time fill it with warm tap water.) This should loosen the fat around the edges just enough to be able to remove the pâté.

Put a baking sheet or flat plate large enough to cover the terrine on top of the terrine and holding the two together, invert the terrine. Give it a gentle shake; the pâté should slide out. If it does not, run a dull kitchen knife around the outside of the pâté to loosen it.

Slice the terrine in half crosswise so that you can see the interior marbling of meat and fat. Wrap each half in plastic and refrigerate for up to 1 week. To serve, cut into ¼-inch-thick slices.

To prepare the duck, in a large saucepan, combine the water with the kosher salt, brown sugar, honey, herbs, peppercorns, pink salt, and garlic and bring to a boil over high heat. Cook for about 2 minutes, or until the salt, sugar, and honey dissolve.

Remove from the heat and set the brine aside to cool. When cool, cover and refrigerate until the brine is very cold, at least 2 hours or up to 24 hours.

Submerge the duck breasts in the brine and weight with a small plate to keep them completely submerged. Refrigerate for 12 hours but not much longer.

Prepare an oven smoker or another smoker according to the manufacturer's instructions. Lift the duck breasts from the brine and rinse under cool, running water. (Do not soak the breasts.) Pat dry. Smoke the duck breasts for 1 to 1½ hours, until an instant-read thermometer inserted in the centers registers 160°F and the breasts are cooked all the way through. Serve immediately or cover and refrigerate for up to 3 days. To serve, slice the duck breast into thin strips.

To serve the charcuterie, arrange 8 to 12 slices of pâté on a platter or wooden board with the sliced duck breasts and salumi. Spoon the pickled onions alongside the meats. Serve with cornichons, olives, pepperoncini, and mustard as well as slices of pretzel or crusty bread.

Note *Pink salt can be a hard-to-find ingredient. Also known as TCM, or tinted curing mix, it is salt with added nitrates. The local butcher is the best place to start when trying to locate it, or try online. I like The Sausage Maker, www.sausagemaker.com. Small oven smokers are sold at kitchen shops and can also be found online.*

PICKLED RED ONIONS
MAKES ABOUT 2 CUPS

2 star anise

1 bay leaf

1½ teaspoons black peppercorns

1½ teaspoons coriander seeds

1½ teaspoons fennel seeds

2 cups red wine vinegar

2 cups Simple Syrup (page 189)

1½ cups thinly sliced red onion (1 to 1½ onions)

Kosher salt and freshly ground black pepper

Lay a double thickness of cheesecloth on a work surface and pile the star anise, bay leaf, peppercorns, coriander, and fennel seeds in the center. Gather the sides of the cheesecloth and tie the opposite corners together (or tie with twine) to make a bundle or sachet.

In a large saucepan, combine the vinegar and syrup. Add the sachet and bring to a boil over medium-high heat. As soon as the mixture boils, remove it from the heat and let cool to room temperature.

Meanwhile, in a mixing bowl, season the onions with salt and pepper and set aside.

Remove and discard the sachet from the pickling liquid and discard. Pour the cooled liquid over the onions. Cover and refrigerate for at least 8 hours, but no longer than 2 days. Serve at room temperature, slightly drained.

Vegetable Spring Rolls with Three Dipping Sauces | Spicy Tuna Rolls | Spicy Shrimp Lettuce Wraps | I love sushi before a steak dinner and I appreciate all Asian foods. These three recipes are sushi-style dishes that are easy to make at home and that taste incredible before a steak meal with all the trimmings. The Vegetable Spring Rolls, super easy to make, are just right before a heavy meal. The dipping sauces I like to serve with them are so cool your guests will be amazed—and will also think you went to a lot of trouble. Not so! The Spicy Tuna Rolls are simple rolls made with my version of spicy tuna simply rolled in sushi rice. Sushi rice is short-grain rice that sticks together and so is perfect for making these little treats. You should be able to find it in most markets. The lettuce wraps are always a crowd-pleaser because most people like to make their own servings. I think of these crunchy treats as "Asian tacos" for just this reason. **SERVES 4**

VEGETABLE SPRING ROLLS WITH THREE DIPPING SAUCES

4 rice paper rounds, each about 8½ inches in diameter (I use Red Rose brand rice paper rounds)

4 medium Bibb lettuce leaves

1 cup julienned carrots

½ cup thinly sliced cucumber

2 ounces sweet or hot red peppers, thinly sliced

12 cilantro sprigs

8 fresh mint leaves

Plum Hoisin Sauce (recipe follows)

Roasted Red Pepper Sweet-and-Sour Sauce (recipe follows)

Lime Vinaigrette (recipe follows)

Soak the rice paper in warm water for about 30 seconds or until soft. Lift from the water and lay on folded kitchen towels to dry.

Lay a sheet of plastic wrap on a work surface and lay a rice paper round on the plastic. Put a lettuce leaf on the rice paper, about 1 inch from the bottom.

Layer one-fourth of the carrots, cucumber, and peppers on the lettuce. Top with one-fourth of the cilantro and 2 mint leaves. Roll the rice paper up and around the filling, using the plastic wrap as a guide. Wrap the plastic around the roll and twist the ends to tightly secure the roll. Repeat with the remaining rice paper rounds, lettuce leaves, and filling.

To serve, unwrap the plastic wrap and discard. Slice the rolls into rounds with a damp, sharp knife. Serve with the three dipping sauces.

PLUM HOISIN SAUCE
MAKES ABOUT ¾ CUP

½ cup plum sauce
⅓ cup hoisin sauce
2 tablespoons plum wine
1 teaspoon finely grated orange zest

In a mixing bowl, whisk together the plum sauce, hoisin sauce, and wine. Cover and refrigerate for up to 1 week.

To serve, sprinkle the grated zest over the sauce.

ROASTED RED PEPPER SWEET-AND-SOUR SAUCE
MAKES ABOUT ¾ CUP

¼ cup water
½ cup sugar
¼ cup prepared chili garlic sauce
2 tablespoons rice vinegar
1 tablespoon diced seeded peeled roasted red pepper

In a saucepan, bring the water and sugar to a boil over medium-high heat and boil for about 3 minutes, or until the sugar dissolves. Let cool.

When cool, add the chili sauce, vinegar, and diced red pepper. Using an immersion blender, puree the sauce until smooth. Alternatively, transfer to a blender or food processor and puree.

Use immediately or transfer to a lidded container and refrigerate for up to 1 week.

LIME VINAIGRETTE
MAKES ABOUT ¾ CUP

½ cup freshly squeezed lime juice
¼ cup packed brown sugar
2½ tablespoons fish sauce
¼ teaspoon chili oil
1 tablespoon torn fresh mint leaves
1 tablespoon chopped fresh cilantro
1 tablespoon chopped roasted peanuts

In a mixing bowl, whisk together the lime juice, sugar, fish sauce, and chili oil. Stir in the mint and cilantro and serve, garnished with the peanuts. The vinaigrette can be refrigerated in a lidded container for up to 3 days.

SPICY TUNA ROLLS

SERVES 4

1 pound sashimi-grade bluefin
or yellowtail tuna, minced

½ cup plus 6 tablespoons Spicy
Mayonnaise (recipe below)

4 tablespoons minced fresh chives

1 shallot, minced

1 tablespoon minced fresh cilantro

4 sheets nori

4 cups cooked sushi rice

¼ pound store-bought pickled ginger

¼ cup fresh wasabi or wasabi paste

In a mixing bowl, stir together the tuna, ½ cup of the mayonnaise, 2 table-spoons of the chives, the shallot, and cilantro. Cover and refrigerate until needed or for up to 3 hours, although this is better if used right away.

Put 1 piece of the nori on a sushi mat. Spread 1 cup of the rice on the nori and spread to make a smooth, even layer. Lay ½ cup of the tuna mixture in an even layer about 1 inch from the bottom, covering most of the rice.

Spoon 1½ tablespoons of the remaining mayonnaise and ½ tablespoon of the remaining chives over the tuna. Fold the nori over the tuna and roll up, using the mat to form a solid roll.

Repeat with the remaining nori sheets and ingredients.

Slice each roll into 6 pieces with a damp, sharp knife. Dip the knife in water between every cut so that the blade is always wet when it is slicing the sushi. Serve with the pickled ginger and wasabi on the side.

SPICY MAYONNAISE
MAKES ABOUT 1¼ CUPS

1 tablespoon Sriracha chili sauce
or another red chili sauce

1 teaspoon dried red chili flakes

1 teaspoon togarashi powder
(Japanese spice blend) or cayenne

1 teaspoon sesame chili oil

1 teaspoon freshly squeezed lemon juice

1¼ cups mayonnaise or Japanese mayonnaise

In a mixing bowl, stir together the chili sauce, chili flakes, and togarashi powder. Stir in the chili oil and lemon juice until combined. Stir in the may-onnaise and mix well.

Serve immediately or transfer to a lidded container and refrigerate for up to 24 hours. Use in sandwiches or salads.

SPICY SHRIMP LETTUCE WRAPS

SERVES 4

16 jumbo shrimp, peeled

2 tablespoons togarashi powder
(Japanese spice mix) or cayenne

2 tablespoons olive oil

½ cup julienned cucumber

½ cup julienned red bell pepper

½ cup julienned daikon radish

Kosher salt

½ cup Spicy Mayonnaise (page 20)

¼ cup chopped cilantro

16 Bibb lettuce leaves

Prepare a clean, well-oiled charcoal or gas grill so that the coals or heating element are medium hot. Or, heat the broiler.

Sprinkle the shrimp with the togarashi powder and then brush with the olive oil. Grill the shrimp, turning once, for about 2 minutes, or until pink and cooked through.

Put the cucumber, red pepper, and radish on a serving plate and season to taste with a little salt. Put the shrimp on another plate or in a dish and then arrange the mayonnaise, cilantro, and lettuce leaves in the middle of the table. Let everyone build their own wraps, flavoring them with the mayo and cilantro.

Cucumber Tonic

BARRING AN AVERSION TO GIN (apparently it is very common), a gin and tonic is one of the classiest thirst quenchers around. The sweet bitterness of tonic water plays nicely with the herbal bitterness of gin. This version matches the refreshment of the classic but adds the elegant touch of cucumber. I use just the skin of the cucumber for a subtle green hue with plenty of flavor and no small bits of pulp, which would be a problem with a whole cucumber.

THE CUCUMBER TONIC
SERVES 1

4 to 5 strips English cucumber peel

1½ ounces (3 tablespoons) gin

½ ounce (1 tablespoon) freshly squeezed lime juice

Ice

Tonic water

Cucumber round, for garnish

In a cocktail shaker, combine the cucumber peel, gin, and lime juice. Shake briskly 9 or 10 times and then strain into an ice-filled glass. Top with tonic water and garnish with the cucumber round.

Riesling Wine

RIESLING IS NEARLY EVERY SOMMELIER'S TRUMP CARD for dishes that prove difficult to pair with wine. A high, bright acidic finish often precedes a magnificent range of stone fruit and citrus, making a wine with such versatility that it works as an aperitif as well as with braised meats. It is also good with green vegetables or when balancing out intense heat. Sweetness levels vary greatly across the multitude of regions and countries where the Riesling grape is grown, but a good rule of thumb is to look for the alcohol content. The lower the alcohol, the more likely the wine is to have a high sugar content.

I was inspired to create this appetizer during a trip to Hawaii. My buddies at Honolulu Fish, a wholesale company in Hawaii, took me to an early-morning auction where the fishermen unload huge whole fish such as tuna and swordfish to sell. Like its counterpart in Japan, this is a world-renowned auction that attracts buyers from Japan, Europe, and the mainland of the United States. I was blown away by the deep-red ahi tuna and decided to showcase it in such a way that both its beauty and intense flavor would shine forth. Because Hawaii is so influenced by Asian cultures, I included Kaffir lime leaves, wasabi, rice vinegar, sesame oil, and Asian pears. But that doesn't mean you should shy away from taking this to another level by spooning a little caviar on top of each serving! **SERVES 4**

AHI TUNA TARTARE WITH ASIAN PEAR, CUCUMBER, AND AVOCADO

WONTON CRISPS

12 wonton wrappers, each about 3 inches in diameter, cut diagonally in half into triangles

Olive oil, for brushing

Sesame seeds, for sprinkling

Kosher salt and freshly ground black pepper

TUNA TARTARE

2 tablespoons soy sauce

1 tablespoon rice vinegar

1 tablespoon freshly squeezed lime juice

1 Kaffir lime leaf, minced very fine (see Note)

1½ teaspoons wasabi paste

¾ teaspoon Asian sesame oil

¾ pound sushi-quality ahi tuna steak, cut into ¼-inch dice

1 medium avocado, cut into ¼-inch dice

1 cup finely diced Asian pear

1 cup finely diced cucumber

1 scallion, white and green parts, finely chopped

Toasted sesame seeds, for garnish

Chopped fresh chives, for garnish

To make the crisps: Preheat the oven to 350°F. Line a baking sheet with parchment or waxed paper.

Arrange the wonton triangles on the baking sheet and brush with olive oil. Sprinkle with sesame seeds and season to taste with salt and pepper.

Bake for about 9 minutes, or until the triangles are golden brown. Let cool on the baking sheet. Use immediately or store at room temperature in a tightly covered container for up to 8 hours.

To make the tartare: In a medium mixing bowl, whisk together the soy sauce, vinegar, lime juice, lime leaf, wasabi paste, and sesame oil. Add the tuna, avocado, pear, cucumber, and scallion. Stir gently to coat the fish and vegetables with the sauce.

Put 4 ring molds, each about 2 inches deep and 3 inches in diameter, on each of 4 chilled plates. (Tuna cans, with the tops and bottoms removed, work well, as do cookie and biscuit cutters.) Spoon the tartare mixture into the molds and pack until firm and tight. Lift the molds straight up and off the tuna. Sprinkle with sesame seeds and chives and serve with the wonton crisps.

Note *Kaffir lime leaves can be found fresh in most Asian supermarkets.*

The recipes in this chapter are a little more formal than those in Chapter 1, but only in how they are presented, not in spirit. They are still meant to be shared with good friends, never too fancy or overwhelming, and always designed to hit the spot before a steak dinner. A few generations ago, no one would think of preparing escargot, foie gras, or even crab cakes at home, but thankfully that has changed so that today we don't blink an eye when we see a recipe for one or the other.

You may not blink but that does not mean you will actually be inspired to try one of these more esoteric-sounding dishes. Please jump in! Your own sense of accomplishment will be eclipsed only by your guests' pleasure and happy comments. The mussels braised in beer should be eaten communally, but the other hot appetizers are usually plated. The escargot is as traditional as can be because I can't imagine improving on the original, but crispy sweetbreads, sautéed scallops, and stuffed artichokes absolutely reveal a Tramonto twist. I love them all, and now that so many of these "specialty" ingredients are easy to acquire, I am sure you will, too.

Hot appetizers demand high-energy music, such as that by:
METALLICA | RUSH | AC/DC | VAN HALEN | ALICE IN CHAINS

HOT APPETIZERS

This is a fantastic dish to serve family style—and actually, I can't think of a better way of serving them than plunking a big bowl overflowing with the shiny black mussels in the middle of the table. And make that an outdoor table, if possible, because this is a messy appetizer (which can easily become a main course when doubled). Don't forget the toast for sopping up the briny, buttery broth at the bottom of the bowl—the best part for some folks! And don't forget the beer, either. I like Belgium-style beer because I associate mussels with that small, coastal country, but any local ale will do just fine. I usually buy one of the ales made by Goose Island when I make this, a local ale from a nearby brewery. **SERVES 4**

ALE-BRAISED MUSSELS, BELGIAN STYLE

2 pounds mussels (I like Prince Edward Island mussels, if you can find them)

2 tablespoons unsalted butter

2 tablespoons extra-virgin olive oil

1 cup diced smoked country ham or prosciutto (about ¼ pound)

1 tablespoon minced garlic

1 shallot, minced

2 sprigs thyme

1 (12-ounce) bottle Belgian-style ale

1 tablespoon chopped fresh flat-leaf parsley

1 tablespoon chopped fresh thyme

1 tablespoon chopped fresh basil

Juice of 1 lemon

Kosher salt and freshly ground black pepper

1 crusty baguette, cut into 1-inch-thick slices

Olive oil, for brushing

1 clove garlic, for rubbing

Holding them under cool water, scrub each mussel's shell with a stiff-bristled brush. Remove the byssal threads (or beard), which connect the mussels to rocks in the water: Grab the fibers with your fingers and pull them out, tugging toward the hinged point of the shell.

In a medium-sized saucepan or skillet, heat 1 tablespoon of the butter and the oil over medium heat. When the butter melts, add the ham and cook for 4 to 5 minutes, until the ham is crispy and the fat has rendered.

Add the minced garlic, shallot, and thyme sprigs to the rendered fat and cook over medium-low heat for about 2 minutes, or until soft. Add the mussels, stir to coat with the vegetables and pan juices, and cook for about 1 minute.

Add the ale, cover the pan, and bring to a boil over medium-high heat. Decrease the heat and simmer for 8 to 10 minutes, until all the mussels open. (Discard any that do not open.)

Add the remaining 1 tablespoon butter, the parsley, chopped thyme, basil, and lemon juice and toss to distribute the herbs and lemon juice and allow the butter time to melt. Season to taste with salt and pepper.

Meanwhile, preheat the oven to 375°F.

Brush both sides of the bread slices with olive oil and lay on a baking sheet. Toast in the oven, turning once, for 7 or 8 minutes, until nicely browned. Rub the toasted bread with the garlic clove. Alternatively, you can grill the bread for 4 to 5 minutes, turning once, and then rub with garlic.

Using a slotted spoon, divide the mussels evenly among 4 bowls or place all in a large bowl for the table. Pour the broth in the pan over the mussels and serve with the bread for dipping in the broth.

How to Buy and Treat a Mussel

ALWAYS BUY FRESH MUSSELS AND PLAN TO COOK AND EAT THEM ON THE SAME DAY—or at the very most within 24 hours. Buy them from a fish guy with good turnover, so you know they are alive and fresh, and choose those with tightly closed shells. If a shell is open, tap it. If the mussel is alive, it will snap shut. If it doesn't, you don't want it. Also, avoid mussels with cracked or chipped shells. When you buy mussels, you buy them by the pound—approximately 22 mussels—and so you may not be able to examine every single one at the market. Luckily, mussels are relatively inexpensive and so you can toss those few that don't meet this criteria when you get home.

As soon as you get them home, remove the mussels from their packaging and wrap them in a moist kitchen towel. Put the bundle in a large bowl or on a rimmed baking sheet and refrigerate until ready to cook. Never store them in plastic because they need to breathe.

This rich, tasty little risotto is a gorgeous appetizer that exemplifies my affection for combining meat and seafood in the same recipe. This could easily be a main course, albeit an opulent one, and could also be employed as a bed for sautéed salmon. Make this at home as a starter for a steak dinner and you won't need more than the steak and a salad for the main event. It is that filling and satisfying. **SERVES 4**

CHORIZO AND ROCK SHRIMP RISOTTO

3 tablespoons extra-virgin olive oil

1 pound rock shrimp or other medium-sized shrimp, peeled

Kosher salt and freshly ground black pepper

½ pound dried chorizo sausage, cut into half-moons

3 tablespoons unsalted butter

½ bulb fennel, cut into medium dice

1 yellow onion, cut into medium dice

1⅔ cups medium-grain rice (such as Carnaroli or Arborio)

½ cup dry white wine

5 cups chicken stock, preferably homemade (page 188)

2 tablespoons grated Parmigiano-Reggiano cheese

1 tablespoon chopped fresh flat-leaf parsley

1 tablespoon chopped fresh tarragon

Juice of ½ lemon

In a sauté pan, heat 1 tablespoon of the olive oil over medium heat. Season the shrimp with salt and pepper and cook in the oil for about 1 minute, or until cooked halfway through. The shrimp will not be opaque all the way through and will still feel springy. Transfer to a plate and set aside.

In a large, deep pot, heat 1 tablespoon of the oil and cook the chorizo, stirring to promote even browning, for about 2 minutes, or until golden brown. Add 2 tablespoons of the butter and cook until the butter melts and foams. Using a wooden spoon, scrape the bottom of the pan to release any solids.

Add the fennel and onion and cook, stirring, for about 2 minutes, or until translucent. Add the rice and cook for about 1 minute, stirring to coat with the fat. Add the wine and cook for about 1 minute, or until the wine is absorbed by the rice.

Meanwhile, in a large saucepan or pot, bring the stock to a boil over medium-high heat. Lower to a simmer and keep simmering while cooking the risotto. Adjust the heat up or down to maintain a very low simmer.

Ladle about ¾ cup of the hot stock into the pot with the rice and stir over medium heat until the liquid is absorbed by the rice. Add another ladleful of stock and stir until absorbed. Repeat this process until all the stock is used. This is a long process—it will take about 20 minutes—but your patience will pay off with a smooth, delicious risotto. When done, the rice will be creamy and tender.

Add the shrimp, stir to combine, and let the shrimp finish cooking, only about 1 minute. Do not overcook the shrimp.

Off the heat, stir in the remaining tablespoon of butter, the Parmesan, parsley, tarragon, and lemon juice. Divide among 4 bowls and drizzle each bowl with one-fourth of the remaining 1 tablespoon olive oil.

Escargot with Garlic Butter | Jumbo Lump Crab Cakes with Rémoulade or Classic Tartar Sauce | Oysters Rockefeller | There's hardly a steakhouse that does not have these three starters on their menus, and so how could I write a book about steak without them? But don't think of these as "restaurant fare"—they are easy to make at home and will impress even the most fastidious guest. I intentionally have not put a Tramonto twist on any of them because I can't think of any way to improve on how they have always been cooked by master steakhouse chefs at legendary eateries such as Delmonico's and The Palm. Clearly, these are made to be part of a steak dinner, at home or in a restaurant.

ESCARGOT WITH GARLIC BUTTER

SERVES 4 TO 6

ESCARGOT

1 (7.5-ounce or 8.25-ounce) can large Burgundy snails (about 2 dozen snails)

¼ cup extra-virgin olive oil

1 shallot, minced

2 cups chicken stock, preferably homemade (page 188)

1 bay leaf

1 sprig thyme

½ cup dry red wine

GARLIC BUTTER

1 cup unsalted butter, softened

1 tablespoon minced garlic

1½ teaspoons chopped fresh flat-leaf parsley

1½ teaspoons fresh thyme leaves

1½ teaspoons chopped fresh chives

1 teaspoon Dijon mustard

1 teaspoon freshly squeezed lemon juice

Freshly ground black pepper

Lemon wedges, for garnish

Preheat the oven to 400ºF.

To prepare the escargot: Put the snails in a colander and rinse with cold water. Pat dry with a kitchen towel and set aside.

In a sauté pan, heat the oil over medium-high heat and cook the shallot for about 1 minute, or until it begins to soften. Add the snails and sauté for about 1 minute longer. Add the stock, bay leaf, and thyme and decrease the heat. Simmer for 4 to 5 minutes, until the snails are hot.

Add the wine, raise the heat to medium-high, and cook for 2 to 3 minutes, until the liquid in the pan reduces by half. Set aside to cool, leaving the snails in the liquid.

To make the garlic butter: In the bowl of a food processor fitted with the metal blade, pulse the butter, garlic, parsley, thyme, chives, mustard, and lemon juice until smooth. Season to taste with pepper and pulse again.

Divide the snails among the indentations in 4 to 6 ovenproof snail dishes and top each serving with 1 tablespoon of garlic butter. Bake for 8 to 10 minutes, until the snails are heated through and the butter melts. Serve immediately, with lemon wedges for garnish.

Note *The garlic butter can be made ahead of time and wrapped into a cylinder in waxed paper. It will keep in the refrigerator for up to 5 days and in the freezer for up to 1 month. It's easy to slice the chilled cylinder into rounds to top the snails. Use it also to spread on bread, toss with pasta, or flavor chicken.*

About Escargot

AS MOST PEOPLE KNOW, the French word *escargot* means "snail," and yes, the dish requires that you eat snails. But these are not your ordinary garden snails; they are delicious, fresh-tasting—some say "lobster-like"—delicacies traditionally served in a garlicky butter sauce. Most snails sold for escargot are imported from France, and most are *Helix pomatia, Helix lucorum,* or *Helix aspersa,* also known as *petit-gris,* or little gray snails. Don't worry about memorizing these terms; you will buy the snails already cleaned, processed, and packed into cans. Some say the best escargot come from the Burgundy region of France. I like the wild Burgundy snails sold on line at www.igourmet.com, where you can also buy the reusable shells, if you want to serve the snails in them. (I don't, but you might like to; it's fun.) Finally, before you can serve escargot, you should buy snail dishes, each with 6 indentations. I recommend Staub enameled cast-iron dishes, but any porcelain snail dish will do.

Mint Julep

THIS IS A GREAT DRINK, EVEN WHEN THE PONIES AREN'T RUNNING. The key is the crushed ice packed like a snow cone in the short, almost bucket-like glass (metal if you are going for Derby style). This version may upset the purist because it is little bit sweeter and mintier than the classic.

MINT JULEP
SERVES 4

20 to 30 fresh mint leaves, plus more for garnish

12 ounces (1½ cups) bourbon

2 tablespoons plus 2 teaspoons Mint Simple Syrup (page 10)

Crushed ice

Bruise the mint leaves with your hands and place in a bowl. Pour the bourbon over the mint and let sit for 10 to 20 minutes (depending on how quickly you want to serve the drinks). Strain the bourbon through a fine-mesh sieve into a pitcher and discard the mint leaves. Add the simple syrup and stir well.

Pack 4 glasses with ice and pour the Julep over the ice. Immediately put more ice in each glass and garnish with fresh mint leaves.

JUMBO LUMP CRAB CAKES WITH RÉMOULADE OR CLASSIC TARTAR SAUCE

SERVES 4

CRAB CAKES

5 tablespoons extra-virgin olive oil

1 yellow onion, finely minced

2 cloves garlic, finely minced

1 teaspoon Worcestershire sauce

1 pound fresh jumbo lump crabmeat, picked and cleaned, or 1 (16-ounce) can pasteurized crabmeat

1 cup panko bread crumbs

¼ cup chopped fresh cilantro

¼ cup chopped fresh flat-leaf parsley

1 tablespoon mayonnaise

1 tablespoon Dijon mustard

1 large egg white

Juice of ½ lemon

½ jalapeño pepper, seeded and finely diced

Kosher salt and freshly ground black pepper

SALAD

Juice of ½ lemon

2 tablespoons extra-virgin olive oil

2 cups mixed greens (such as frisée and watercress)

1 tablespoon torn fresh flat-leaf parsley

4 radishes, shaved

Kosher salt and freshly ground black pepper

Rémoulade (page 189) or Classic Tartar Sauce (page 190)

To make the crab cakes: In a sauté pan, heat 3 tablespoons of the oil over medium heat and cook the onion and garlic for about 3 minutes. Add the Worcestershire sauce and cook for about 2 minutes longer, or until transparent. Set aside to cool for 10 minutes.

In a bowl, mix the crabmeat with ½ cup of the bread crumbs, the cilantro, parsley, mayonnaise, mustard, egg white, lemon juice, and jalapeño pepper until well blended. Season to taste with salt and pepper. Form into 4 equal-sized crab cakes.

Spread the remaining ½ cup of bread crumbs in a shallow dish and coat each crab cake with crumbs on both sides. Set the coated crab cakes on a waxed paper–lined baking sheet and refrigerate for about 10 minutes.

In a large sauté pan, heat the remaining 2 tablespoons oil over medium heat and cook the crab cakes, turning once, for about 4 minutes, or until golden brown.

To make the salad: In a mixing bowl, whisk together the lemon juice and oil to create an emulsion. Add the greens, parsley, and radishes and toss to coat. Season to taste with salt and pepper.

Divide the salad evenly among 4 serving plates. Put 1 crab cake on top of each salad and spoon a dollop of rémoulade or tartar sauce next to it on the plate.

OYSTERS ROCKEFELLER

SERVES 4 TO 6

1 cup panko bread crumbs

¼ cup grated Parmigiano-Reggiano cheese

¼ cup extra-virgin olive oil

1 tablespoon chopped fresh flat-leaf parsley

1½ teaspoons fresh tarragon

Kosher salt and freshly ground black pepper

6 tablespoons unsalted butter

2 cloves garlic, minced

1 shallot, chopped

2 pounds fresh spinach, stemmed, roughly chopped, and rinsed, with some water clinging to the leaves

¼ cup Pernod

½ cup heavy cream

Pinch of cayenne

8 cups rock salt

8 tablespoons star anise

8 tablespoons pink peppercorns

8 tablespoons black peppercorns

8 cinnamon sticks, broken into 2 or 3 pieces

24 fresh, shucked oysters (see page 36)

Grated zest of 1 lemon

2 tablespoons chopped fresh flat-leaf parsley

2 lemons, cut in wedges

Preheat the oven to 450°F.

In a mixing bowl, toss the bread crumbs and cheese with the oil, parsley, and tarragon and season to taste with salt and pepper. Set aside.

In a sauté pan, melt 4 tablespoons of the butter over medium-low heat. When hot, add the garlic and shallot and cook for about 2 minutes. Add the spinach and cook for 3 to 4 minutes, until wilted. Add the Pernod and cook for about 2 minutes, or until very little liquid remains. Add the cream and bring to a boil. Decrease the heat and cook for about 5 minutes, or until reduced by half. Remove the pan from the heat and add the remaining 2 tablespoons butter and the cayenne. Season to taste with salt and pepper.

In a mixing bowl, mix the salt with the star anise, pink and black peppercorns, and cinnamon sticks. Spread a thick layer of the salt mixture in a shallow roasting pan or jelly roll pan. Arrange the oysters, nestled in the bottom shells, on top of the salt. Spoon about 1 teaspoon of the spinach mixture on top of each oyster and sprinkle with a generous amount of the bread crumb mixture. Be sure the oysters are pushed into the salt to anchor them. Bake for about 15 minutes, or until golden brown on top.

Spread a layer of salt on each of 4 serving plates. Put 6 oysters on the salt, garnish with the zest and parsley, and serve with the lemon wedges.

A Little More about Oysters

OYSTERS GROW IN ALL OCEAN BODIES AND ARE BELOVED THE WORLD OVER FOR THEIR BRINY SWEETNESS. They also are famous for creating pearls as they grind sand in their shells, and so between that and their indescribable flavor, it's no wonder they are considered a special treat by most of us.

Oysters are not easy to shuck, or open. I describe how to do so in great detail on page 5, and with practice you will soon be shucking them like a guy working at an island raw bar! They have a natural hermetic-type seal that keeps them closed tight and also seals in their fresh flavor. Always buy oysters that are securely closed, which, as with all bivalves (oysters, clams, mussels), means they are alive. If a slightly opened shell closes with a snap when you tap it, the oyster is alive and healthy.

Keep the oysters cold when you get them home and plan to eat them within 24 to 32 hours of purchase. I put the oysters on a bed of cracked ice and push the dish to the back of the fridge where it is the coldest. Not only does this insure their freshness, but a cold oyster is easier to shuck. Some people even put them in the freezer for about 10 minutes before shucking (but it's not advisable to store them in the freezer). Shuck them no more than 2 hours before serving.

When you shuck the oysters, use a sturdy oyster knife and a protective glove or thick kitchen towel to protect your hands from the sharp ridges on the shell and any barnacles still attached to the oyster. The towel or glove also insures that the oyster does not slip from your hands and the shucking knife does not stab your other hand. Safety first!

Don't shake your head at the idea of foie gras at home! A little goes a long way and everyone will be ecstatic that you thought of it. Of course, you don't have to make this dish with foie gras; you can serve the peaches and mint salad with pork chops or grilled pork tenderloin. I got the idea for the recipe when I visited Charleston, South Carolina, one of our most beautiful cities and truly steeped in history and graceful charm—and also the home to some great food. I was there during peach season and had a pork chop with peaches and mint, inspiring me to use foie gras instead, one of my very favorite foods. **SERVES 4**

PAN-SEARED FOIE GRAS WITH PEACHES AND MINT

Juice of 1 orange

1 tablespoon honey

¼ cup extra-virgin olive oil

4 ripe peaches, peeled, pitted, and cut into medium dice

¼ cup sliced fresh mint leaves

Kosher salt and freshly ground black pepper

4 (3-ounce) portions foie gras, each about 1 inch thick (I suggest foie gras from Hudson Valley Foie Gras)

1 teaspoon chopped fresh lavender, for garnish

In a mixing bowl, whisk together the orange juice and honey. Still whisking, slowly add the oil in a drizzle until the dressing emulsifies. Add the peaches and mint and season with salt and pepper to taste. Set aside at room temperature for about 15 minutes to give the peaches time to macerate in the dressing.

With a sharp knife, lightly score the foie gras so that each shallow score is about ¼ inch apart. Season on both sides with salt and pepper.

In a dry skillet heated over high heat, sear the foie gras on both sides. The total cooking time should be no longer than 4 minutes.

Scoop the peaches from the dressing with a slotted spoon and distribute evenly among 4 serving plates. Top the peaches with the foie gras. Drizzle with the honey-orange juice dressing and serve, garnished with the lavender.

Blown Away by Foie Gras

THE FIRST TIME I TASTED FOIE GRAS I WAS BLOWN AWAY. It was an experience that has stayed with me over the years so that I harbor a soft spot for the creamy, rich livers. You will, too.

Culinary historians believe Egyptians may have made it, and there is good evidence that the Romans fed their geese figs to sweeten the meat. Foie gras is the livers of fattened geese and ducks, and while goose foie gras is richer than duck, both are excellent. I usually cook with duck foie gras, buying it from Hudson Valley Foie Gras, a supplier in New York State that treats the animals humanely. They supply many of the gourmet stores and i-commerce sites in the country. Very good foie gras is imported from Europe, too.

Always buy fresh, grade A foie gras livers. They should be pale beige and firm when you touch them. Clean them by removing all veins, blood clots, and sinews (use needle-nose pliers or tweezers, if necessary). When they are cooked, they will have a silken texture that cannot be mistaken for anything else! Believe me, once you taste foie gras, you will understand why it's been considered a delicacy for centuries.

The union of scallops, mushrooms, and balsamic is a joyous one,

and when served before a steak dinner, it's a golden celebration. Scallops cook quickly, and so take care not to overcook them. If you go to the trouble of buying plump fresh sea scallops, or more expensive and even better diver scallops, cook them only until medium or medium-rare. Look for creamy or pinkish sea scallops, not those that are bright white. The former are fresh; the latter have been soaked in a preservative. While I urge you to be picky about the scallops you buy for this, be flexible when it comes to the mushrooms. Use whatever are in season and fresh in your market or at the farm stand. **SERVES 4**

SAUTÉED SEA SCALLOPS WITH MUSHROOMS AND BALSAMIC

12 large sea scallops

Kosher salt and freshly ground black pepper

4 tablespoons extra-virgin olive oil

4 shallots, thinly sliced

1 clove garlic, minced

½ pound mixed mushrooms (such as oyster, chanterelle, and cremini), sliced ¼ inch thick

Juice of ½ lemon

¼ cup aged balsamic vinegar

2 tablespoons unsalted butter

1 tablespoon chopped fresh basil

1 tablespoon chopped fresh flat-leaf parsley

Season the scallops with salt and pepper.

In a 10- to 12-inch nonstick skillet, heat 2 tablespoons of the olive oil until very hot and nearly smoking. Cook the scallops for about 1 minute, or until crisp and golden brown on one side. Turn over and cook for 2 minutes longer, or until golden brown. Take care not to overcook the scallops. I like them medium or medium-rare. When cooked to medium, they are cloudy, opaque and look a little raw. They are not bright white on the outside. Remove from the heat and set aside.

In the same or another skillet, heat the remaining 2 tablespoons oil until very hot. Add the shallots and sauté over medium heat for 3 to 4 minutes, until softened. Add the garlic and cook for 1 minute. Add the mushrooms and toss in the oil for 3 to 4 minutes, until softened. Add the lemon juice and cook for 1 minute. Add the vinegar and butter, swirling the pan to mix. Toss in the basil and parsley and season to taste with salt and pepper.

Put 3 scallops on each of 4 serving plates and spoon the mushroom sauce over them. Serve right away.

When I think of eating steak, particularly in a steakhouse, I think of artichokes because the vegetable is a great match for beef. Yet, I am far more apt to cook and eat artichokes at home, rather than order them in a restaurant, because they are deliciously messy and shareable, and they make any family meal a happy, giggly one. If you haven't cooked artichokes before, start now. This is an easy way to prepare them and one that tastes so good, you will be sold. Let's face it: The dish makes a statement and has a discernible "wow!" factor.

SERVES 4

STUFFED ARTICHOKES WITH LEMON-GARLIC BREAD CRUMBS

ARTICHOKES

4 large globe artichokes

1 lemon, halved

1 cup dry white wine

¼ cup olive oil

½ cup chopped onion

2 teaspoons minced garlic

1 bay leaf

2 sprigs thyme

1 tablespoon kosher salt

Freshly ground black pepper

STUFFING

3 cups homemade or store-bought bread crumbs

1 cup grated Parmigiano-Reggiano cheese

1 cup chopped fresh flat-leaf parsley

1 cup julienned salumi (such as finocchiona or calabrese), optional

2 tablespoons chopped garlic

1 tablespoon finely grated lemon zest

Juice of ½ lemon

Kosher salt and freshly ground black pepper

¼ cup extra-virgin olive oil, plus more for drizzling

2 teaspoons unsalted butter

4 lemon wedges

To prepare the artichokes: Cut the stems from the artichokes and discard. Slice about ½ inch off the tops and then, using scissors, cut the remaining leaf tips. Rub the cut leaves with a lemon half.

Separate the leaves with your thumbs and pull out the purple leaves from the centers along with enough of the yellow leaves to expose the fuzzy chokes. Scoop out the chokes and squeeze lemon juice into the cavities.

In a 4- to 6-quart pot, stand the artichokes upright and add enough cold water to cover. Add the wine, oil, onion, garlic, bay leaf, thyme, and salt. Season with a little pepper and toss the squeezed lemon halves into the pot. Lay a clean kitchen towel directly on top of the artichokes to keep them submerged. Bring to a boil over high heat. Leave the towel in place, cover the pot, and simmer for about 1 hour, or until tender. Adjust the heat up or down to maintain a medium simmer. Drain, reserving 2 cups of the cooking liquid. Let the artichokes cool for 15 to 20 minutes, until they are cool enough to handle.

To make the stuffing: Preheat the oven to 350°F.

If using homemade bread crumbs, spread them in a shallow baking pan and bake, stirring frequently to prevent sticking and burning, for about 10 minutes, or until lightly golden brown. Set aside to cool completely. Do not turn off the oven.

In a mixing bowl, toss the cooled bread crumbs or the store-bought crumbs with ½ cup of the cheese, ½ cup of the parsley, ½ cup of the salumi, the garlic, lemon zest, lemon juice, and salt and pepper to taste. Drizzle the oil over the crumbs and toss to coat evenly.

Spoon about 2 tablespoons of the stuffing into the cavity of each artichoke. Spread the leaves as much as possible without breaking them and spoon more stuffing between the leaves. Top each artichoke with ½ teaspoon of butter.

Arrange the artichokes in a shallow baking dish and pour the reserved poaching liquid into the dish. Bake for 15 to 20 minutes, until golden brown. Remove the dish from the oven and sprinkle each artichoke with

the remaining ½ cup cheese and ½ cup salumi. Return to the oven for about 5 minutes, or until the cheese is lightly browned.

Using tongs, transfer an artichoke to each of 4 shallow bowls. Pour any remaining liquid into the bowls and serve the artichokes garnished with the remaining ½ cup parsley, lemon wedges, and drizzles of olive oil.

Note *A 6- to 8-quart pressure cooker is a great place to cook artichokes. Put the artichokes in the cooker with 2 cups of water and the remaining ingredients. Seal the cooker with the lid and cook for about 10 minutes at high pressure, following the manufacturer's instructions. When done, put the still-covered pressure cooker in the sink and run cold water over it to cool it. Do not remove the lid until the pressure reduces.*

Vodka-Thyme Sour

A VODKA SOUR IS ONE OF THE SIMPLEST CLASSIC COCKTAILS THERE IS, and the refreshing tang of the sour mix that carries the near flavorless kick of vodka can't be beat. This subtle turn on the cocktail adds thyme to the mix. Soda can be poured in as a finish to cut the sweetness without losing the flavor of the thyme, technically making this a Vodka Collins.

VODKA-THYME SOUR
SERVES 1

1½ ounces (3 tablespoons) vodka

1½ ounces (3 tablespoons) Thyme Sour Mix (recipe follows)

Club soda (optional)

In a cocktail shaker, combine the vodka and sour mix, Shake vigorously 9 or 10 times and then pour the cocktail into an ice-filled glass. Top off with club soda and serve with a straw.

THYME SOUR MIX
MAKES ABOUT 3 CUPS

1 cup sugar

1 cup water

20 sprigs thyme

2 cups strained freshly squeezed lemon juice

In a saucepan, combine the sugar and water and bring to a simmer over medium heat. Cook for a few minutes, stirring, until the sugar dissolves and the syrup is clear. At this point the syrup should be beginning to bubble.

Remove from the heat and add the thyme. Cover and set aside for about 10 minutes. Strain the syrup through a fine-mesh sieve into a bowl. Let the syrup cool and then stir in the lemon juice.

Use immediately or refrigerate in a tightly lidded container for up to 3 days.

I like to start a steak dinner with another kind of meat, and sweetbreads are one of my favorites. I think of them as the "ultimate nugget" because they are so lush. Their friendliness with steak is akin to how well foie gras goes with steak. I am simply a sucker for sweetbreads when they are cooked right. And this recipe does them right! **SERVES 4**

CRISPY SWEETBREADS WITH PECANS AND HONEY

SWEETBREADS

1 pound fresh veal sweetbreads

¼ cup distilled white vinegar

1 bay leaf

1 tablespoon whole black peppercorns

2 teaspoons kosher salt

2 cups quick mix flour (such as Wondra) or all-purpose flour

½ teaspoon freshly ground black pepper

¼ teaspoon cayenne

1 tablespoon unsalted butter

1 tablespoon olive oil

SAUCE

½ cup finely chopped onion

4 shallots, finely chopped

¼ cup high-quality dry Spanish sherry

Juice of 1 orange

2½ tablespoons sherry vinegar

1½ cups chicken stock or veal jus, preferably homemade (page 188)

1 cup chopped pecans

1 tablespoon honey

1 tablespoon unsalted butter

1 tablespoon chopped fresh chervil

1 tablespoon chopped fresh tarragon

To prepare the sweetbreads: Place the sweetbreads in a bowl and cover with cold water. Refrigerate for 6 to 8 hours, or overnight, changing the water twice. Drain well.

In a large saucepan, combine the white vinegar, bay leaf, peppercorns, and 1 teaspoon of the salt. Add the sweetbreads and enough cold water to cover. Bring to a boil over medium-high heat and immediately remove from the heat. Set aside for 10 minutes. Using a slotted spoon, lift the sweetbreads from the liquid and transfer to a shallow pan. Refrigerate for about 30 minutes.

Sweetbreads Have Nothing to Do with Sweets or Bread— But They Are Delicious!

THE THYMUS GLANDS OF CALVES OR LAMBS, sweetbreads have two lobes, one more elongated than the other but both with the same rich, sweet flavor and creamy, delicate texture. Most people prefer veal sweetbreads over lamb sweetbreads, and in fact, it can be tricky to find lamb sweetbreads for sale.

When buying sweetbreads, look for plump, compact lobes with no darkening. Nearly every recipe for sweetbreads calls for soaking them in water or milk and then draining them. Don't skip this step, and be sure to cook them shortly after soaking. They are fragile and don't keep too well.

With a sharp knife, cut the white-colored center membrane, tough fibrous pieces, and connective tissue from the sweetbreads. Slice the sweetbreads into ¾-inch-thick pieces.

In a mixing bowl, whisk the flour with the remaining 1 teaspoon salt, the black pepper, and cayenne. Toss the chilled slices of sweetbread in the mixture to coat lightly and evenly.

In a skillet large enough to hold the sliced sweetbreads in a single layer, heat the butter and olive oil over medium heat. When hot, cook the sweetbreads for about 3 minutes without turning the slices. Turn the slices over and cook for about 5 minutes longer, or until golden brown. Transfer with a slotted spoon to a plate and set aside. Wipe out the pan with paper towels.

To make the sauce: In the same wiped-out pan, sauté the onion and shallots over medium heat for about 5 minutes, or until lightly browned. If needed, add a little more oil to the pan, but if it's simply wiped out, it probably won't be necessary. Add the sherry, orange juice, and sherry vinegar, increase the heat to high, and deglaze the pan by stirring and scraping the bottom and sides with a wooden spoon to dislodge any browned bits. Cook for about 2 minutes, or until reduced by about half.

Add the stock, reduce the heat, and simmer for about 5 minutes, or until reduced to just under 1 cup. Whisk in the pecans, honey, and butter.

Return the sweetbreads to the pan and turn them in the sauce until heated through and nicely glazed. Sprinkle the chervil and tarragon over the sweetbreads and sauce and serve immediately, evenly divided among 4 serving plates.

Because I love to experience a wide range of textures and tastes in a single forkful, I am a major fan of salads. Just about anything goes when you prepare one of these often raw, usually cold, dishes. This does not mean a good salad is not a carefully constructed dish with complementing flavors and consistencies that make up a totally satisfying experience. And yet my recipes are casual and fun, meant to be served in big bowls or on platters set in the center of the table for everyone to enjoy. I love to serve food this way—not only is it a refreshing change from the restaurant fare I am most used to preparing, but it encourages a sense of familiarity and conviviality.

When I was growing up, salad was not a separate course but was still part of nearly every meal. My wife, Eileen, often starts her meal with a salad, and many of those here could be first courses: Think about The Wedge salad, the Lyonnaise Salad, and the Chicago-Style Garbage Salad. Others can be main courses served with wine or a pale ale, such as the Caesar salad with steak, the chopped salad made with seafood, or the crab salad. Read through the recipes and decide how you want to serve salad. There is no "wrong way" to do it. It's all good.

A salad, with its myriad ingredients, is a symphony of tastes and texture. When I make them, I turn to the mellow sounds of:
NORAH JONES | BOB SEGER | ROD STEWART | AMY WINEHOUSE

SALADS

It doesn't get any more quintessentially steakhouse than a wedge of iceberg topped with creamy blue cheese dressing. In addition, my mother made a similar salad with regular frequency when I was growing up, so this brings back fond memories for me. It is so simple, it should top the list when you make a steak dinner at home.

Back in the day, when iceberg lettuce was just about all you could get at a lot of restaurants, Roquefort was the cheese of choice for the dressing, but I prefer to splurge on real Stilton, imported from one of the three counties in the United Kingdom permitted to make regulation Stilton. It's a heady blue, with deep, true flavor. And because I lived and cooked in Leicestershire County in England, where they make Stilton, I have a soft spot for the cheese. You can, of course, use another blue if you prefer.

I realize some people might be put off by the iceberg lettuce and decide to substitute another, more trendy green, but for the authentic experience, try iceberg. I love good iceberg, especially the tender baby heads you can find at farmers' markets and some grocery stores. **SERVES 4**

THE WEDGE

8 slices thick-cut bacon

1 cup mayonnaise

1 cup crumbled Stilton or another blue cheese

¼ cup buttermilk

¼ cup sour cream

2 tablespoons freshly squeezed lemon juice

½ teaspoon Worcestershire sauce

4 small, densely packed heads baby iceberg lettuce, outer leaves removed, inner core quartered; or 1 large head iceberg, quartered, each quarter cut into 4 pieces

1 carrot, peeled and julienned

3 scallions, white and green parts, thinly sliced on the diagonal

2 cups diced cucumber

8 to 10 cherry tomatoes, halved or quartered

4 radishes, thinly sliced

Salt and freshly cracked black pepper

In a large skillet, cook the bacon over medium heat until just crispy. Drain on paper towels. When cool, break into small pieces.

In the bowl of a food processor fitted with the metal blade, mix together the mayonnaise, cheese, buttermilk, sour cream, lemon juice, and Worcestershire. Pulse until blended but with some chunks of cheese remaining.

Divide the wedges of lettuce among 4 chilled plates. Dress each wedge with the dressing and top with generous scatterings of the bacon, carrot, and scallions. Sprinkle the cucumbers, tomatoes, and radishes around the lettuce and season to taste with salt and cracked black pepper.

A Bar in the Garden

A FANTASTIC OFFSHOOT OF THE MICROBREWERY CRAZE has been a rise in the number of artisanal sodas—a crazy mix of organic root beers, cream sodas, ginger beers, and fruit colas. These boutique drinks have their own little section at the end of the aisle, beyond the name-brand sodas, in my local supermarket, and very likely in yours. We love to grab three or four six-packs of these thirst quenchers to offer friends as an alternative to alcohol. I throw them in a cooler for anyone to grab, and also set up a bar with a variety of rums (spiced, white, and dark) to mix with the sodas. This encourages guests to experiment with their own versions of the classic rum and cola. You could also decorate the bar with a collection of fruit garnishes, from the classic lime and lemon to pineapple chunks and star fruit, for the risk takers in the crowd!

Is this guy serious? Does he really think anyone wants to make something called "garbage salad"? If you are from Chicago, you know the answer is a resounding "Yes!" This salad is similar to a chopped salad, but with more protein than that venerable American offering, in the form of salumi and cheese—not unlike antipasti. I make this at home all the time with whatever veggies, salumi, and cheese we have in the house and the boys scarf it right up. The work is in the prepping—chopping, trimming, slicing—but once that's done (and it can be done a little ahead of time), it's just a matter of pitching everything into a big bowl and tossing with dressing. Use as many of the ingredients here as you can, or add your own. My "garbage" may not be your "garbage"! **SERVES 4**

CHICAGO-STYLE GARBAGE SALAD

½ head iceberg lettuce, chopped

1 head romaine lettuce, chopped

1 cup diced cucumber

1 cup thinly sliced radishes

1 roasted red bell pepper, seeded and julienned

1 roasted yellow bell pepper, seeded and julienned

1 rib celery, thinly sliced

1 cup cherry tomatoes, halved or quartered

½ red onion, thinly sliced

3 ounces provolone cheese, thinly sliced into julienne

3 ounces salumi (such as finocchiona, Calabrese, or sopressata), thinly sliced and julienned

1 cup garbanzo or chi chi beans

½ cup pitted kalamata olives

4 pepperoncini or banana peppers

2 cups Garlic Croutons (page 58)

¼ cup grated Parmigiano-Reggiano cheese

1 cup Tramonto's House Dressing (page 190)

2 tablespoons chopped fresh flat-leaf parsley

Kosher salt and cracked fresh black pepper

Extra-virgin olive oil, for drizzling

In a large mixing bowl, mix together the iceberg and romaine lettuce, cucumber, radishes, red and yellow roasted peppers, celery, tomatoes, and onion. Add the provolone and salumi and toss to mix. Add the beans, olives, pepperoncini, croutons, and half of the Parmesan and toss again.

Spoon the dressing over the salad and toss to coat. Sprinkle with the remaining Parmesan, the parsley, salt, pepper, and a drizzle of olive oil. Serve immediately.

Warm, slightly wilted spinach tossed with a mild vinegary dressing, crispy pancetta, and creamy goat cheese . . . just thinking about it makes my mouth water. This is so easy to make at home, although you do have to make the dressing just before serving. As with most simple preparations, details count: Use tender young spinach from a farmers' market if you can, pancetta from a good Italian deli, and artisanal goat cheese. Because I am a junkie for texture, the pecans do it for me here. Finally, a word about pancetta: It's sometimes called Italian bacon because it's cured, although not smoked. It is heavily seasoned with black pepper and not quite as salty as bacon. Need I add that it is one of my favorites? **SERVES 4**

WARM SPINACH SALAD WITH PANCETTA, GOAT CHEESE, AND SPICED PECANS

6 cups baby spinach, picked over to remove any stems

¼ pound fresh goat cheese, crumbled

Spiced Pecans (recipe follows)

¼ cup extra-virgin olive oil

6 ounces pancetta, cut into ½-inch dice

2 cloves garlic, thinly sliced

3 ounces good-quality apple cider vinegar

Kosher salt and freshly cracked black pepper

In a large salad bowl, toss the spinach with the goat cheese and pecans.

In a skillet or sauté pan, heat the olive oil over medium heat. When hot, sauté the pancetta for about 10 minutes, or until golden brown and crispy. Lift the pancetta from the pan, leaving the fat behind, and set aside on a plate.

Add the garlic to the pan and cook for 15 to 30 seconds, until browned. Watch it carefully because it will cook very quickly in the hot fat. Add the vinegar and cook, stirring, for about 1 minute. Return the pancetta to the pan.

Pour the dressing over the spinach salad, tossing well until the leaves are coated and the cheese begins to melt and become creamy. Season to taste with salt and pepper. Serve immediately.

SPICED PECANS
MAKES ABOUT 2 CUPS

1 tablespoon light brown sugar

¼ teaspoon cayenne

¼ teaspoon ground cumin

2 teaspoons olive oil

2 cups pecan halves

Preheat the oven to 350°F. In a mixing bowl, mix together the brown sugar, cayenne, and cumin. Add the oil and mix thoroughly. Add the pecans and toss until thoroughly coated.

Spread the pecans out on a baking sheet. Bake for 8 to 10 minutes, then stir once. Continue baking for 7 to 10 minutes longer, until the nuts are toasty, browned, and aromatic. Watch carefully to make sure they do not burn. Set aside to cool.

The pecans can be made up to 1 day ahead and kept in an airtight container.

Salad Greens

WHEN YOU MAKE A GREEN SALAD, START WITH CLEAN, CRISP GREENS. Shortly before you toss the salad, rinse the greens gently—even those in packages labeled "pre-washed"—in cool water (you might even want to rinse them twice). Drain them and dry with paper towels or in a salad spinner. Make sure the greens are dry before you dress them. Soggy leaves mean sodden salads.

Don't be shy about trying all different kinds of greens, from the familiar heads of iceberg, romaine, and red-leaf lettuces to the more unusual mâche, watercress, radicchio, and mesclun mixes. I like to pick herbs from my garden or buy bunches from the farmers' market in the summertime and toss good handfuls of their aromatic leaves in salad for explosions of flavor.

This classic bread and tomato salad, so beloved in Italy, is fantastic with roast chicken and just about any grilled meat—especially in the summer when vegetables and herbs are at their very best. You can also serve it as a first course or a light lunch. Whichever you choose, try to find great tomatoes for the salad.

SERVES 4

PANZANELLA SALAD

VINAIGRETTE

½ cup extra-virgin olive oil

3 tablespoons sherry vinegar

1 teaspoon finely minced garlic

½ teaspoon Dijon mustard

Kosher salt and freshly ground black pepper

SALAD

1 small ciabatta or rustic sourdough loaf

3 tablespoons olive oil

Kosher salt

2 large, ripe tomatoes (preferably heirloom, local, or organic), cored and cut into 1-inch cubes

1 seedless cucumber, peeled and sliced into ½-inch-thick rounds

1 red bell pepper, seeded and thinly sliced

1 yellow bell pepper, seeded and thinly sliced

½ red onion, thinly sliced

20 large fresh basil leaves, roughly torn

2 tablespoons drained capers

Freshly ground black pepper

To make the vinaigrette: In a small bowl, whisk together the olive oil, vinegar, garlic, and mustard. Season to taste with salt and pepper. Whisk well before using.

To make the salad: Tear or cut the bread into 1-inch cubes. You should have about 4 cups of bread cubes.

In a large sauté pan, heat the olive oil over low heat and when hot, add the bread. Season well with salt and cook over low to medium-low heat, tossing frequently, for about 10 minutes, or until nicely browned. Add more oil as needed.

In a large bowl, mix together the tomatoes, cucumber, peppers, onion, basil, and capers. Add the bread cubes and toss with the vinaigrette. Season liberally with salt and pepper and serve immediately.

Rum Runner Punch

A PUNCH BOWL IS A LOST TRADITION AT BACKYARD GET-TOGETHERS, so I say it's time to revive the happy custom. To begin, freeze fruit juices in various ice molds (or any appropriate bowl or container) to keep the punch chilly. This way, as the ice melts it adds flavor to the punch, rather than watering it down. Don't worry about diluting the alcohol; this recipe calls for ½ ounce of dark rum to be floated on top of each drink, so you won't notice the slightly watered-down alcohol. This punch packs a punch!

RUM RUNNER PUNCH
SERVES 1

1 ladleful Punch (recipe follows)

½ ounce (1 tablespoon) dark rum

Slice of pineapple, for garnish

Maraschino cherry, for garnish

Fill a rocks glass with ice. Ladle enough punch into the glass to fill it, but leave enough room to top it off with rum. Pour the rum into the glass so that it floats on the top. Garnish the glass with the pineapple and a cherry.

THE PUNCH
SERVES 20

2 cups Jamaican white rum

2 cups fresh pineapple juice

2 cups freshly squeezed orange juice

1 cup freshly squeezed lime juice

1 cup grenadine

1 cup banana liqueur

2 dashes of freshly ground nutmeg

Juice ice cubes

In a large punch bowl, combine the rum, pineapple juice, orange juice, lime juice, grenadine, and banana liqueur. Season with the nutmeg.

When you're in the mood for a main-course salad, try this one on for size. A perfect fit, I am sure. If you want a side salad, leave off the steak and enjoy the classic Caesar salad—or add grilled chicken, shrimp, or salmon for an entirely different dish. I prefer crispy romaine hearts—the inner leaves of the large heads—rather than the darker, outer leaves, but both work well. When you make the salad with steak, be sure to pepper the meat generously and get a nice char on it as it grills. Just about any cut of steak works with Caesar salad, but my favorites are skirt steak, filet, and sirloin. Cut the meat across the grain and enjoy a feast of cheesy, garlicky, meaty, peppery, lemony flavors. If you really don't like anchovies, you can forget about them, but they add such depth I hope you don't. I use white anchovies, called *boquerones* all across Spain and pretty easy to find on this side of the Atlantic, too. **SERVES 4**

GRILLED STEAK CAESAR SALAD

STEAK AND MARINADE

1 cup olive oil

½ cup white wine vinegar

½ red onion, diced

½ cup finely chopped cilantro

½ cup finely chopped
fresh flat-leaf parsley

6 cloves garlic, crushed

2 jalapeño peppers, coarsely chopped

1 tablespoon kosher salt

1½ teaspoons toasted
fennel seeds, crushed

1 teaspoon cracked fresh black pepper

½ teaspoon cayenne

4 steaks (such as skirt, filet, or
sirloin), 6 to 8 ounces each

DRESSING

1½ cups grated Parmigiano-
Reggiano cheese

2 large eggs

6 white anchovy fillets,
drained and chopped

3 cloves garlic, minced

Juice of 2 lemons

1 tablespoon red wine vinegar

1 teaspoon Dijon mustard

1 teaspoon Worcestershire sauce

⅔ cup extra-virgin olive oil

To marinate the steaks: In the bowl of a food processor fitted with a metal blade, mix together the olive oil, vinegar, onion, cilantro, parsley, garlic, jalapeños, salt, fennel seeds, black pepper, and cayenne and process until smooth. Reserve 3 tablespoons for later use.

Put the steaks in a large, shallow glass or ceramic dish or pan, cover with the marinade, and turn to coat. Cover and refrigerate for at least 2 hours or up to 8 hours.

Prepare a clean, well-oiled charcoal or gas grill so that the coals or heat element are medium hot. Or, heat the broiler.

Meanwhile, make the dressing: In the bowl of a food processor fitted with the metal blade, mix together the Parmesan, eggs, anchovies, garlic, lemon juice, vinegar, mustard, and Worcestershire. Process for about 30 seconds. With the food processor running, slowly drizzle the olive oil through the feed tube until the sauce is emulsified. Use right away or transfer to a lidded glass jar and refrigerate until ready to use.

To grill the steaks: Remove the steaks from the marinade and let the excess drip off into the pan. Discard the marinade. Grill the steaks, turning once, for a total of 10 to 15 minutes for medium rare, or to the degree of doneness you prefer. The cooking time will depend on the thickness of the steak. (For more on cooking steak, see page 121.) Let the steaks rest on a cutting board for about 10 minutes before slicing.

To make the salad: Fill a deep skillet or saucepan about halfway with water and bring to a simmer over medium-high heat. Cook the haricots verts for about 2 minutes, or just until blanched and bright green. Drain, plunge into a bowl of ice and water, and drain again.

In a mixing bowl, toss the haricots verts, croutons, romaine, tomatoes, and anchovies with the dressing, being sure to coat the lettuce evenly.

Slice the steaks against the grain and on the diagonal to ensure tenderness.

SALAD

2 cups halved haricots verts

Garlic Croutons (recipe follows)

3 romaine hearts, cut
into 2-inch pieces

1 cup halved cherry tomatoes

4 white anchovy fillets,
drained and chopped

5 to 6 fresh basil leaves, torn

Cracked fresh black pepper

Extra-virgin olive oil, for drizzling

Divide the salad evenly among 4 plates or bowls and top with the sliced steak. Drizzle each serving with the 3 tablespoons reserved marinade and sprinkle with the basil and pepper. Drizzle olive oil over the steaks and serve.

GARLIC CROUTONS
MAKES ABOUT 4 CUPS

1½ cups olive oil

½ cup freshly grated Parmigiano-Reggiano cheese

½ clove garlic, minced

2 tablespoons chopped fresh thyme

Leaves from 6-inch sprig
rosemary, chopped

Kosher salt and freshly
ground black pepper

1½-pound loaf focaccia or any crusty
bread, cut into ½-inch cubes

Preheat the oven to 350ºF.

In a mixing bowl, stir together the olive oil, Parmesan, and garlic. Add the thyme and rosemary and season to taste with salt and pepper.

Add the bread cubes and toss gently to coat. Spread the bread cubes in a baking dish, leaving a little space between the cubes. Bake, stirring several times to insure even browning, for 12 to 15 minutes, until golden brown and crisp.

Transfer the croutons to a cool plate or pan and let cool to room temperature. Store in a tightly lidded container at room temperature for up 2 weeks.

Basil Margarita

THE MARGARITA HAS A UNIQUE BLEND OF INGREDIENTS that makes the thirst quencher satisfying on multiple levels. The intensity of the salt on the rim of the glass, followed by the stark contrast of the sweet lime and triple sec leads to the smoky finish of the *reposado* ("rested," or aged) tequila. This progression of flavors pleases whatever you crave. Fooling with perfection can seem harebrained, but infusing the simple syrup with basil adds just another level of refreshment. The basil offers a savory component that takes the edge off the sweetness before the misty tequila takes over.

BASIL MARGARITA
SERVES 1

2 lime wedges

Kosher or other large-grain salt

1½ ounces (3 tablespoons) reposado tequila

1 ounce (2 tablespoons) freshly
squeezed lime juice

½ ounce (1 tablespoon) triple sec

½ ounce (1 tablespoon) Basil
Simple Syrup (recipe follows)

Ice

Basil tops or flowers (optional)

Rub a margarita glass with a lime wedge. Spread the salt in a saucer and roll the outer moistened rim of the glass in the salt (this technique keeps the salt on the *outside* of the glass, so that it does not salt the cocktail).

In a cocktail shaker, combine the tequila, lime juice, triple sec, and simple syrup. Fill the shaker with ice and shake briskly 9 or 10 times. Fill the prepared glass with ice and then strain the cocktail over the ice. Garnish with a lime wedge and basil top or flower.

BASIL SIMPLE SYRUP
MAKES ABOUT 1 CUP

1 cup water

1 cup sugar

1 bunch fresh basil (20 to 25 leaves)

In a saucepan, mix together the water and sugar and heat over medium heat. Let the syrup cook until the sugar dissolves and the syrup is clear, which will be about the time the syrup starts to bubble. Remove the pan from the heat.

Add the basil to the syrup, cover, and let sit for about 1 minute. Strain through a fine-mesh sieve and discard the basil. Refrigerate the syrup in a covered container for up to 1 week.

When it comes to creating an out-of-the-ordinary atmosphere at home, I often rely on my memories from a number of years ago when I lived in Britain and often traveled through France. This small salad is one of my all-time favorites, a crisp mixture of frisée and endive mingled with crunchy bacon and topped with a poached egg. In its hometown of Lyon, it's served in bistros—or *bouchons,* as the casual eateries found in that charming French city are called. I think it makes perfect sense before a steak dinner. Seriously: Who doesn't like steak and eggs? **SERVES 4**

LYONNAISE SALAD

½ pound bacon, cut into thin strips

2 cups haricots verts

2 quarts water

¼ cup white vinegar

2 heads frisée or curly endive

2 heads Belgian endive, chopped

1 cup shredded Gruyère cheese, plus additional for garnish

Sherry Vinaigrette (page 192)

Garlic Croutons (page 58)

2 tablespoons chopped fresh flat-leaf parsley

1 tablespoon chopped fresh tarragon

Kosher salt and freshly cracked black pepper

4 large eggs

In a skillet, cook the bacon over medium heat for 5 to 7 minutes, until golden brown. Drain on paper towels.

In a deep skillet filled about halfway with boiling, salted water set over medium-high heat, blanch the haricots verts for about 3 minutes. Plunge them into a bowl filled with cold water and ice and drain.

In a large saucepan, bring the water and vinegar to a gentle boil over medium-high heat.

Meanwhile, in a mixing bowl, toss together the bacon, haricots verts, frisée, Belgian endive, Gruyère, vinaigrette, croutons, parsley, and tarragon. Season to taste with salt and pepper and divide evenly among 4 chilled plates.

One at a time, break the eggs into a large spoon or small bowl and slip gently into the gently boiling liquid. After about 3 minutes, the whites should be cooked through and the yolks still soft. Using a slotted spoon, lift each egg from the poaching liquid and center on top of a salad. Serve immediately, garnished with more Gruyère.

Dressing a Salad

WHEN YOU DRESS THE SALAD, use only enough dressing to moisten the greens and other ingredients with a few tosses. Too much dressing causes the greens to wilt and the salad will taste too heavily of the dressing and not enough of all the delicious tastes and textures of the fresh ingredients.

I usually mix up a vinaigrette just before using it, but there are times when it makes sense to double or triple the amount and keep the dressing in a lidded jar in the refrigerator. This way, you can shake the jar and dress a midweek salad in a flash.

I love that this crab salad is dressed with olive oil and lemon juice, rather than the more expected mayonnaise. While there are times I love the creaminess of mayo, the undiluted tang and lightness of a vinaigrette-tossed salad is just right to precede a steak dinner with all the trimmings. For texture, I toss in apple, celery, and fennel, then for contrast serve it over tender mesclun greens.

Peekytoe crab has gotten a lot of attention in recent years. It's an extraordinarily sweet, succulent crab from Maine, where the cold Atlantic waters contribute to the incredible flavor of both crab and lobster. There are conflicting stories about where the name comes from: Some say "peekytoe" comes from "picked toe," the name Mainers have long used for this sand crab (in Maine "picked" means sharp). Because "picked" is pronounced as two syllables (*pick-ed*) by Mainers, the name morphed into "peekytoe." Others claim "peekytoe" refers to the configuration of the crabs' legs, which are crooked like a picket fence. Regardless of which theory you subscribe to, the crabmeat is rich, pink, and succulent. You can substitute another kind of crabmeat for peekytoe, as long as it's fresh and unpasteurized. **SERVES 4**

PEEKYTOE CRAB SALAD WITH APPLE, FENNEL, AND CELERY

1 pound peekytoe crabmeat or other high-quality crabmeat

1 cup extra-virgin olive oil

1 tablespoon grated lemon zest

¼ cup freshly squeezed lemon juice

Kosher salt and freshly cracked black pepper

1 Fuji apple or other sweet apple, peeled, cored, and thinly sliced (use a mandoline, if you have one)

2 ribs celery, thinly sliced (use a mandoline, if you have one)

1 bulb fennel, thinly sliced (use a mandoline, if you have one)

1 tablespoon chopped fresh tarragon

1 tablespoon thinly sliced scallion

2 cups mesclun greens

Pick through the crabmeat to remove any remaining shell.

In a mixing bowl, whisk together the olive oil and the lemon zest and juice and season to taste with salt and pepper.

Add the crabmeat and toss gently. Add the apple, celery, fennel, tarragon, and scallion and toss gently until well coated.

Divide the mesclun greens evenly among 4 chilled plates and top each bed with the crab salad. Spoon any dressing in the bottom of the bowl over the crab salad.

Given my affection for Chicago-Style Garbage Salad (page 51), it's no surprise I would include another version of chopped salad in the book, one that Chicagoans like equally well. Adding seafood to a classic chopped salad turns a simple dish into a glorious creation that can be a small appetizer or, in larger amounts, a main course. I like to create an even more substantial meal by adding mussels. On the other hand, you can omit the seafood and make this a far less complicated, yet equally satisfying, salad.

The Gribiche Sauce, a traditional French mayonnaise-based sauce, is perfect here. If you can't find cornichons (crisp, tangy pickles made from tiny gherkin cucumbers), substitute another sort of gherkin. **SERVES 4**

CHOPPED SEAFOOD SALAD

RED WINE VINAIGRETTE

2 tablespoons red wine vinegar

1 teaspoon Dijon mustard

¼ cup extra-virgin olive oil

Kosher salt and freshly cracked black pepper

SEAFOOD SALAD

2 tablespoons extra-virgin olive oil

1 clove garlic, minced

12 mussels, scrubbed clean

Kosher salt and freshly ground black pepper

¼ cup dry white wine

4 cooked large shrimp, cut into large dice

¼ pound jumbo lump crabmeat

½ cup sliced hearts of palm

½ cup ½-inch-diced seedless cucumber

1 avocado, cut into ½-inch dice

1 tablespoon chopped fresh tarragon

1 tablespoon chopped fresh flat-leaf parsley

½ cup Gribiche Sauce (page 192)

Juice of 1 lemon

2 hard-cooked eggs, chopped

1 cup red and yellow cherry tomatoes, halved or quartered

¼ cup chopped scallions

¼ cup finely diced celery

¼ cup cooked sweet corn kernels

1 head Bibb lettuce, chopped into ½-inch pieces

To make the vinaigrette: Whisk the vinegar with the mustard and then whisk in the olive oil until smooth and emulsified. Season to taste with salt and pepper and set aside.

To make the salad: In a large sauté pan, heat the olive oil over medium heat and cook the garlic for 30 or 40 seconds, until softened. Add the mussels and season with salt and pepper. Toss gently to coat with the oil and garlic. Add the wine, cover, and cook for about 5 minutes, or until the mussels open. Discard any that do not open. Set the pan aside to allow the mussels to cool.

In a mixing bowl, toss the shrimp with the crabmeat, hearts of palm, cucumber, avocado, tarragon, and parsley. Add the Gribiche Sauce and lemon juice. Add the chopped hard-cooked eggs, tomatoes, scallions, celery, and corn and mix gently. Season to taste with salt and pepper.

Sprinkle the vinaigrette over the seafood salad and toss gently.

Divide the lettuce among 4 plates. Spoon the seafood salad on the lettuce and garnish each plate with 3 mussels.

The beauty of this salad is its simplicity—and when you are preparing a meal at home that's what you want. I have always been especially fond of the cool, clean flavor of cucumbers and so was excited to try a salad using Japanese mini cukes. Eileen and the kids agreed it was one of the best accompaniments to grilled steak, chops, and fish. I have a Japanese mandoline, which makes slicing the cucumbers into paper-thin slices a breeze. If you don't have one, use a very sharp knife and do the best you can.

Japanese cucumbers are similar to slender English cucumbers in that they do not require peeling and have very few, if any, seeds. The difference is that Japanese cukes have bumps, while English cucumbers are smooth. For this salad, I like to use the minis, which often are sold in packs of eight and look something like Kirbys, or pickling cukes. **SERVES 4**

CUCUMBER SALAD

6 Japanese mini cucumbers or other small, seedless cucumbers

1 cup cooled Simple Syrup (page 189)

½ cup rice wine vinegar

1 teaspoon sesame oil

1 teaspoon olive oil

1 tablespoon toasted white sesame seeds

1 tablespoon black sesame seeds

Grated lemon zest, for garnish

Slice the cucumbers on a mandoline into very thin rounds. Transfer to a glass or ceramic bowl.

Whisk together the simple syrup, rice vinegar, sesame oil, and olive oil. Pour over the cucumbers, mix well, and refrigerate for at least 1 hour or up to 2 hours.

Divide the cucumbers and soaking liquid evenly among 4 bowls. Sprinkle with the white and black sesame seeds and mix well. Garnish with lemon zest and serve at once.

When I decided to try my hand at a peanut dipping sauce, I discovered the mixture was also great as a noodle sauce and even a vinaigrette. And so, here is my version of a favorite cold noodle salad. Although the sauce has sesame oil, I don't rely on sesame elsewhere, but instead use ground peanuts for a lot of the great flavor, as well as soy sauce that I doctor to make it taste even better. All in all, a great cold starter salad or accompaniment to grilled meats. My kids love this one! **SERVES 4**

PEANUT NOODLE SALAD

1 pound Chinese egg noodles

¾ cup Peanut Salad Dressing
(recipe follows)

½ cup hot brewed Chinese black tea

¼ cup chopped peanuts

1 cup chopped cucumber

1 cup finely sliced red bell pepper

1 red jalapeño pepper or
another mildly spicy pepper,
seeded and thinly sliced

2 scallions, thinly sliced

1 tablespoon sesame seeds

8 lime wedges

Fill a large saucepan about two-thirds with water and bring to a boil over high heat. Add the noodles and cook according to the package directions. Drain.

In a large mixing bowl, whisk the peanut dressing with the hot tea. Add the hot noodles and toss to mix well.

Serve garnished with peanuts, cucumber, red pepper, jalapeño, scallions, sesame seeds, and lime wedges.

PEANUT SALAD DRESSING
MAKES ABOUT 2½ CUPS

1 cup raw unsalted peanuts

¼ cup peanut oil

½ cup sugar

6 tablespoons rice vinegar

5 tablespoons Rick's Soy Sauce (page 193), or
other high-quality soy sauce

1-inch knob fresh ginger, peeled and chopped

1 clove garlic, minced

1 small red chile pepper, seeded and coarsely chopped

½ teaspoon dried red chili flakes

½ teaspoon ground toasted Szechuan pepper

Kosher salt

6 tablespoons sesame oil

1 tablespoon chili oil

In the bowl of a food processor fitted with the metal blade, process the peanuts until finely ground. Add the peanut oil and pulse to moisten slightly. Add the sugar, vinegar, soy sauce, ginger, garlic, chile pepper, chili flakes, Szechuan pepper, and salt to taste and process until smooth. Transfer to a bowl.

Stir the sesame oil and chili oil into the sauce. Use immediately or cover and refrigerate for up to 4 days. Use for other salads, even tossed green salads, and for other pasta salads.

Soups are always part of a steakhouse menu, and so I could not imagine writing a book about steak without including them. I borrowed some steakhouse standards such as onion soup and clam chowder and put my own spin on them. I selected others to reflect the part of the country where I live. We are close to Wisconsin and so a cheese soup was appropriate, and because we have wonderful local corn and squash, I include a corn bisque and a pumpkin soup. Gazpacho is a warm-weather soup I could eat all year long, but because I figured your grill probably would already be fired up, I didn't think tossing a few shrimp on it to add to the soup would be a hassle. Soups are great starters but also serve as light meals.

Sandwiches clearly are not first courses. They are meals in and of themselves and all my life I have been intrigued and nourished by them. I started my professional cooking career at Wendy's when still a teenager and came away from the experience truly loving hamburgers. I still do and the three boys and I eat them often during the week. Sandwiches are great quick meals, and between sports, music lessons, and schoolwork, our household—like yours, I am sure—is pretty busy during the week. Of course, a great sandwich, such as the Chicago Italian Beef Sandwich or the Tempura Soft-Shell Crab Sandwich, makes a terrific weekend lunch, too.

Making soups and sandwiches is long and slow or production cooking. For these tasks I like the bluesy tones of:
BONNIE RAITT | BUDDY GUY | STEVIE RAY VAUGHAN | ERIC CLAPTON

SOUPS AND SANDWICHES

As much as crocus and daffodils, asparagus is a harbinger of spring. And when I first see tender young stalks in the market, I can't wait to make this light, pretty soup and celebrate the end of winter. This is also the time of year when the Chicago farmers' market reopens, much to my delight! If you live in a region where ramps are available, use them in place of the leeks; their mild onion and garlic notes add another layer of flavor to the soup. **SERVES 4**

CHILLED ASPARAGUS SOUP

2 leeks

2 Yukon Gold potatoes, peeled and roughly chopped

3 tablespoons unsalted butter

1 clove garlic, minced

Kosher salt and freshly cracked black pepper

3 cups vegetable stock, preferably homemade

2 bunches fresh asparagus, bottoms snapped off, stalks cut into ½-inch-long pieces

1 cup half-and-half

Juice of 1 lemon

¼ cup extra-virgin olive oil

¼ cup shaved Parmigiano-Reggiano cheese

Trim and discard the root ends and dark green leaves from the leeks. Cut the leeks in half lengthwise and slice into half-moons. Submerge in a bowl of ice-cold water. Let the leeks soak for a few minutes and separate the layers to remove any dirt or sand.

In a separate bowl of ice-cold water, submerge the chopped potatoes.

In a medium-sized stockpot, melt the butter over medium heat and cook the garlic for 1 to 2 minutes, until softened. Drain the leeks and potatoes and add to the pot. Season lightly with salt and pepper and cook for about 1 minute.

Add the vegetable stock to the pot, bring to a simmer, and simmer for about 30 minutes.

Add the asparagus and simmer for about 10 minutes, or until tender when pierced with a small, sharp knife.

In a blender, purée the hot soup in batches until very smooth. As each batch is puréed, pour it into a glass or rigid plastic container. Cover the soup and refrigerate until chilled, at least 2 hours, or up to 6 hours.

When cold, stir in the half-and-half and lemon juice and season to taste with salt and pepper.

Serve the soup in chilled bowls. Drizzle each serving with olive oil and sprinkle with the shaved Parmesan.

This soup needs long, slow cooking to ensure that the beef becomes tender. During the hours the soup simmers on the stove, the house fills up with such rich, inviting aromas that anyone who walks in the door feels immediately welcome. I often make this a day or two ahead of time and then heat it up and settle back to enjoy the experience. The robust, full-bodied soup belongs in a steakhouse, and so as far as I am concerned belongs at home, too—particularly on a brisk fall or winter weekend, accompanied by a big glass of red and some crusty bread. **SERVES 4 TO 6**

BEEF AND BARLEY SOUP

1 pound boneless beef short ribs, cut into 1-inch cubes

Kosher salt and freshly ground black pepper

2 tablespoons extra-virgin olive oil

1 yellow onion, diced

2 carrots, peeled and diced

2 ribs celery, diced

2 cloves garlic, chopped

6 cups beef stock, preferably homemade (page 187)

⅓ cup pearl barley

½ teaspoon fresh thyme leaves

½ pound cremini mushrooms, quartered

2 tablespoons unsalted butter

3 tablespoons chopped fresh flat-leaf parsley

4 to 6 teaspoons sour cream

Season the beef with salt and pepper. Heat a heavy-bottomed stockpot over high heat. When hot, add the olive oil. Cook the meat in the oil, turning with a wooden spoon, until browned on all sides. Do this in batches so that you don't crowd the pot and the pot does not lose too much heat from trying to cook too much at one time. Lift the meat from the pot as it is browned and set aside on a plate.

Add the onion, carrots, celery, and garlic to the pot and cook over low heat, stirring, for about 15 minutes, or until softened.

Return the beef and any accumulated juices on the plate to the pot. Add the stock, cover, and bring to a simmer over medium heat. Partially cover and simmer the soup for 2½ to 3 hours, until the meat is extremely tender. Adjust the heat up or down to maintain the simmer.

Add the barley and thyme and simmer, uncovered, for about 1 hour longer, or until the barley is tender. Adjust the heat up or down to maintain the simmer.

Meanwhile, season the mushrooms with salt and pepper. Heat a sauté pan over medium-high heat and melt 1 tablespoon of the butter. Sauté the mushrooms just until golden brown.

Add the mushrooms to the soup and simmer for 15 to 20 minutes. Stir in 1½ tablespoons of the parsley and season to taste with salt and pepper. Let the soup cool a little. Transfer to the refrigerator and chill until cold, at least 2 hours or up to 24 hours. This soup is best made a day ahead of time.

To serve, reheat the soup over medium heat. If the barley has absorbed too much of the broth, add more broth or water. Stir in the remaining 1 tablespoon butter. Ladle the soup into bowls and garnish each serving with sour cream and the remaining parsley.

I make a lot of friends with this soup during the long, cold Chicago winters. It's a warm, filling, and welcoming choice when you plan to stay home and watch a Bears game. While it's a great starter, it can also be a main course—we like it for lunch in our house. Living close to Wisconsin, I have access to amazing Cheddar cheeses and usually choose those that have been aged for three or four years. Use one that suits your taste and that you know will taste incredible with bacon. And when it comes to the beer, reach for a Guinness if you can; but if not, any dark, boldly flavored stout will do well. If you don't mind going to the trouble, do as I often do and fire up the grill—even on the coldest Chicago day—and grill some great bakery bread instead of making croutons. Very little trouble, actually, for a big payoff. **SERVES 4**

CHEDDAR AND GUINNESS SOUP WITH BACON AND CROUTONS

1 tablespoon extra-virgin olive oil

1 tablespoon minced garlic

½ cup unsalted butter

½ yellow onion, roughly chopped

2 ribs celery, minced

¼ cup all-purpose flour

½ cup Guinness beer or another stout, plus more for drinking

6 cups chicken stock, preferably homemade (page 188)

2 cups heavy cream

1 tablespoon dry mustard

1 pound shredded sharp Cheddar cheese

1½ teaspoons Worcestershire sauce

8 slices thick-cut bacon, chopped and cooked until crisp

2 cups Garlic Croutons (page 58)

In a large saucepan, heat the oil over medium heat and sauté the garlic for 2 to 3 minutes, taking great care not to let it burn. Add the butter and when it melts, stir in the onion and celery and cook for about 10 minutes, or until the onion is translucent. Sprinkle the flour over the vegetables, stir well, and cook for 3 to 4 minutes.

Add the beer and bring to a simmer. Scrape up any browned bits sticking to the bottom of the pan with a wooden spoon and continue to cook for about 2 minutes.

Add the stock, cream, and dry mustard and bring to a simmer, stirring occasionally to insure a smooth soup. When the soup is smooth and simmering steadily, whisk in the cheese until melted. Stir in the Worcestershire.

Ladle the soup into 4 soup bowls and garnish with the bacon and croutons. Serve with cold Guinness.

Beer

WHEN IT COMES TO BEER, the rule of thumb is "drink what you like." There is no doubt that the icy cold refreshment of beer goes hand in hand with grilled foods. A pilsner is the most popular and forgiving style of beer and can accompany a wide range of flavors. Seafood is especially nice opposite the floral complexity of a well-hopped beer—look for an India pale ale (IPA). Spicy foods work well with wheat beers that typically have a citrusy sweetness to their finish. Braised food is perfect paired with rich and dark ales and stouts.

Beer is less of a financial commitment than most wines or liquors, so there's never a reason not to try something new. Even at major chain grocery stores, the beer selection is huge, and is even more mind boggling and exciting at specialty liquor stores. If you happen to be in one of those specialty stores, tell an employee what kind of beer you like. He or she will show you a wide selection of similar options (and believe me, will love making suggestions).

The most important ingredients in this soup are patience and faith. Patience because the soup needs long, slow cooking; faith because you have to believe all those onions really will cook down. You just need patience! (You can see where this line of reasoning is going, right?) While you can make onion soup with just about any kind of onion—even the sharpest sweeten with long, slow cooking—I like sweet onions such as Vidalia. When they cook, their natural sweetness is enhanced, and then they are mixed with beef stock and a little dry sherry and topped with a cheesy, bready crust—wow! Simple and hearty and elegant, all at the same time. **SERVES 4**

VIDALIA ONION **SOUP**

6 pounds Vidalia or other sweet onions (about 6 large onions)

6 tablespoons unsalted butter

Kosher salt

¼ cup dry sherry

2 quarts light beef stock, preferably homemade (page 187)

Freshly ground black pepper

4 slices baguette, each about ½ inch thick

2 tablespoons extra-virgin olive oil

1 large clove garlic

2 cups shredded Gruyère cheese

1 tablespoon grated Parmigiano-Reggiano cheese

1 tablespoon chopped fresh flat-leaf parsley

Peel and remove the top and bottom of the onions. Cut the onions into julienne, or very thin strips.

In a large stockpot or Dutch oven, melt the butter over low heat. Add the onions and a pinch of salt. Let the onions cook over very low heat, stirring often with a wooden spoon and scraping any bits stuck to the bottom of the pot, for about 4 hours, until a deep, rich brown.

Add the sherry and stir with the wooden spoon to deglaze. Raise the heat to medium and cook for 4 to 5 minutes, until the sherry reduces by half. Add the beef stock and bring to a simmer over medium heat. Taste, season with salt and pepper, and simmer for about 20 minutes to give the flavors time to blend. At this point, you can cool the soup and refrigerate it for up to 2 days. I think it tastes best if made ahead of time.

When you are ready to serve the soup, preheat the oven to 500°F. Brush the bread slices with olive oil and toast in the oven on one side for about 2 minutes, or until lightly browned. While still hot, rub each slice with the garlic clove. Do not turn off the oven.

Meanwhile, heat the soup over medium-high heat until boiling.

Ladle the soup into oven-safe bowls or classic onion soup crocks and top each with a slice of toasted baguette. Sprinkle evenly with the Gruyère. Put the bowls on a baking sheet and bake for 1 to 2 minutes, until the cheese is golden brown and bubbly.

Serve immediately, sprinkled with the Parmesan and parsley.

Most people know the difference between New England and Manhattan clam chowders: The former is milky, while the latter is made with a tomato-rich broth. Within New England itself—a very small region of the country comprised of six states—good-natured debates still rage about the relative merits of Boston chowder, Rhode Island chowder, and Maine chowder. Luckily, I live in Illinois and so can make chowder any way I like. This is one of our favorite soups: creamy, briny, and chock-full of clams and chunks of potatoes. A pretty straightforward rendition of an American classic. **SERVES 4 TO 6**

NEW ENGLAND CLAM CHOWDER

CLAM BROTH

12 to 15 cherrystone or quahog clams, scrubbed (about 4 pounds)

1 bay leaf

3 sprigs thyme

1 cup water

CHOWDER

6 tablespoons unsalted butter

6 slices bacon, chopped

1 onion, minced

2 ribs celery, minced

1 clove garlic, minced

1 teaspoon chopped fresh thyme

1 bay leaf

½ cup all-purpose flour

1 (32-ounce) bottle clam juice

3 Yukon Gold potatoes, cut into small dice

1 cup heavy cream

2 tablespoons chopped fresh flat-leaf parsley

Kosher salt and freshly ground black pepper

Minced scallion, for garnish

To make the broth: Put the clams in a large bowl and cover with cold water. Cover and refrigerate for at least 4 hours or up to 12 hours.

Lay the bay leaf and thyme sprigs on the bottom of a large, heavy saucepan and top with the clams. Add the water, cover the pan, and bring to a boil. Cook for about 5 minutes. Stir the clams, cover, and cook for about 5 minutes longer, or until the clams open. Discard any that do not open. Using a slotted spoon or tongs, remove the clams from the pan. Strain the cooking liquid through a double thickness of cheesecloth into a bowl. Repeat to insure that all sand is strained from the broth.

Set aside 4 to 6 nice-looking clams to use for garnish. Pull the meat from the rest of the clams and chop roughly. Transfer to a bowl and refrigerate until ready to use.

To make the chowder: In a heavy stockpot or Dutch oven, melt the butter over medium heat. Add the bacon and cook for about 5 minutes, or until golden brown and crispy. Lift the bacon from the pot and drain on paper towels. Leave the fat behind.

Add the onion, celery, and garlic to the bacon fat in the pot and cook for 4 to 5 minutes, until the onion is translucent. Add the thyme and bay leaf and cook for about 3 minutes longer, or until the flavors blend. Sprinkle the flour over the vegetables and stir to combine. Whisk in the reserved clam broth and bottled clam juice, taking care the vegetables don't clump together. Bring to a simmer over medium heat and cook for about 10 minutes.

Add the potatoes and cook for about 15 minutes, or until the potatoes are tender. Stir in the reserved clams and bacon, the cream, and parsley. Season the chowder to taste with salt and pepper. Be careful when adding the salt as the clams and bacon are quite salty. Discard the bay leaf.

Ladle the soup into 4 bowls and garnish each with a reserved clam and minced scallion.

I must have made a hundred different gazpachos during my career and never tire of the fresh, uncooked vegetable soup. When I decided to make a version I knew everyone in the household would like, I turned to perfectly ripe melons and tomatoes for the basis of the soup and then garnished it with grilled shrimp. What a perfect little appetizer before a grilled chicken or steak dinner! **SERVES 4**

MELON AND TOMATO GAZPACHO WITH GRILLED SHRIMP

1 pound medium shrimp, deveined with shells on (20 to 25 shrimp)

Extra-virgin olive oil

Kosher salt and freshly ground black pepper

2 ripe heirloom or other tomatoes, seeded and cut into large cubes

2 ripe red beefsteak tomatoes or 4 yellow tomatoes, cut into large cubes

2 ripe yellow beefsteak tomatoes, cut into large cubes

2 cucumbers, peeled, seeded, and cut into large cubes

1 small red onion, diced

1 rib celery, chopped

½ ripe cantaloupe, seeds removed, flesh scooped from rind and diced

½ ripe honeydew melon, seeds removed, flesh scooped from rind and diced

1 teaspoon minced jalapeño pepper

Juice of ½ lemon

1 tablespoon sherry vinegar

2 tablespoons chopped fresh chives

Pinch of smoked paprika

Sugar

1 red tomato, finely diced, for garnish

1 yellow tomato, finely diced, for garnish

Prepare a clean, well-oiled charcoal or gas grill so that the coals or heating element are at medium-high heat. Alternatively, you can use a stovetop grill. Soak 4 bamboo skewers in cool tap water for about 20 minutes. This will prevent them from charring.

In a mixing bowl, toss the shrimp with enough oil to coat lightly. Season with salt and pepper. Thread the shrimp equally on the skewers. Grill, turning once, for 2 to 3 minutes total, until the shrimp turn pink and are cooked through. Remove 4 shrimp from the skewers and set all the shrimp aside to cool.

In the bowl of a food processor fitted with the metal blade, mix the 3 types of cubed tomatoes with the cucumbers, onion, celery, cantaloupe and honeydew melons, and jalapeño and pulse until nearly smooth but with some chunks remaining.

Transfer the soup to a bowl and add the lemon juice and vinegar. Stir in 1 tablespoon of the chives and the paprika and stir well. Season to taste with salt and pepper and a little sugar, if needed. Cover the bowl and refrigerate for at least 1 hour or until well chilled.

Ladle the soup into chilled bowls. Chop the 4 reserved shrimp and sprinkle over the top of each bowl. Garnish each bowl with the diced red and yellow tomatoes, remaining 1 tablespoon chives, and a drizzle of olive oil. Serve, with a full skewer of shrimp next to or balanced on top of each bowl.

Muscat Wine

NO MATTER THE STYLE OF WINE MADE FROM THIS GRAPE, the exotic aromatics stand out; fruit blossom floral notes are the foundation for its syrupy apricot and lychee flavors. The dry styles, although hard to find, are certainly worth seeking out. The sweet styles vary from fortified to late-harvest. Moscato d'Asti, a sweeter version from Northwestern Italy and a favorite with summer lunch dishes, is a light sparkling wine. It has a relatively low alcohol content, which makes it good to serve alongside bold spicy flavors and a real hit with barbecued food as well. The vintage of the wine should be the year before the summer you are drinking it; this is not a wine for aging.

Because a bisque is defined as a creamy soup of puréed crustaceans or vegetables, I suppose this creamy corn soup topped with a luscious crab salad is the real thing! I puree the corn to provide creamy texture and garnish the soup with magnificent Alaskan king crabmeat. Illinois sweet corn is as good as any corn anywhere; I suggest you buy the freshest local corn you can from a farm stand or farmers' market. I especially like Silver Queen corn, which has small, white, super-sweet kernels. The crabmeat will be cooked when you buy the legs and just needs to be picked from the shells. This is a terrific soup to serve before just about any meal.

SERVES 4 TO 6

SWEET CORN BISQUE WITH ALASKAN KING CRAB

2 tablespoons unsalted butter

4 cups fresh corn kernels
(from about 8 ears)

1 cup coarsely chopped peeled carrot

1 cup coarsely chopped onion

1 cup coarsely chopped celery

2 tablespoons sugar

Kosher salt and freshly
ground black pepper

½ cup brandy

2 cloves garlic, crushed

Leaves from 2 sprigs thyme, chopped

Leaves from 2 sprigs
tarragon, chopped

1 bay leaf

3 cups vegetable stock,
preferably homemade

1 cup heavy cream

½ pound Alaskan king crabmeat
(1½ to 2 pounds whole crab legs)

1 avocado, chopped

1 tablespoon chopped cilantro

1 tablespoon fresh lime juice

1 tablespoon extra-virgin olive oil

In a large stockpot or Dutch oven, melt 1 tablespoon of the butter over low heat and add the corn, carrot, onion, celery, and sugar. Season to taste with salt and pepper and cook very slowly for about 30 minutes, or until the vegetables are soft.

Add the brandy and cook for about 2 minutes, deglazing the pan by scraping the bottom with a wooden spoon to release any browned bits. Add the garlic, thyme, tarragon, and bay leaf and cook for 2 minutes longer.

Add the vegetable stock, raise the heat to medium-high, and bring to a boil. Lower the heat so that the soup is at a low simmer and simmer for 30 to 45 minutes, until the flavors have blended. Adjust the heat up or down to maintain the gentle simmer.

Discard the bay leaf. Add the heavy cream and let the soup come to a low simmer. Cook for about 10 minutes longer, adjusting the heat to maintain the simmer.

In a blender, puree the soup in batches. As each batch is pureed, pour it through a sieve back into the pot or a bowl. Adjust the seasonings with salt and pepper.

Reheat the soup over low heat, stirring often to prevent sticking or scorching. Stir in the remaining 1 tablespoon butter until it is fully incorporated into the soup.

Make sure the crabmeat is cleaned of all bits of shell. In a mixing bowl, gently toss the crabmeat with the avocado, cilantro, lime juice, and olive oil and season to taste with salt and pepper.

Ladle the hot soup into bowls and garnish each serving with the crab mixture.

I can't think of a better soup to serve in the fall, and if you serve it in small pumpkins, all the better! But if you don't have the time or energy to scoop out six pumpkins, the soup tastes just as good in traditional bowls.

I am a devotee of foie gras and find its lusciousness adds a richness and depth to the soup you can't get otherwise. I have also made this with grilled shrimp in place of the foie gras with stunning results. When we took the photograph of this soup for the book, I garnished it with both green and toasted pumpkin seeds. **SERVES 6**

PUMPKIN SOUP WITH FOIE GRAS

1 (5-pound) ripe pumpkin or 3 (29-ounce) cans unseasoned pumpkin puree

Kosher salt and freshly ground black pepper

6 (1-pound) pumpkins, for serving bowls (optional)

1 tablespoon olive oil

1 Spanish onion, chopped

1½ teaspoons crushed fennel seed

Pumpkin cooking liquid, or 3 cups chicken stock, preferably homemade (page 188)

Juice of 1 orange

½ cup packed light brown sugar

½ cup maple syrup

1½ teaspoons ground allspice

1½ teaspoons ground cinnamon

½ teaspoon cayenne

1 bay leaf

1 cup heavy cream

¼ cup unsalted butter, diced

6 (1-ounce) portions foie gras, each about 1 inch thick (I like Hudson Valley foie gras), optional

Truffle oil, for drizzling

1 tablespoon chopped chives, for garnish

3 tablespoons toasted pumpkin seeds (see Note), for garnish

Grated zest of 1 orange, for garnish

Fleur de sel and cracked black pepper

If using fresh whole pumpkin, cut into quarters. Remove and discard the seeds, or save them for toasting, and peel off the skin. Cut the pumpkin flesh into large cubes and transfer to a large saucepan. Cover with water and add a pinch of kosher salt. Bring to a boil over medium-high heat, reduce the heat, and simmer for 30 to 40 minutes, until very soft.

Meanwhile, if using the small pumpkins for serving bowls, cut off their tops as if you were cutting a jack-o'-lantern. Scoop out the seeds and membranes. Reserve the seeds for toasting (see Note). Scrape the insides well to make the pumpkins as clean as possible. These will be the serving bowls. Set the pumpkins and their lids aside.

Drain the cooked pumpkin and reserve both the cooking liquid and cubed pumpkin. You should have about 3 cups of liquid.

In a large saucepan, heat the oil until hot over medium heat. Reduce the heat to medium-low and cook the onion very slowly for about 10 minutes, or until softened but not browned. Add the fennel seed and cook for about 2 minutes longer. Add the cubed pumpkin (or canned pumpkin puree) and cook for about 5 minutes. Add the reserved cooking liquid or chicken stock, orange juice, brown sugar, maple syrup, allspice, cinnamon, cayenne, and bay leaf and cook for 3 to 4 minutes, stirring. Discard the bay leaf.

Off the heat and using a hand mixer set on medium speed or an immersion blender, puree the soup until smooth. Add the cream, return the soup to the stove, and cook for 2 to 3 minutes longer. Work the cream into the soup with the blender (this is where an immersion blender is great). Add the butter a piece at a time and mix with the blender. At this point, the soup will be creamy. Season to taste with kosher salt and ground pepper. Cover to keep hot.

Preheat the oven to 250°F.

If using pumpkin bowls, put the reserved pumpkins on a baking sheet. Lay their lids on the sheet, too. Warm them in the oven for about 10 minutes.

If using foie gras, with a sharp knife, lightly score each piece so that each shallow score is about ¼ inch apart. Season on both sides with kosher salt

and ground pepper. Heat a dry skillet over high heat. When hot, sear the foie gras on both sides. The total cooking time for the foie gras should be no longer than 4 minutes.

Pour the hot soup into the pumpkin bowls (or 6 warmed soup bowls) and top each with a piece of foie gras. Drizzle with truffle oil and garnish with the chopped chives, pumpkin seeds, and a drizzle of the foie gras pan fat. Finish with the orange zest, fleur de sel, and cracked pepper.

Note *To toast pumpkin seeds, spread them on a baking sheet or shallow baking pan. Season lightly with kosher or sea salt. Bake in a 250°F oven, shaking the pan 3 or 4 times to promote even toasting, for about 30 minutes, or until crispy and browned. Remove from the oven and set aside to cool. Store in an airtight container for up to 1 week.*

If you've heard of a Philly cheesesteak, you will "get" this sandwich. It's a sinfully delicious meal meant to be eaten out of hand, wrapped as it is in foil. It's important to buy a high-end cut of meat for the sandwich, which is why I suggest rib eye, because it is well marbled and will stay juicier than other cuts. The horseradish spread and provolone cheese add a nice sharp-smooth taste and texture element, although if you prefer a sharper cheese, use Cheddar or another favorite. **SERVES 4**

STEAK SANDWICHES

1 pound boneless rib eye steak

½ cup olive oil

1 cup sliced cremini mushrooms

1 cup red onion, sliced into half-moons

Kosher salt and freshly ground black pepper

4 hoagie or sub rolls

About 4 tablespoons Horseradish Spread (page 189)

¼ pound provolone cheese, sliced

Put the steak in the freezer for 15 minutes. This will help you slice it thinly.

Preheat the oven to 400ºF.

Using a sharp knife, slice the chilled meat as thinly as you can. Set aside.

Heat a large skillet over high heat. When hot, add ¼ cup of the olive oil. When the oil is hot, sauté the mushrooms and onion for about 3 minutes, or until golden brown. Transfer to a plate and set aside.

Return the skillet to high heat. When hot, add the remaining olive oil. Lightly season the steak with salt and pepper. When the oil is hot, sauté the beef slices for about 2 minutes, or until nearly cooked through. Add the mushrooms and onion and toss to combine with the meat.

Slice the rolls nearly all the way through but do not split into 2 halves. Spread the inside of each roll with horseradish spread.

Arrange 4 rectangles of aluminum foil on the countertop, making sure each rectangle is large enough to enfold a roll. Lay an open roll on each piece of aluminum foil.

Pile each roll with equal amounts of the meat and mushroom mixture and then top with the provolone. Close the rolls and wrap each sandwich in the foil.

Put the foil packets in the oven for 10 minutes to give the cheese time to melt. Remove from the oven, carefully unwrap the sandwiches, and serve.

Chenin Blanc Wine

THE VERSATILE CHENIN BLANC GRAPE makes nearly every style of white wine. It is grown with much success in South Africa, and a few producers have experimented with it here in the United States. But the Loire Valley of France is where the art of growing Chenin blanc grapes was perfected. Melon and citrus flavors dominate the palate at the outset, but the finish moves toward crystallized honey and roasted nuts. Vouvray is the easiest village label to locate, yet quality varies immensely. Discuss the differences with the proprietor of your wine shop (I'm sure he or she will appreciate a discussion of this sort).

This is not a roast beef sandwich—far from it. It is a hot sandwich made with slices of meat from a slow-cooked beef roast and giardiniera (an Italian vegetable relish), which is splashed with a little beef stock and encased in a crusty Italian roll. Ever since I moved to Chicago, I have loved these sandwiches—and when I say that, I mean it: I indulge at least once a week! When I learned that they are attributed to the Italian union workers who manned the stockyards on Chicago's South Side many years ago, I was not surprised. The laborers must have brought home the less desirable pieces of meat and, being Italian, figured out ways to make them not only palatable but totally delicious. The tradition lasts to this day in local restaurants and everyone has their favorite, whether it's the sandwich at Mr. Beef, Al's Beef, Johnnie's Beef, Tony's Italian Beef, or Max's Italian Beef. Sounds like names from an episode of *The Sopranos* or an old Jimmy Cagney flick. **SERVES 4**

CHICAGO ITALIAN BEEF SANDWICHES

2 cloves garlic, chopped

¼ cup dried oregano

1 teaspoon dried basil

1 teaspoon dried thyme

3 pounds boneless beef top round, inside round, or rump roast, trimmed of fat

Kosher salt and freshly ground black pepper

1 onion, sliced

4 cups beef stock, preferably homemade (page 187)

4 pepperoncini, left whole or coarsely chopped

¼ cup pepperoncini juice (from the jar)

Juice of 1 lemon

4 hard rolls or Italian-style rolls, each about 6 inches long

About 2 cups Giardiniera (recipe follows)

In a small bowl, mix together the garlic, oregano, basil, and thyme. Lightly season the roast with salt and pepper and then rub the spice mixture over the meat. Transfer to a shallow dish, cover with plastic, and refrigerate for at least 8 hours or up to 12 hours.

Preheat the oven to 350°F.

Scatter the onion slices over the bottom of a roasting pan and then put the roast on top of them. Pour the stock into the pan. Roast, uncovered, for about 1½ hours, or until medium and a meat thermometer inserted in the thickest part of the roast registers 140°F. Transfer the roast to a platter or cutting board and let cool to room temperature. Reserve the roasting liquid and onion.

When the roast is cool, slice against the grain as thinly as possible. Place the sliced meat in a Dutch oven or other heavy-bottomed pot. Pour the roasting liquid and onion over the meat. Add the pepperoncini, pepperoncini juice, and lemon juice. Bring to a simmer over medium-high heat. As soon as the liquid simmers, remove the pot from the heat.

Slice the rolls nearly all the way through but do not split in half. Open the rolls and dip the cut sides (the insides) into the stock just to moisten them.

Lay the open rolls on each of 4 plates and using tongs, divide the beef, onion, and pepperoncini evenly among them. Top each sandwich with the giardiniera, press gently to close, and serve. Reserve the juice for dipping or pouring over the meat in the sandwich.

GIARDINIERA
MAKES ABOUT 5 CUPS

MARINADE

1 cup Champagne vinegar

1 cup water

½ cup olive oil

½ cup sugar

1 teaspoon celery seed

1 teaspoon mustard seed

1 bay leaf

VEGETABLES

½ cup olive oil

1 clove garlic, minced

1 teaspoon dried red pepper flakes

1 teaspoon fennel seed

1 teaspoon dried oregano

1 cup cauliflower florets

1 red bell pepper, seeded and cut into ½-inch dice

1 yellow bell pepper, seeded and cut into ½-inch dice

1 cup diced carrots

2 cups diced celery

1 cup sliced red onion

1 cup stemmed and quartered small white mushrooms

1 cup pimiento-stuffed green olives, halved

Kosher salt and freshly ground black pepper

To make the marinade: In a large saucepan, combine the vinegar, water, olive oil, sugar, celery seed, mustard seed, and bay leaf. Bring to a boil over medium-high heat and cook for 1 to 2 minutes, stirring to blend the ingredients and make sure the sugar dissolves. Remove from the heat and cover to keep warm.

To prepare the vegetables: In a large pot, heat the olive oil over medium heat. When hot, add the garlic, red pepper flakes, fennel seed, and oregano and cook, stirring, for 1 minute. Add the cauliflower, red and yellow peppers, carrots, celery, red onion, mushrooms, and olives. Cook, stirring, for 8 to 10 minutes, until the mushrooms release their moisture and begin to soften. Pour the marinade over the vegetables and stir well. Remove the pot from the heat and allow to cool. Cover and refrigerate for 24 hours.

Taste the giardiniera and season with salt and black pepper. Serve right away, or refrigerate, tightly covered, for up to 7 days. To serve hot, heat gently over medium heat.

When I make these sandwiches, people come running! This is the real deal. A luxurious triple-decker sandwich that replaces the expected turkey or ham with a delicious New England—style lobster salad, the sort of salad you would find in a lobster roll on the coast of Maine. But I have not overlooked the bacon, which tastes great with lobster. You could grill the lobster for the salad to get some smoke on it, which will complement the smokiness of the bacon. I have long loved club sandwiches and it's a not-so-well-kept secret that I order one from room service whenever I arrive at a hotel late in the evening. Most are very good, some are outstanding, and only very rarely, a sandwich does not inspire! **SERVES 4**

LOBSTER CLUBS

6 scallions, trimmed

1½ pounds cooked lobster meat (canned, pasteurized lobster meat works fine here), cut into bite-sized pieces

1¼ cups Lemon Aioli (page 193)

1 tablespoon chopped fresh flat-leaf parsley

½ tablespoon chopped fresh tarragon

Kosher salt and freshly ground black pepper

12 slices thick-cut bacon

12 slices brioche bread, each about ½ inch thick

2 avocados, pitted, peeled, and sliced

1 large beefsteak tomato, cut into 4 thick slices

2 cups mixed field greens

Prepare a clean and well-oiled charcoal or gas grill so that the coals or heat element are medium hot. Or, heat the broiler or stovetop grill. Grill the scallions for about 5 minutes, turning once, or until nicely charred. Slice the scallions into discs. In a mixing bowl, stir the lobster meat with the aioli, scallions, parsley, and tarragon. Season to taste with salt and pepper, cover, and refrigerate until ready to use and for up to 3 hours.

Preheat the oven to 375°F. Lay the bacon in a single layer on a baking sheet and bake for about 10 minutes, or until crispy. Do not turn the bacon during cooking. Drain on paper towels. Toast the brioche in a toaster or toaster oven and then lay 4 of the pieces on each of 4 plates. Spread aioli on each of the 4 slices of toast and then divide the lobster salad evenly among the 4 slices and gently spread the salad over the toast. Top each sandwich with sliced avocado and another piece of toast. Lay the tomato and bacon over the second piece of toast. Top with the greens. Spread half the aioli on 4 of the remaining slices of toast (you will still have 4 more slices) and arrange these, aioli side up, on top of the lobster salad. Lay 3 slices of bacon on each sandwich, topped with a tomato slice and the greens. Spread the remaining aioli on the final 4 pieces of toast and lay these on top of the sandwiches, aioli side down.

With your hand pressing gently on the top of each sandwich, cut each one in half on the diagonal or into quarters or 2 triangles. Skewer each sandwich section with a toothpick or small wooden skewer to hold it together. Serve immediately.

As soon as soft-shell crabs hit the market in the spring, I buy them and race home to make these sandwiches. Their season is so fleeting, I want to take every advantage of it. Even my kids, who aren't crazy about crabmeat or the idea of eating whole crabs, are nuts about these crispy, crunchy sandwiches doctored with a crisp Asian slaw. If you're entertaining in the spring and looking for an excuse to sit outside and enjoy the afternoon sunshine, bring a plate of these outside and watch them disappear in minutes. You could also season the crabs with salt and pepper and grill them instead of frying. Up to you! **SERVES 4**

TEMPURA SOFT-SHELL CRAB SANDWICHES

ASIAN SLAW

2 cups finely shredded napa cabbage

½ cup julienned red onion

½ cup julienned carrot

½ cup julienned red bell pepper

½ cup julienned yellow bell pepper

1 tablespoon finely chopped scallion

1 tablespoon chopped cilantro

¼ cup soy sauce

¼ cup freshly squeezed lemon juice

¼ cup sesame oil

Kosher salt and freshly
ground black pepper

CRAB SANDWICHES

Vegetable or canola oil, for frying

2 cups rice flour

1 tablespoon white sesame seeds

1 tablespoon black sesame seeds

1 teaspoon chili powder

4 cups cold soda water

4 cleaned soft-shell crabs (ask your
fishmonger to prepare these for you)

Kosher salt and freshly
ground black pepper

4 large sesame-seed
hamburger buns, split

To make the slaw: In a large mixing bowl, toss together the cabbage, onion, carrot, red and yellow peppers, scallion, and cilantro. In a separate bowl, whisk together the soy sauce, lemon juice, and sesame oil and then drizzle over the cabbage mixture. Toss well and season to taste with salt and pepper. Use immediately or cover and refrigerate for up to 3 days.

To make the sandwiches: Fill a deep heavy pot, Dutch oven, or deep-fat fryer about halfway with oil. Heat over medium-high heat until a deep-fry thermometer registers 375ºF or a small cube of bread or a little flour sizzles and bubbles when tossed in the hot oil.

Preheat the broiler.

Meanwhile, in a mixing bowl, stir together the rice flour, white and black sesame seeds, and chili powder. Whisk in the soda water. The tempura batter should be the consistency of pancake batter.

One at a time, dip 2 soft-shell crabs into the tempura batter, making sure they are completely coated. Carefully lift them from the batter and, with a long-handled slotted spoon, gently submerge in the hot oil and fry for 2 to 3 minutes, until they rise to the top and are golden brown. Fry only 2 crabs at a time and let the oil regain its heat between batches.

Transfer the crabs to a paper towel–lined baking sheet or shallow pan. Season with salt and pepper as quickly as you can.

Meanwhile, toast the buns under the broiler for 1 to 2 minutes, until golden brown. Put a whole bun on each of 4 plates. Put a crab on each one and top with the Asian slaw. Serve immediately.

I have proudly served this decadent version of a cheeseburger for more than 15 years and in fact won an award from *Gourmet* magazine back in 1999 for making the "best burger of the year" when I was the chef at Brasserie T. The secret lies in the interior garlic butter, tucked into the beef so that it bastes the meat from the inside and creates the juiciest burger you've ever tasted. Try it—you'll like it. And seriously, would you expect anything else from someone who learned to cook professionally at Wendy's? I don't think so!

SERVES 4

TRAMONTO BURGERS

GARLIC BUTTER

½ cup unsalted butter, cubed and softened

2 cloves garlic

1 teaspoon garlic powder

1 teaspoon chopped fresh flat-leaf parsley

ROASTED GARLIC AIOLI

1 whole head garlic

1½ teaspoons olive oil

Kosher salt

1 cup good-quality store-bought mayonnaise

1 teaspoon freshly squeezed lemon juice

Cracked black pepper

CARAMELIZED ONIONS

1 tablespoon unsalted butter

2 large Spanish onions, thinly sliced

Kosher salt

BURGERS

2 pounds ground beef chuck, preferably 80 percent lean

Kosher salt and freshly ground black pepper

4 brioche buns or other hamburger buns, split

4 (1-ounce) slices Gruyère or provolone cheese

1 cup shredded iceberg lettuce

1 large beefsteak tomato, cut into 4 thick slices

To make the garlic butter: Put the butter in a bowl and grate the garlic cloves over it, using a Microplane grater. Add the garlic powder and parsley and stir until well mixed.

Pull about 10 inches of plastic from a roll of plastic wrap, but do not tear it from the roll. Lay the 10 inches on a clean work surface, still attached to the roll, with the free end facing you. While this is not totally necessary, keeping one end of the plastic attached to the roll holds it taut and makes rolling up the butter easier. Spread the garlic butter over the plastic wrap to about 1 inch from the edge of the plastic wrap. Fold the plastic over the butter mixture and roll it to form a small cylinder that is about 7 or 8 inches long. Roll the butter as tightly as you can and when you reach the roll of plastic wrap, tear it off. Transfer to the freezer.

To make the aioli: Preheat the oven to 300°F. Pull the outer layers of papery skin from the garlic head but leave the cloves intact at the root end. Put the head in the center of a sheet of aluminum foil, drizzle with the olive oil, and sprinkle with a pinch of salt. Fold the foil over the top of the garlic to make a loose package. Put the package on a baking sheet and roast for about 35 minutes, until the garlic is soft. Unwrap and set aside to cool.

When cool, squeeze the softened garlic pulp from each clove into the bowl of a food processor fitted with the metal blade. Discard the remaining skin. Add the mayonnaise and lemon juice to the food processor and pulse until smooth. Season to taste with salt and pepper. Use immediately or store in a lidded container in the refrigerator for up to 3 days.

To caramelize the onions: In a large sauté pan, melt the butter over medium heat. When bubbling, add the onions and cook, stirring every 5 minutes or so with a wooden spoon, for 20 to 30 minutes, or until medium brown and very soft. Scrape the browned bits from the bottom of the pan as the onions cool slowly. Season lightly with salt and set aside.

To make the burgers: Remove the garlic butter from the freezer and when thawed enough to cut, slice into 4 discs.

Prepare a clean, well-oiled charcoal or gas grill so that the coals or heat element are medium-hot. Or, heat the broiler.

Form the ground beef into 8 patties. Top 4 patties with a disc of butter, then with the remaining 4 patties. Seal the edges with your fingertips and then, with the palm of your hand, lightly flatten the double burgers. Take care you cannot see any butter along the edges of the patties. Any you see will leak during cooking and the burgers will lose valuable juices. Finally, season the burgers generously with salt and pepper.

Lay a piece of foil on the coolest part of the grill and pile the caramelized onions on the foil to warm while you grill the burgers.

Grill the burgers, turning once, for a total of about 6 minutes for rare burgers, 8 minutes for medium, or 10 to 12 minutes for well done. Turning the burgers only once during cooking allows them to develop a nice crust. Do not press on the meat with a spatula or you will squeeze out the juices and butter.

Meanwhile, lay the buns on the grill, cut sides down, to toast lightly.

Top each burger with onions and then with cheese. Cover the grill for about 1 minute so that the cheese melts fully.

Put a burger on the bottom half of each bun, top with lettuce, a tomato slice, aioli, and then the top of the bun, and serve.

Gamay Noir Wine

THIS GRAPE HAS A LONG HISTORY OF A BAD REPUTATION. From its association with the questionable quality of the Beaujolais Nouveaus of today all the way back to 1395 when the Duke of Burgundy dramatically banished it from that region, the Gamay Noir grape has been viewed as a scoundrel. But for anyone keeping the budget in mind, this grape definitely deserves another look. By choosing wines from one of the ten cru villages of Beaujolais, quality greatly improves and the wine boasts light peppercorn and ripe, fresh strawberry and raspberry flavors. This can be a versatile wine with lighter dishes, especially those using some heat in their preparation.

I don't think there is a better sandwich than this in August and September when tomatoes are at their best. When they pop with juicy flavor, I scoop them up at the farmers' market and take them home to make BLTs. Indeed, Eileen and I enjoy these sandwiches for lunch two or three times a week. Who could get tired of them?

If you haven't tried Calabrian chiles yet, you are in for a treat. They are a little sweet, a little spicy, a little smoky, and completely delicious! If you can't find them at the supermarket, try a gourmet shop or order them online. They are sublime stirred into the aioli. I realize you may have more aioli than you will need, but I suggest this much as some folks like more than others—and you can refrigerate it for 2 or 3 days and use it on other sandwiches, dolloped on salads, or served alongside grilled meat. **SERVES 4**

RICK'S BLTS

2 Calabrian chiles in oil or any red chile packed in oil, minced

1¼ cups Lemon Aioli (page 193)

24 slices double-cut applewood bacon

2 to 3 assorted heirloom tomatoes or other vine-ripened tomatoes, cored and cut into ½-inch-thick slices

Kosher salt and freshly ground black pepper

½ cup unsalted butter, softened

8 slices whole-grain or sourdough bread

2 cups arugula leaves

In a small mixing bowl, stir the minced chiles into the aioli. Cover and refrigerate until ready to use.

Preheat the oven to 350°F. Line a baking sheet or jelly roll pan with parchment or waxed paper and lay the bacon on the paper. Bake in the oven, without turning, for about 15 minutes, or until crisp. Drain on paper towels.

Season the tomato slices with salt and pepper.

Spread butter evenly on 1 side of each slice of bread. Lay the bread, buttered side up, on 2 baking sheets and bake for 2 to 3 minutes, until golden brown. Remove the bread from the oven and while hot, spread each slice with aioli.

Build the sandwiches with the bread, tomatoes, bacon, and arugula. Slice in half and serve.

Cook Bacon Like a Chef

ONE OF THE EASIEST WAYS TO COOK BACON is in a 350°F oven. Lay the bacon slices in a shallow baking pan lined with parchment paper and let it cook in the oven: No turning, no tending, no worry. After 10 or 12 minutes, the bacon is done and all you have to do is drain it on paper towels. I find this a lot easier than standing over a frying pan, fussing with the strips of bacon as they cook. Most chefs I know cook bacon this way. The only trick is to remember you have bacon in the oven. If you forget, it will burn to a crisp! This method works well for pancetta, too. P.S. Save the bacon fat to cook with later. It makes nearly anything taste great.

This sandwich originated in New Orleans, along with so many other good things to eat. The story goes that Italian immigrant workers carried lunch buckets to work filled with cold meat, cheese, olive salad, and a Sicilian bread called *muffuletta.* They happily munched on their lunch until one day someone decided to turn the whole thing into a sandwich. It caught on big time, which is no surprise if you've ever tasted one of these masterpieces. I add some grilled chicken to the olive salad for an update. **SERVES 4**

GRILLED CHICKEN MUFFULETTA

2 boneless, skinless chicken breasts, 6 to 8 ounces each

1 cup extra-virgin olive oil, plus additional for brushing

Kosher salt and freshly ground black pepper

1 tablespoon plus 1 teaspoon red wine vinegar

2/3 cup chopped pimiento-stuffed green olives

2/3 cup pitted chopped Niçoise or kalamata olives

2/3 cup diced red bell pepper

1 tablespoon drained capers, chopped

1 tablespoon chopped fresh basil leaves

1 tablespoon chopped fresh flat-leaf parsley

1 clove garlic, minced

1 Italian bread boule or any rustic round loaf

2 teaspoons red wine vinegar

1 teaspoon dried oregano

¼ pound Genoa salami, thinly sliced

¼ pound hot capicola (also known as coppa), thinly sliced

¼ pound mortadella, thinly sliced

¼ pound prosciutto di Parma, thinly sliced

¼ pound provolone cheese, thinly sliced

¼ pound Swiss or Gruyère cheese, thinly sliced

Prepare a clean, well-oiled charcoal or gas grill so that the coals or heat element are medium-hot. Or, heat the broiler.

Lay the chicken breasts in a shallow dish and pour ⅓ cup of the olive oil over them. Season the chicken with salt and pepper.

Grill the chicken breasts, turning 2 or 3 times, for 12 to 15 minutes, until cooked through and an instant-read thermometer inserted in the thickest part registers 165°F. Let cool, then cut into ½-inch pieces.

In a mixing bowl, toss the chicken with the remaining ⅔ cup olive oil, 1 tablespoon of the vinegar, the pimiento, Niçoise olives, red pepper, capers, basil, parsley, and garlic.

Cut the bread in half crosswise, as if you were slicing a large hamburger bun. Brush the insides with olive oil and grill for 3 to 4 minutes. Begin with the crust side down and turn about halfway through so that the oil-brushed sides are down. Remove from the grill and sprinkle the cut sides with the remaining 2 teaspoons vinegar and the oregano.

Spread half of the chicken salad over the bottom half of the loaf. Make sure to include all of the delicious juices. Layer all the cured hams, sausages, and cheeses on top of the salad. Top with the remaining chicken salad. Place the top half of the bread on the sandwich. Wrap tightly in plastic and refrigerate for 2 to 3 hours.

To serve, slice into 4 wedge-shaped sandwiches.

Chefs love to cook fish and

seafood because they are so accommodating to so many techniques and flavor combinations. I am no exception, and not only do I serve fish at Tru and Tramonto's Steak and Seafood, but I cook it at home as often as I can. I have always liked surf and turf—dating back to my childhood—and for me, serving fish and meat at the same meal is not a stretch. I look for reasons to splurge on king crab legs, for instance, which can be put in the middle of the table, a little for everyone to savor, and then enjoy a small steak or chop to round out the meal. If you don't like meat, or want to cut back on it, fish is a great go-to protein. Try the cioppino as a main course or in smaller amounts as a first course. Give the frog legs a go; you will be happy you did. And don't miss the Lobster Pot Pie—it is sensational and well worth the effort.

Speaking of effort, it's important to go the extra mile to buy fresh-as-can-be and sustainable fish and seafood. Buy what looks best on any given day and don't be a slave to the type of fish called for in the recipe. Most can be switched out for another as long as they have similar textures.

When I cook fish and seafood, I like the energy and power ballads of:
MICHAEL JACKSON | LED ZEPPELIN | JOURNEY |
PRINCE | BON JOVI

FISH AND SEAFOOD

Tips on Buying Fish

REGARDLESS OF WHERE YOU BUY FISH, ask the guy behind the counter when they get their deliveries and try to buy fish on those days. This will ensure you get the freshest fish you can. If you are lucky enough to have a reputable fish store in your town or city, work on establishing a relationship with the owner. He will take care of you and help you choose the right fish for your recipe. For instance, if the sea bass is not too good (or he has none), he will help you select another kind of bass or a fish with a similar texture.

All the standard advice about selecting fish you have read before is worth revisiting: Look for moist, fresh-looking fish; any scales should glisten and never look dull; whole fish should have clear eyes and red gills. The fish store or counter should never smell fishy but instead should smell just a little bit briny—like the sea. It should be spotless with fresh ice cradling the fish.

I like to buy whole sides of fish and butcher them at home, or even whole fish (already gutted and clean) that I cut up at home. This way, I have fish bones and can use them to make a light fish stock to use in the dish I am cooking or to freeze in small amounts to use later.

How to Store Fish at Home

IT'S A GOOD IDEA TO COOK AND EAT FISH ON THE DAY YOU BUY IT, but unless you purchase it right before dinnertime, you will have to refrigerate it for a period of time. Put the fish in the fridge as soon as you can after buying it. Don't unwrap it. Too many people drown the fish in ice, laying it directly on top of ice cubes or crushed ice in a shallow dish. I prefer to put the ice in a pan and then lay the fish over it, on a perforated top or rack. Shove the pan to the back of the refrigerator, which is the coldest part of the box.

I have yet to find a seafood stew I don't love, but I think cioppino might be my all-time favorite. As you can see when you run your eye down the page, this is one of those recipes with a lot of ingredients, but very little preparation. Once you have gathered the ham, tomatoes, crab, shrimp, halibut, and mussels, it's just a matter of assembling the stew. Cioppino is a fish stew that was developed by immigrant Italian fishermen who settled in San Francisco, and, perhaps not surprisingly, resembles a lot of rustic European fish stews. Dungeness crabs are found on the West Coast—a good clue as to the origin of the dish. I like to serve this with good sourdough bread—another San Francisco triumph—because the bread lets me sop up the last drop.

SERVES 6

CIOPPINO, TRAMONTO STYLE

¼ cup unsalted butter

¼ cup olive oil

½ cup finely chopped serrano ham or another cured ham (such as prosciutto)

1 rib celery, cut into ½-inch dice

1 yellow onion, cut ½-inch dice

1 (28-ounce) can whole peeled tomatoes (I like San Marzano tomatoes)

2 cups bottled clam juice

2 cups white wine

4 cloves garlic, minced

Juice of 1 lemon

1 teaspoon chopped fresh basil

1 teaspoon chopped fresh oregano

1 teaspoon Worcestershire sauce

1 bay leaf

½ teaspoon crushed red pepper flakes

Kosher salt

1 Dungeness crab (about 2 pounds), cracked and cleaned, or 1 pound thawed frozen crabmeat

12 large shrimp, peeled and deveined

2 pounds halibut fillet or other firm-fleshed white fish, cut into 1-inch chunks

24 mussels (I like Prince Edward Island mussels)

½ bunch flat-leaf parsley, chopped

Sourdough bread, for serving (optional)

In a large pot, melt the butter in the olive oil over medium heat. When hot, sauté the ham, celery, and onion for about 10 minutes, or until soft.

Add the tomatoes, crushing them with a wooden spoon or your hands. Add the clam juice, wine, garlic, lemon juice, basil, oregano, Worcestershire, bay leaf, pepper flakes, and salt and simmer on low heat, uncovered, for about 1 hour.

Add the crab, shrimp, and halibut, cover, and simmer for 5 minutes. Add the mussels, cover, and simmer for 3 minutes more, or until the mussels open. Discard any mussels that don't open.

Remove the cioppino from the heat, stir in the parsley, and discard the bay leaf. Ladle into bowls and serve hot with sourdough bread.

Sparkling Wine Cocktails

SPARKLING WINE AND CHAMPAGNE ARE FANTASTIC AND REFRESHING APERITIFS ON THEIR OWN, but they can be amazing if you add a little bit of flavor to enhance their elegance, whether served alone or alongside fish and seafood dishes. Less is certainly more when it comes to adding ingredients: Too much will flatten the bubbles (which is the most distinctive part). Apart from the traditional Angostura bitters, there is a wealth of producers who make flavored syrups and juices to add to the sparkling wine—peach, orange, mint, and celery. Try experimenting with these flavors in place of Angostura in the traditional Champagne Cocktail.

TRADITIONAL CHAMPAGNE COCKTAIL

Put a sugar cube in the bottom of a Champagne flute. Add 5 to 8 dashes of bitters. Top with Champagne or sparkling wine.

MIMOSA

In a Champagne flute, combine 2 parts sparkling wine or Champagne and 1 part desired fruit juice (most often orange juice).

The Italians have poached fish in olive oil for hundreds of years and no wonder—it works wonders with the texture and flavor of a sturdy, oily fish such as salmon. Olive oil poaching has gained favor here, too, in recent years and while you may think of it as the province of restaurant chefs, it's super easy to do at home. The only trick is to use a deep-frying thermometer to make sure the oil's temperature is low enough that the fish is gently poached. While it's easiest to cook the fish on top of the stove, if you want to taste something amazing, set the oil-filled pan on the grill and poach the fish there. The result is smoky and delicious. **SERVES 4**

OLIVE OIL–POACHED SALMON WITH ROASTED BEETS

2½ quarts extra-virgin olive oil

3 sprigs thyme

1 sprig rosemary

½ orange, cut into ¼-inch-thick slices

1 lemon, cut into ¼-inch-thick slices

4 skinless salmon fillets, each about 6 ounces and 2 inches thick

Kosher salt and freshly ground black pepper

Roasted Beets with Charred Fennel and Orange (page 242)

In a Dutch oven or other large pot, heat the olive oil over medium-low heat until a thermometer registers 150°F. Add the thyme and rosemary sprigs and the orange and lemon slices.

Season the salmon fillets with salt and pepper. Using a slotted spoon or spatula, lower them gently into the oil. Let the oil regain its temperature and then poach the fish for 8 to 10 minutes for rare salmon that is still a little raw in the center. If you prefer your salmon fully cooked, cook for an additional 2 minutes.

Lift the salmon from the oil and drain on paper towels. Divide the beets among 4 plates and set a fillet on top of each serving. Serve immediately.

I am extremely fond of mahimahi any way it is cooked, but my favorite method for the firm white fish is grilling. This means I am most apt to cook it during the summer when the backyard grill hardly has a chance to cool down between meals. I serve it with a great salad of raw fennel, lemon, and olives, which makes this very Mediterranean in style. The salad is good on its own or with other kinds of fish, too. **SERVES 4**

GRILLED MEDITERRANEAN-STYLE MAHIMAHI WITH OLIVES AND SHAVED FENNEL

4 boneless, skinless mahimahi fillets, each about 7 ounces

1 cup Tramonto's House Dressing (page 189)

2 fennel bulbs, trimmed, fronds reserved

1 cup pitted picholine olives

½ cup extra-virgin olive oil

½ cup sliced red onion

¼ cup torn fresh basil leaves

1 tablespoon chopped fresh cilantro

1 tablespoon chopped fennel fronds, plus more for garnish

Grated zest and juice of 3 lemons, a little zest reserved for garnish

Kosher salt and freshly ground black pepper

Lay the mahimahi fillets in a glass or other nonreactive dish and pour the dressing over them. Cover and refrigerate for 2 hours.

Prepare a clean, well-oiled charcoal or gas grill so that the coals or heat element are medium-hot. I like to work with a very well-oiled grill so I can lay the fish directly on the grate.

Meanwhile, shave the fennel bulbs into a mixing bowl with a mandoline or Microplane grater. Add the olives, olive oil, onion, basil, cilantro, fennel fronds, and lemon zest and juice. Toss together and season to taste with salt and pepper. Set aside for about 20 minutes for the flavors to develop.

Remove the fillets from the dish and wipe off any excess dressing with a paper towel. Season the fish on both sides with salt and pepper.

Grill the fillets, covered and turning just once, for about 8 minutes, or until nearly opaque and moist.

Divide the fennel and olive salad evenly among 4 shallow bowls. Top with the grilled mahimahi. Garnish with the reserved lemon zest, fennel fronds, and a spoonful of the dressing from the salad.

Few meals are more fun than a relaxed crab dinner, with newspaper spread on the table and topped with a platter of crabs so that no matter how messy it gets, cleanup is a breeze. *Deadliest Catch,* the Discovery Channel's reality show about harvesting Alaska's king crab, has made a lot of people interested in these superb creatures, and I hope has also given them more appreciation for how valuable the crabs are. The crabs are already cooked when you buy them, so the most difficult part of this meal is making the piquillo butter—and that's pretty much a breeze. The sweetness of the peppers melds with the richness of the butter to complement the brininess of the crabs. **SERVES 4**

KING CRAB LEGS WITH PIQUILLO PEPPER BUTTER

1 cup unsalted butter, softened

8 whole piquillo peppers (see Note), plus additional for garnish

1 clove garlic, minced

Juice of ½ lemon

¼ teaspoon crushed red pepper flakes

Kosher salt and freshly ground black pepper

2 pounds cooked king crab legs, split

2 tablespoons chopped fresh flat-leaf parsley, for garnish

1 lemon, cut into 4 wedges, for garnish

In the bowl of a food processor or a blender, process the butter with the peppers, garlic, lemon juice, and red pepper flakes until smooth. Season to taste with salt and pepper and pulse again. Use the piquillo butter immediately or cover and refrigerator for up to 2 days.

When ready to serve, transfer the piquillo butter to a small saucepan and heat over medium-low heat until melted.

Put the crab legs on a platter and pour about two-thirds of the warm butter over them, reserving the rest for dipping. Garnish the crab legs with parsley, lemon wedges, and whole peppers.

Note *Piquillo peppers, grown in northern Spain, are nearly always packed in jars or cans after being hand picked and roasted. They are slightly sharp, yet also sweet and so please everyone who likes roasted red peppers. Because the peppers are not rinsed before packing, they usually have small specks of charred skin still on the red flesh. If you must, you can substitute other jarred roasted red peppers, but try to find piquillos for their outstanding flavor.*

If you haven't cooked frog legs, what are you waiting for? They are easy to handle, quick to cook, and taste great, especially when served with garlic and tomatoes as I do here. Some markets carry frog legs, and you can always buy them online. Imagine the conversation when you serve these! *Bon appétit!* **SERVES 4**

ROASTED FROG LEGS WITH GARLIC AND TOMATOES

½ cup olive oil

2 large onions, diced

2 cups chicken stock, preferably homemade (page 188)

2 cups white wine

¾ cup Garlic Confit (page 181)

⅔ cup Stewed Tomatoes (page 251)

2 bay leaves

Salt and freshly ground black pepper

1 tablespoon chopped fresh flat-leaf parsley

1 tablespoon chopped fresh thyme

1 tablespoon chopped fresh chives

2 pounds frog legs, cleaned and skinned

2 tablespoons unsalted butter

In a large saucepan, heat ¼ cup of the olive oil over medium heat. When hot, sauté the onions for about 5 minutes, or until lightly browned. Add the stock, wine, confit, tomatoes, and bay leaves and season to taste with salt and pepper. Bring to a simmer and cook for about 1 hour, adjusting the heat up or down to maintain the simmer. Stir in the parsley, thyme, and chives. Discard the bay leaf and set the sauce aside.

Preheat the oven to 400ºF.

In a large ovenproof sauté pan or another pan that can go from stovetop to oven, heat the remaining ¼ cup oil. Season the frog legs very well with salt and pepper. When the oil is hot, put the legs in the pan and then transfer to the oven to roast for 7 to 8 minutes, until cooked through, moist, and lightly browned. The texture will be similar to that of cooked chicken.

Transfer the frog legs to a platter or divide among 4 serving plates.

Pour the tomato-confit sauce into the hot pan and set it over medium-low heat. Whisk in the butter, a tablespoon at a time, not adding the second tablespoon until the first is fully incorporated. Spoon the hot sauce over the frog legs and serve.

Cooking salmon on a cedar plank imbues the fish with a subtle, smoky, woody flavor that is unmistakable but never overwhelming. The tradition comes from coastal Northwestern Native Americans, whose diet has long been rich in salmon. They lashed large sides of fish to the damp planks and propped them over open fires for what no doubt were matchless feasts. When you do this at home, you don't have to tie the fish to the plank, but your friends will love the pageantry of your effort if you serve it on an untreated cedar plank. You can find the planks at most cookware shops. **SERVES 4**

CEDAR-PLANK SALMON WITH MUSTARD AND MAPLE

6 tablespoons Dijon mustard

2 tablespoons maple syrup

1 teaspoon cayenne

Grated zest and juice of ½ orange

4 salmon skin-on fillets,
each 7 to 8 ounces

Kosher salt and freshly
ground black pepper

3 tablespoons unsalted butter, melted

2 tablespoons chopped fresh
flat-leaf parsley, for garnish

A Fish Cutting Board

WHEN YOU CUT UP FISH at home, do so on a cutting board reserved solely for this purpose. No matter how many times you run the board through the dishwasher or wipe it down with bleach, it will retain its fishy smell, which is not something you want to impart to onions or fruit, or anything else you chop. I like plastic cutting boards for both fish and poultry and always use them only for their specific purposes. This is where colored boards come in handy.

Soak an untreated cedar plank, about 6 by 14 inches, in well-salted water for about 1 hour, making sure the plank is immersed completely.

Meanwhile, in a bowl, mix together the mustard, maple syrup, cayenne, and orange zest and juice. Set aside 2 tablespoons of the marinade for finishing the dish.

Rinse the salmon under cold running water and pat dry with paper towels. Season liberally on both sides with salt and pepper. Lay the fillets, skin sides down, in a shallow glass or ceramic dish and spread the marinade over the fish. Let marinate for 15 to 20 minutes at room temperature.

Prepare a clean, well-oiled gas or charcoal grill so that the heating element or charcoal is medium-hot. Put the wet cedar plank on the grill for 3 minutes and then turn it over.

Lift the fillets from the marinade, being very careful that they do not fall apart, and lay, skin sides down, on the plank. Cover the grill and cook for 12 to 15 minutes, until the salmon is just barely opaque in the center and an instant-read thermometer registers 135°F when inserted in the center. Check the plank occasionally to make sure the edges don't catch fire. If they start to smolder, mist them with water or move the plank to a cooler part of the grill.

Transfer the salmon and the plank to a platter. Mix the reserved 2 tablespoons marinade with the melted butter and drizzle over the salmon. Garnish with parsley and serve right from the plank.

There's not a lot to say about this lovely, colorful dish—far better to pick up some sea bass, juicy cherry tomatoes, and fresh herbs and fire up the grill. This is a summery meal, one that I make as often as I can in July and August when the living is easy. Make sure the grilling grid is well oiled to prevent sticking and that the coals are hot, hot, hot. **SERVES 4**

GRILLED SEA BASS WITH TOMATILLO-TOMATO RELISH

TOMATILLO-TOMATO RELISH

1 pound tomatillos, husked, washed, and chopped

½ pint red cherry tomatoes, quartered

½ pint yellow cherry tomatoes, quartered

1 large red onion, chopped

1 red bell pepper, seeded and chopped

4 cloves garlic, minced

1 jalapeño pepper, seeded and diced

½ cup olive oil

⅓ cup sherry vinegar

¼ cup sugar

1 bunch cilantro, chopped

2 tablespoons torn fresh basil leaves

Juice of ½ lime

Kosher salt and freshly ground black pepper

SEA BASS

4 skin-on boneless sea bass fillets, each about 8 ounces; or a 1½- to 2-pound skin-on, boneless whole side of fish

3 tablespoons olive oil

Kosher salt and freshly ground black pepper

8 whole scallions, trimmed

To make the relish: In a large bowl, mix together the tomatillos, red and yellow tomatoes, onion, bell pepper, garlic, jalapeño, olive oil, vinegar, sugar, cilantro, basil, and lime juice. Set aside for about 20 minutes for the flavors to blend. Season to taste with salt and pepper.

To cook the sea bass: Prepare a clean, very well-oiled charcoal or gas grill so that the coals or heat element are hot. Or, heat the broiler.

Rub both sides of the fish liberally with about 2 tablespoons olive oil and then season generously with salt and pepper. Score the skin of the fillets in 1 or 2 places and then turn over and score the other side in 3 or 4 places.

Place the fillets on the grill, skin side down, and grill, turning once, for 6 minutes, or until cooked through. Grill the whole side of fish for 8 minutes on the skin side with the grill covered, then turn and grill for 3 to 4 minutes, until cooked through.

Brush the whole scallions with the remaining 1 tablespoon oil and season well with salt and pepper. Grill the scallions, turning once, for about 2 minutes, until lightly browned. Remove from the grill and roughly chop.

To serve, put 1 fillet on each plate or the whole side on a large platter, skin side up. Spoon the relish over the top and garnish with the chopped grilled scallions. Spoon the dressing from the relish over the fish and serve.

Sauvignon Blanc Wine

THIS GRAPE MAKES THE "GIN AND TONIC" OF THE WINE WORLD—a marvelously universal drink that appeals to just about everyone. Sauvignon blanc wines are bursting with ripe citrus notes and finishing with green herbal ones that vary from fresh-cut grass to tomato leaves. The real difficulty comes in deciding which region of the world your Sauvignon blanc should come from. The most noted Sauvignon blancs come from France, from the central vineyards of the Loire Valley (Sancerre, Menetou-Salon, and Pouilly-Fumé), where the ancient soil plays a huge role in the chalky mineral finish of the wines. In the Americas (both North and South), the grape runs the gamut from showing up in light aperitifs to bolder wines that may see a bit of oak treatment. A good rule of thumb is to search out cool climate wines. New Zealand is quickly emerging as the crowd favorite for SBs; there the wines boast an herbal and fruit blend with a tinge of sweetness to balance out the acidity.

In the Tramonto household, we eat a lot of Chinese broccoli, which also is called Chinese kale or *kai-lan*. I grill it, blanch it, steam it, and stir-fry it, and we're never disappointed. It's pretty much underutilized in this country, but once you discover it, you'll like it, too. I pretty much think any sort of grilled tuna served with soy brown butter is a classic and this is no exception, particularly with the broccoli alongside it. Nothing fancy going on, just good, solid fish cookery that results in a spectacular dish. I like to cook tuna only until it's done on the outside but still rare in the center. You might like it a little more done. **SERVES 4**

GRILLED TUNA WITH CHINESE BROCCOLI AND SOY BROWN BUTTER

SOY BROWN BUTTER

2 cups balsamic vinegar

½ cup unsalted butter

1 tablespoon soy sauce

Freshly ground black pepper

BROCCOLI AND TUNA

1 tablespoon sesame oil

⅓ cup sugar

1 large shallot, sliced

4-inch knob fresh ginger, peeled and grated

6 cloves garlic, sliced

3 bunches Chinese broccoli

4 sushi-grade tuna steaks, each 7 to 8 ounces, cut into 4 squared-off logs (4 sides approximately equal)

¼ cup olive oil

Ginger-Curry Rub for Fish (page 171)

To make the browned butter: In a medium saucepan set over medium-high heat, bring the vinegar to a boil, reduce the heat to medium-low, and simmer for about 30 minutes, or until the vinegar reduces to about ½ cup.

In a medium skillet set over medium heat, heat the butter until It melts and turns light brown. Remove from the heat and let cool to room temperature.

Slowly whisk the browned butter Into the reduced balsamic vinegar. Whisk in the soy sauce and season with pepper to taste. Reserve the emulsion at room temperature.

To cook the broccoli and tuna: Heat a large sauté pan over medium heat. When hot, add the sesame oil and cook the sugar, shallot, ginger, and garlic for 3 to 4 minutes, until the shallot Is translucent.

Add the broccoli and sauté for 7 to 10 minutes, until wilted. Stir the broccoli as it cooks and take care that it does not burn. Remove from the heat, cover to keep warm, and set aside.

Prepare a clean, well-oiled charcoal or gas grill so that the coals or heat element are medium-hot. Or, heat the broiler.

Brush all sides of each tuna steak with olive oil and rub the rub into all sides. Grill the tuna for a total of 6 to 8 minutes for rare to medium-rare tuna. Cut into thick slices.

Divide the warm broccoli among 4 plates and top with the sliced, grilled tuna steaks. Drizzle each serving with the brown butter.

If you like the flavors of soy, garlic, and ginger, you will love this. My kids sure do—I can't grill enough shrimp to satisfy them! The shrimp is amazing served alongside a juicy steak, although you could serve it as a main dish on its own. Be sure to soak the bamboo skewers so that they don't burn on the grill. **SERVES 4**

GRILLED SHRIMP WITH GARLIC AND GINGER

¼ cup olive oil

¼ cup soy sauce

2 tablespoons toasted sesame oil

Juice of 1 lemon

2 teaspoons honey

1 (4-inch) knob fresh ginger, peeled and grated (I use a Microplane grater, which works very well)

3 cloves garlic, minced

1 tablespoon minced shallot

¼ teaspoon dried red pepper flakes

¼ cup unsalted butter, softened

1 pound large shrimp, deveined, shells and tails intact

Kosher salt and freshly ground black pepper

1 tablespoon chopped fresh basil

1 tablespoon chopped fresh cilantro

Soak 4 long bamboo skewers in cool water for about an hour, or use metal skewers.

In a small bowl, whisk together the olive oil, soy sauce, sesame oil, lemon juice, honey, ginger, garlic, shallot, and red pepper flakes. Transfer to the bowl of a food processor fitted with the metal blade and process until smooth. Add the softened butter and pulse until thoroughly combined.

Prepare a clean, well-oiled charcoal or gas grill so that the coals or heat element are medium-hot. Or, heat the broiler.

Thread the shrimp on the damp bamboo skewers and arrange in a shallow glass dish so that they lie flat. Spoon the marinade over the shrimp. Let stand at room temperature for about 20 minutes.

Grill the shrimp, turning once, for 2 to 4 minutes, until just cooked through. Baste the shrimp with the butter as they grill. Season generously with salt and pepper.

Serve the shrimp right off the grill, garnished with basil and cilantro.

I love to serve this to my friends as a super-indulgent side dish to steak, although it also stands on its own as a main dish. Steak and lobster are great friends and so when you are in the mood for a different sort of surf and turf, whip this up. Lobster pot pie is not unusual in Maine, where lobster is plentiful, but everywhere else in the United States it is pretty exotic. If you've ever had the pleasure of stopping at the Maine Diner on Route 1 in Wells, Maine, you might have tasted their lobster pot pie. I like mine just as much. Because it's topped with biscuits instead of pie crust, it's easy to make as well as homey and rustic. Dig in! **SERVES 6**

LOBSTER POT PIE

LOBSTER FILLING

4 live lobsters, each 1½ to 2 pounds, or about 2 pounds cooked lobster meat

2 cups diced potatoes

1 cup diced carrots

6 tablespoons unsalted butter

1 cup chopped onions

½ cup chopped celery

Kosher salt and freshly ground black pepper

6 tablespoons unbleached all-purpose flour

3 cups lobster stock or chicken stock, preferably homemade (page 188)

1 cup heavy cream

1 cup sweet peas

1 tablespoon chopped fresh flat-leaf parsley

1½ teaspoons chopped fresh tarragon

BISCUIT DOUGH

2 cups unbleached all-purpose flour

1 tablespoon baking powder

1 teaspoon kosher salt

¼ teaspoon baking soda

6 tablespoons cold unsalted butter, cut into chunks

¾ cup buttermilk

To prepare the lobster filling: If cooking live lobsters, fill a large pot about halfway with water and bring to a boil over high heat. Drop the lobsters headfirst into the boiling water and cover the pot. When the water returns to a boil, cook the lobsters for 8 to 10 minutes, until the shells turn bright red. Lift the lobsters from the pot and set aside to cool. When cool, crack the claw and tail shells and remove the meat. You should have about 2 pounds of lobster meat.

Fill a saucepan or deep skillet about halfway with water and bring to a simmer over medium-high heat. Add the potatoes and blanch for 10 to 12 minutes. Drain and set aside.

Fill the same saucepan or deep skillet about halfway with water and bring to a simmer over medium-high heat. Add the carrots and blanch for 10 to 12 minutes, until fork-tender. Drain and set aside.

Preheat the oven to 375°F. Grease an 11 by 13-inch glass baking dish.

In a large sauté pan, melt the butter over medium-high heat. Sauté the onions and celery for 2 minutes, then season with salt and pepper to taste. Stir in the flour and cook, stirring, for 3 to 4 minutes to make a roux.

Stir in the stock and bring to a boil over high heat. Reduce the heat to medium and simmer for 8 to 10 minutes, until the sauce starts to thicken. Stir in the cream and continue to simmer for about 4 minutes. Season to taste with salt and pepper.

Stir in the lobster meat, potatoes, carrots, and peas. Return to a simmer and stir in the parsley and tarragon. Pour the filling into the prepared baking dish and set aside.

To make the biscuit dough: In a mixing bowl, whisk together the flour, baking powder, salt, and baking soda. With your fingers, a pastry blender, or a fork, cut the butter cubes into the dry ingredients until the mixture resembles coarse crumbs. Add the buttermilk and stir just until combined. Do not overmix.

Chardonnay Wine

STRONG FEELINGS ABOUND in regard to the varying styles of wines made from the Chardonnay grape. Most people expect a slightly sweet, pineapple-driven fruit with buttery and coconut-y oak flavors, but in the hands of the French, the grape makes a wine with lemon-curd type fruit, light hazelnut-oak flavors, and a dusty limestone finish. Versions of the wine with no oak contact are popping up all over the world, offering steely bright Granny Smith apple and Meyer lemon flavors not weighed down by oak. No matter what style is preferred, the velvety mouthfeel of Chardonnay is perfect with rich dishes—especially shellfish.

Turn the dough out onto a lightly floured surface and gently pat into a disk about ½ inch thick. Do not roll the dough, but use your fingertips to pat it very gently. Use a 2½- to 3-inch biscuit cutter or an upturned glass to cut out rounds of dough.

Shingle the dough rounds over the lobster filling to cover the casserole completely but with gaps here and there. Bake for 10 to 15 minutes, until the biscuit topping is golden brown and crispy and the filling bubbles. Let the casserole rest for about 5 minutes before spooning in shallow dishes or bowls.

When I was a kid, we ate sausage with peppers and onions several times a month—or more—and I was never sorry to see it on the supper table. When I started cooking professionally, I fell in love with grilled fish, and so now two of the loves of my life come together in this remarkable recipe. Meaty fish such as swordfish stand up extremely well to peppers and onions. I add some olives and salt for a stronger flavor profile and then grill the fish just until it's medium. It's a beautiful, summery dish. **SERVES 4**

GRILLED SWORDFISH WITH PEPPERS, ONIONS, AND OLIVES

3 tablespoons olive oil

3 anchovy fillets (optional)

1 large yellow onion, thinly sliced

2 red bell peppers, seeded and thinly sliced

2 yellow peppers, seeded and thinly sliced

3 cloves garlic, minced

1 cup kalamata olives, pitted and halved

½ cup white wine

Kosher salt and freshly ground black pepper

4 swordfish steaks, 7 to 8 ounces each

2 tablespoons torn fresh basil leaves, for garnish

1 lime, quartered, for garnish

Prepare a clean, well-oiled charcoal or gas grill so that the coals or heat element are medium-hot. Or, heat the broiler.

In a sauté pan, heat 2 tablespoons of the olive oil over medium heat. If using anchovies, sauté the fillets for about 30 seconds so that they "melt" or almost disappear. Add the onion and red and yellow peppers and cook for about 3 minutes, or until softened. Add the garlic and sauté for about 1 minute. Take care so the garlic does not burn.

Add the olives and white wine and cook for 3 to 4 minutes, until the wine is reduced by half. Season to taste with salt and black pepper.

Season the fish generously with salt and pepper and drizzle with the remaining 1 tablespoon olive oil. Grill the steaks, turning only once, for about 10 minutes, or until the fish is opaque all the way through.

Lay 1 piece of swordfish on each of 4 plates and top with the pepper and onion mixture. Garnish with the basil and lime wedges and spoon the liquid from the peppers and onions over the fish. Serve immediately.

The steaks in this chapter

are just the ticket for those times you want to "fire up the grill and throw on a steak." They are the quintessential steaks on a plate—nothing fussy or complicated and guaranteed to please your dinner guests and family members alike. These steaks are the reason I wrote the book. Simply put, I love to grill and I especially love to grill steak. I have been known to be outside on New Year's Eve, manning the grill as the icy wind whips off Lake Michigan and turns southern Illinois into a winter wonderland. I agree, it's more fun in the summer. But grilled meat tastes awfully good on a cold night, too.

The trick to these recipes is to buy the best beef you can afford, and to take great care when you cook it. I have peppered the chapter with hints and tips for doing both these things, so I don't think you'll have any problems. Whether you like a charcoal or gas grill, the steaks will be amazing. I promise.

High energy is the order of the day for grilled steaks and so I pump up some good outdoor music:
AEROSMITH | U2 | THE ROLLING STONES | THE BEATLES |
SANTANA

AND WE KNOW THAT ALL THINGS WORK TOGETHER FOR GOOD TO THOSE WHO LOVE GOD, TO THOSE WHO ARE THE CALLED ACCORDING TO HIS PURPOSE.   — ROMANS 8:28

STEAK ON A PLATE

Notes on the Steak Recipes

YOU WILL FIND THAT THE RECIPES in this chapter are quite similar to each other. This is because it's all about the steak, the cut, and how it's cooked, rather than any extra ingredients. These steaks are unadorned for good reason. I suggest a marinade with a few of them, but even the marinades are simple ones.

When you go to the expense of buying a superior cut of beef, you want to cook it to perfection and serve it simply—perhaps with a sauce, perhaps not. I see no reason to fool around with a great cut when it can very easily speak for itself.

Before you start, take the steak from the refrigerator and let it reach room temperature, which should take no more than 30 minutes (and if the day is hot, it will take only about 15 minutes). Pat the meat dry with a paper towel and then season it according to the recipe. You never want to grill or roast cold meat straight from the refrigerator because it won't cook properly. The exception to this is ground meat, which should be left in the fridge until you are ready to cook it.

How to Choose a Great Steak

DON'T BE AFRAID OF FAT WHEN YOU BUY STEAK. It is fat that provides beef with its glorious flavor and juicy texture. The marbling—the strands of fat running through the meat in a web-like network, which also is called "graining"—should be delicate and uniformly even. Avoid thick, ropy marbling and thick layers of outer fat. The fat itself should look creamy and moist and the meat should be light red—not dark, apple red. Don't be tempted by bright red steak without marbling. It will be tough and tasteless.

When the steak cooks, the fat dissolves and lubricates the meat and conducts Its great flavor throughout the meat. Narrow, even threads of fat melt evenly, while thick strands do not melt at the same rate and will leave the steak tough and tasting of fat.

BEEF CUTS

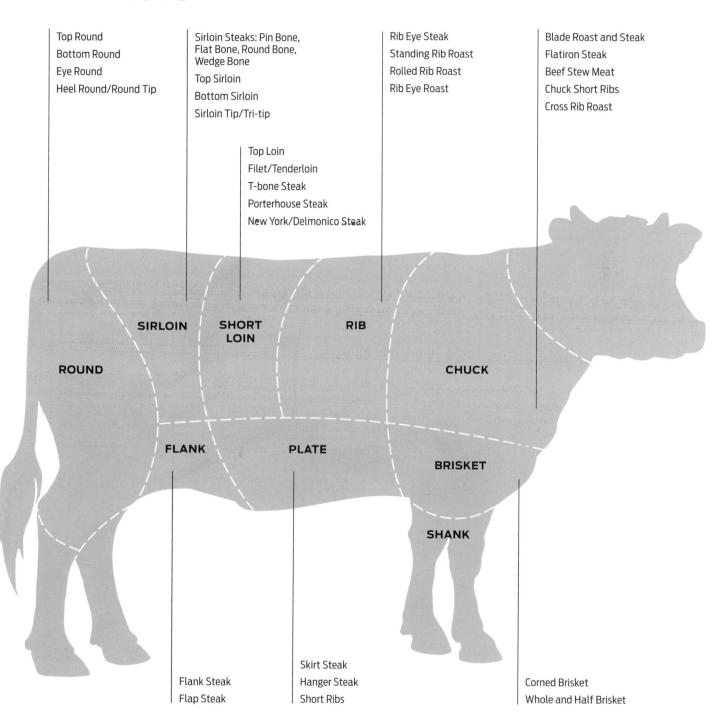

Top Round
Bottom Round
Eye Round
Heel Round/Round Tip

Sirloin Steaks: Pin Bone,
Flat Bone, Round Bone,
Wedge Bone
Top Sirloin
Bottom Sirloin
Sirloin Tip/Tri-tip

Rib Eye Steak
Standing Rib Roast
Rolled Rib Roast
Rib Eye Roast

Blade Roast and Steak
Flatiron Steak
Beef Stew Meat
Chuck Short Ribs
Cross Rib Roast

Top Loin
Filet/Tenderloin
T-bone Steak
Porterhouse Steak
New York/Delmonico Steak

SIRLOIN

SHORT LOIN

RIB

ROUND

CHUCK

FLANK

PLATE

BRISKET

SHANK

Flank Steak
Flap Steak

Skirt Steak
Hanger Steak
Short Ribs

Corned Brisket
Whole and Half Brisket

It's easy to spot a strip steak: It looks like a T-bone without the tenderloin. This is because this steak is created when the tenderloin is removed from the short loin and the loin is cut into steaks. Strip steaks are also called shell steaks because they refer to the meat surrounding the tenderloin. I call them New York strips, but some folks call them Kansas City strips. Whatever you call them, cook them carefully and enjoy a great piece of beef. If you can find dry-aged strip steaks you are in for a treat. The aging improves the flavor, making the steak more intense, more tender, and completely irresistible. **SERVES 4**

DRY-AGED NEW YORK STRIP

4 dry-aged boneless New York strip steaks, about 12 ounces each and 1½ inches thick

½ cup olive oil

Kosher salt and freshly ground black pepper

Cognac Sauce (page 176) or Bordelaise Sauce (page 176)

Prepare a clean, well-oiled charcoal or gas grill so that the coals or heat element are medium-hot. Or, heat the broiler.

Brush both sides of the steaks with the olive oil and season liberally with salt and pepper.

Grill the steaks, turning once, for a total of 15 minutes for rare meat or 18 minutes for medium-rare. Let the steaks rest for about 5 minutes before serving.

Meanwhile, in a saucepan, heat the Cognac or the bordelaise sauce over medium heat for 3 to 4 minutes, until hot.

Put the steaks on each of 4 serving plates and pass the sauce on the side.

How to Grill a Perfect Steak

A BIG, THICK STEAK ON THE GRILL should be treated with great care. If you overcook it, there is nothing for it. You will have to eat dry, gray meat. It may taste okay but it will not be as amazing as a well-cooked, juicy steak, charred on the outside and temptingly pink on the inside. I understand that not everyone likes rare meat but most folks appreciate medium-rare steak. Below are guidelines for how long to grill a steak. But first, a few caveats:

- Clean the grill and oil the grilling grid well so that the meat does not stick. Use any vegetable oil for this, such as canola or safflower.

- Make sure the coals have reached the right temperature or the heating elements are nice and hot.

- Lay the steak on the grill using tongs. You do not, under any circumstances, want to pierce the steak and release the valuable juices.

- Only turn the steak once and use tongs.

- Be sure to let the steak rest for at least 5 minutes once it's done.

I have provided total cooking times for the steaks in each recipe, and suggest that you turn the steak about halfway into that time—no more. As a rule, the first side should cook slightly longer than the second because by the time the meat is turned, it has already taken on some heat.

THICK STEAKS
(ABOUT 1 INCH THICK)

FOR RARE MEAT:
cook for about 10 minutes

FOR MEDIUM-RARE:
cook for about 15 minutes

FOR MEDIUM-WELL:
cook for about 20 minutes

REALLY THICK STEAKS
(1¼ TO 1½ INCHES THICK)

FOR RARE MEAT:
cook for about 12 minutes

FOR MEDIUM-RARE:
cook for about 17 minutes

FOR MEDIUM-WELL:
cook for about 22 minutes

SUPER THICK STEAKS
(ABOUT 2 INCHES THICK)

FOR RARE MEAT:
cook for about 15 minutes

FOR MEDIUM-RARE:
cook for about 20 minutes

FOR MEDIUM-WELL:
cook for about 25 minutes

Filet mignon, cut from the tenderloin, is considered the most tender cut of all—it also seems to be America's favorite cut. Because this muscle gets little exercise, the meat is yielding but also milder tasting than other cuts. Some folks prefer this, while others would rather eat a strip or club steak for a more robust flavor. The filet should be cooked using a dry method such as grilling, roasting, or sautéing—never braising—and served with a luxurious sauce, such as the classic Béarnaise or red wine sauce that so many people associate with it. **SERVES 4**

FILET MIGNON

4 filet mignons, 6 to 8 ounces each and about 2 inches thick

¼ cup olive oil

Kosher salt and freshly ground black pepper

Fleur de sel and cracked black pepper

Béarnaise Sauce (page 175) or Red Wine Sauce (page 183)

Prepare a clean, well-oiled charcoal or gas grill so that the coals or heat element are medium-hot. Or, heat the broiler.

Brush both sides of the filets with olive oil and season liberally with kosher salt and ground pepper.

Grill the steaks, turning once, for a total of 14 minutes for rare meat or 16 minutes for medium-rare. Let the steaks rest for about 5 minutes before serving.

Put each filet on each of 4 serving plates and finish with the fleur de sel and cracked pepper. Pass the sauce on the side.

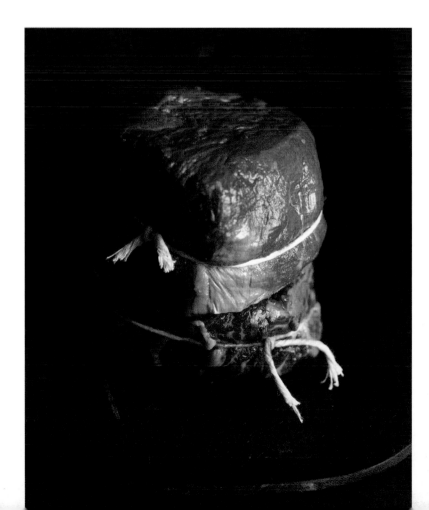

This is one of my favorite cuts—well, unless I am offered a bone-in rib eye, which is also one of my favorites. Hanger steak is not very pretty and comes in two lumpy pieces connected by a tough sinew that should be disconnected and discarded. Hangers are also known as butcher's steaks because in the old days no one wanted such a homely-looking piece of meat and so the butchers took them home for their own families—much to their delight. Today these cuts are extremely trendy and popular, and for good reason: Hanger steak is full bodied and downright delicious. It takes very well to being marinated. **SERVES 4**

HANGER STEAK

2 hanger steaks, about 1 pound each, cleaned, trimmed, and jacquarded by a butcher

Balsamic Marinade (page 191)

Olive oil

Kosher salt and freshly ground black pepper

Mushroom Jus (page 186)

In a shallow baking dish, cover the steaks with the marinade. Gently rub it into the meat. Cover and refrigerate for at least 24 hours or up to 36 hours.

Prepare a clean, well-oiled charcoal or gas grill so that the coals or heat element are medium-hot. Or, heat the broiler.

Lift the steaks from the marinade and let the marinade drip into the dish. Brush the steaks with olive oil and season generously with salt and pepper.

Grill the steaks, turning 2 or 3 times, for a total of 12 to 14 minutes for medium-rare meat. Brush the steaks with the marinade during the first half of grilling. If the thin ends of the steaks are getting done before the thicker, turn the steaks so that the thin sections are on the outer, or cooler, part of the grill. Let the steaks rest for about 5 minutes before serving.

Meanwhile, in a saucepan, heat the jus over medium heat until very hot.

Slice the steaks against the grain, and divide among 4 serving plates or arrange on a platter. Spoon the jus over the steak and serve.

Thick, Juicy Steaks

I LIKE TO COOK STEAKS that are 1½ to 2 inches thick so that the outside of the meat has time to develop a nicely charred crust before the interior cooks through. To ensure that the juices remain inside the meat, never, never pierce a steak with a fork or slice it open with a knife. Use tongs to move it on and off the grill and to maneuver it over the heat. Then always, always let the meat rest for 5 to 8 minutes before slicing it.

A few years ago, Kobe beef from Japan was all the rage. It is an especially tender steak from Wagyu beef cattle who are raised with tender, loving care that sometimes includes daily massages and a ration of beer. In the United States, breeders crossed Angus cattle with domestically raised Wagyu to meet the demand and so you will see domestic steaks that are labeled "Kobe style." Another way to satisfy the demand for Wagyu is to serve a less expensive cut of meat from a Wagyu steer, as I do here with flatirons, also known as top blade steaks. The steak is very rich and well marbled—so if you like tender steaks, try this. **SERVES 4**

KOBE FLATIRON STEAK

4 Kobe or Kobe-style flatiron steaks, 10 to 12 ounces each and about 1 inch thick

¼ cup olive oil

Kosher salt and freshly ground black pepper

1 cup Red Wine Sauce (page 183)

Prepare a clean, well-oiled charcoal or gas grill so that the coals or heat element are medium-hot. Or, heat the broiler.

Brush both sides of the steaks with the oil and season generously with salt and pepper.

Grill the steaks, turning once, for a total of 10 minutes for rare meat or 15 minutes for medium-rare. Let the steaks rest for about 5 minutes before serving.

Meanwhile, in a small saucepan, heat the sauce over medium heat for 3 to 4 minutes, until hot.

Slice the steaks against the grain, and divide among 4 serving plates or arrange on a platter. Spoon the warm sauce over the steak and serve.

How to Tell When the Steak Is Done

MANY HOME COOKS FEEL MOST COMFORTABLE relying on an instant-read thermometer to determine when the steak is done. I agree that it's far more preferable to insert a thermometer into a thick section of the steak than to slice it open with a paring knife. If you cut it, the juices will spill out, and that's no good!

Experienced cooks and chefs judge doneness by feel. Press the steak where it is thickest and if it feels like the pad of flesh at the base of your thumb, it's rare. If it feels like the area between the base of your thumb and the center of the palm, it's medium-rare. If it feels like the center of your palm, it's medium.

If you prefer to use the thermometer, here are the USDA-approved internal temperatures for beef:

130°F = rare
140°F = medium-rare
150°F = medium
160°F = well done

Everyone loves these large steaks, which are cut from the short loin where it meets the rump. Depending on where the steak is cut, it may be called a top sirloin or a bottom sirloin: The top is more desirable. Look for steaks with good marbling as you don't want a tough steak. Sirloin is the cut used for classic steak au poivre, and also does very well when marinated. **SERVES 4**

SIRLOIN STEAK

4 top sirloin steaks, 6 to 8 ounces each and about 1½ inches thick

Balsamic Marinade (page 191)

¼ cup olive oil

Kosher salt and freshly ground black pepper

Au Poivre Sauce (page 174)

In a shallow baking dish, cover the steaks with the marinade. Gently rub it into the meat. Cover and refrigerate for at least 8 hours or up to 24 hours.

Prepare a clean, well-oiled charcoal or gas grill so that the coals or heat element are medium-hot. Or, heat the broiler.

Lift the steaks from the marinade and let the marinade drip into the dish. Brush the steaks with the olive oil and season generously with salt and pepper.

Grill the steaks, turning once, for a total of 12 to 14 minutes for rare meat or 16 to 18 minutes for medium-rare. Let the steaks rest for about 5 minutes before serving.

Meanwhile, in a saucepan, heat the sauce over medium heat until very hot.

Slice the steaks against the grain, and divide among 4 serving plates or arrange on a platter. Spoon the sauce over the steak and serve.

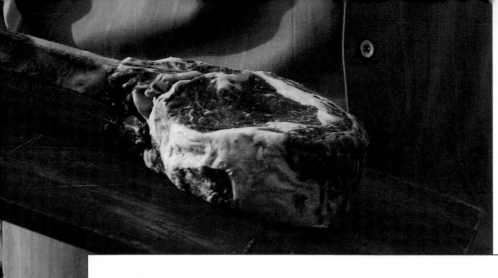

What Is Prime Beef?

AS ITS NAME SUGGESTS, PRIME BEEF IS THE BEST THERE IS. It's not always easy to find USDA prime beef because only 1 or 2 percent of the beef sold in the entire United States can be labeled "prime." It's exceptional beef with fine-grain marbling, even color, and firm texture. A trained butcher or chef can recognize prime beef, but not every home cook can. This is why it's important to establish a relationship with a butcher, should you be lucky enough to have one. He or she will steer you in the right direction.

Just below prime is choice. USDA choice beef is a lot easier to come by than prime and is very, very good. The best choice beef is Angus, although other varieties of choice beef are tasty, too.

Dry-Aged Versus Wet-Aged Steak

VERY LITTLE BEEF IS DRY AGED ANYMORE—but when it is, it is unbelievably tasty and tender. To dry age, raw beef is hung in a temperature-controlled meat locker for four to six weeks. During this time the low-humidity environment is maintained at 34° to 36°F and the meat loses moisture and blood as enzymes break down fibers in the muscle. The final result is that the meat is intensely flavored and so tender "you can cut it with a fork." (Not really, but you get the idea!)

Understandably, most meat purveyors don't dry age their meat. Not only do they need the requisite meat lockers, but the meat loses about 30 percent of its original size when dry aged. That's a direct hit to the bottom line. High-end butchers, such as Lobel's of New York, dry age their steaks and it's worth buying it at least once for the experience. Go to www.Lobels.com. Other sources are Meyer Natural Beef, www.meyernaturalbeef.com and Allen Brothers, www.allenbrothers.com.

Most butchers, if they age beef at all, wet age it for two or three weeks. While this helps the texture of the beef, it does not improve its flavor. This is the industry norm, where the beef is left in the Cryovac wrapping In which it's shipped to age. This kind of aging is better than nothing; most supermarkets don't age beef at all but instead sell it as soon as it arrives. However, some of the more upscale and progressive supermarkets may have it from time to time. Get to know the butchers at your market; they could become your best allies.

I am so pleased skirt steaks have enjoyed a comeback in recent years because they are just delicious. All skirt steaks are cut from under the breast, the lower part of the brisket, whether they are labeled as an inside or outside skirt. Both are long, flat pieces of meat that, when properly cooked, are full flavored. Outside-cut skirts are more tender and juicy and preferred for grilling. The inside-cut skirts are similar in size but tend to be a little tougher, which could be why they often are used for fajitas. Be sure to slice skirt steaks across the grain when you serve them. **SERVES 4**

SKIRT STEAK

4 outside-cut skirt steaks, 10 to 12 ounces each and about ¾ inch thick, cleaned and trimmed by a butcher

¼ cup olive oil

Kosher salt and freshly ground black pepper

T:1 Sauce (page 184)

Prepare a clean, well-oiled charcoal or gas grill so that the coals or heat element are medium-hot. Or, heat the broiler.

Brush both sides of the steaks with the olive oil and season generously with salt and pepper.

Grill the steaks, turning once, for a total of 10 minutes for rare meat or 15 minutes for medium-rare. Let the steaks rest for about 5 minutes before serving.

Slice the steaks against the grain, and divide among 4 serving plates or arrange on a platter. Top with the sauce.

Tempranillo Wine

THIS GRAPE IS GROWN THROUGHOUT THE IBERIAN PENINSULA, but every region seems to call it by a different name: Cencibel, Oja, and Tinto Fino, to name a few. The Rioja region of Spain uses Tempranillo traditionally as the cornerstone of their red blends. Leathery smoky earthiness lifts up bright red fruit notes of dates and strawberries. The classic style is also marked by the use of American oak barrels, which give the wines a bourbon-like quality in their youth and a smooth dill flavor when it ages.

Bone-in rib eyes are large and robust steaks cut from the forequarter, rib section of the animal. But because of the bone, there is not an excessive amount of meat. When you remove the bone from the steak, it becomes a rib eye steak. I love bone-in rib eye and consider it my favorite cut, along with hanger steak. There is nothing more primal than cutting into one of these beauties. **SERVES 4**

BONE-IN RIB EYE

4 bone-in rib eye steaks, about 20 ounces each and 1½ inches thick

½ cup olive oil

Kosher salt and freshly ground black pepper

Bordelaise Sauce (page 176)

Prepare a clean, well-oiled charcoal or gas grill so that the coals or heat element are medium-hot. Or, heat the broiler.

Brush both sides of the steaks with the olive oil and season liberally with salt and pepper.

Grill the steaks, turning once, for a total of 12 to 14 minutes for rare meat or 16 to 18 minutes for medium-rare. Let the steaks rest for about 10 minutes before serving.

Meanwhile, in a saucepan, heat the sauce over medium heat for 3 to 4 minutes, until hot.

Slice the rested steaks against the grain, and divide among 4 plates or arrange on a platter. Top with the sauce, making sure there are pieces of marrow with each steak. Serve.

When the bone of a very thick rib eye is frenched (all the meat scraped off), it becomes a tomahawk steak—also known as a cowboy steak. When I was a judge on *Top Chef,* the contestants cooked these to recreate one of my signature dishes. At the restaurant, I broil the meat at temperatures of 800° to 900°F, but you will get good results on a hot grill. **SERVES 4**

TOMAHAWK STEAK

2 tomahawk steaks (frenched bone-in rib eye steaks), 1½ to 2 pounds each and 2¼ inches thick

½ cup olive oil

Kosher salt and freshly ground black pepper

Prepare a clean, well-oiled charcoal or gas grill so that the coals or heat element are hot. Or, heat the broiler.

Brush both sides of the steaks with the olive oil and season liberally with salt and pepper.

Set the steaks on the hottest part of the grill and sear each side for about 5 minutes. Move to a slightly cooler part of the grill, cover, and cook, turning once, for 30 to 35 minutes total for medium-rare. Let the steaks rest for about 10 minutes before serving.

Slice the rested steaks, and divide among 4 plates or arrange on a platter and serve.

Natural Beef, Organic Beef, Grass-Fed Beef

MORE AND MORE PEOPLE ARE INTERESTED IN NATURAL, ORGANIC, AND GRASS-FED BEEF, either because they are concerned about the environment or about how the animals are raised and slaughtered—or both. There are differences in these kinds of beef.

NATURAL BEEF: This beef comes from cattle raised without antibiotics or hormones. Otherwise, the cattle are fed in feedlots similarly to traditional cattle.

ORGANIC BEEF: The cattle that yield organic beef are fed certified-organic feed from the time they are weaned. They, too, are not given antibiotics or hormones.

GRASS-FED BEEF: These cattle eat only grass since they graze in pastures all their lives. They are not fed corn, as are other cattle, and so take longer to reach their optimal weight. Often they are a little older than other cattle at the time of slaughter. Grass-fed beef is leaner than other beef and has a slightly different, yet still appealing, flavor.

These small steaks are cut from the short loin, near the rib end. When correctly cut and with a fine-grained eye (center nugget of meat), they can be absolutely tender and delicious. I like to cook relatively thick club steaks, although some people like them cut quite thin so that they cook very quickly. If boned, these steaks may be called boneless top loin steaks or Delmonico steaks and most likely were the original Delmonico steak, made famous by the legendary New York restaurant in the 1800s. **SERVES 4**

CLUB STEAK

4 club steaks, 12 to 14 ounces each and about 1½ inches thick

½ cup olive oil

Kosher salt and freshly ground black pepper

Prepare a clean, well-oiled charcoal or gas grill so that the coals or heat element are medium-hot. Or, heat the broiler.

Brush both sides of the steaks with the olive oil and season liberally with salt and pepper.

Grill the steaks, turning once, for a total of 12 to 14 minutes for rare meat or 16 to 18 minutes for medium-rare. Let the steaks rest for about 5 minutes before serving.

Slice the rested steaks, and divide among 4 plates or arrange on a platter.

Malbec Wine

MALBEC IS A GRAPE THAT OFFERS AN INKY COLOR AND ROBUST TANNINS: a combination made in heaven for the bold flavors of just-off-the-grill steak. Malbec is grown all over the world and is often used as a blending grape to make use of its intense color. Argentina stands out as the country that has put the grape in a bottle, with delicious results. The high altitude of Argentina's Mendoza region contributes to the acidity to balance those firm tannins. This juicy balance makes this wine perfect for intense flavors like burgers, crusted steaks, and dry-rubbed pork. But the real beauty of the wine is its value, which is true of many of the awesome wines from South America. There are a multitude of bottles of Malbec that sell for less than $15 that you can purchase with confidence.

The porterhouse is a generous steak when it comes to flavor and size. It is extremely popular in steakhouses, but there's no reason not to cook it at home. It is cut from the short loin near the sirloin and contains a sizable amount of tenderloin—the perfect steak to share with friends. **SERVES 4**

PORTERHOUSE STEAK

1 porterhouse steak, 3 to 3½ pounds and 1½ to 1¾ inches thick

½ cup olive oil

Kosher salt and freshly ground black pepper

Prepare a clean, well-oiled charcoal or gas grill so that the coals or heat element are medium-hot. Or, heat the broiler.

Brush both sides of the steak with olive oil and season liberally with salt and pepper.

Grill the steak, with the grill covered, turning once, for a total of 18 to 20 minutes for rare meat or 20 to 24 minutes for medium-rare. Let the steak rest for about 5 minutes before serving.

Slice the rested steak, and divide among 4 plates or arrange on a platter.

I love flank steak, as do most people who have enjoyed a well-cooked one. These lean, flat cuts of meat, cut from the lower section of the short loin, are full of flavor and deliciously tender. Known as inexpensive cuts of meat and less costly than other steaks, they are not exactly cheap! Flank steak is the cut most often used for London broil, which is not an actual cut but a preparation. Flank is terrific for marinating and once cooked, must be sliced across the grain, or to put it another way, sliced on the diagonal, crossway to the fibrous grain of the meat. **SERVES 4**

FLANK STEAK

4 flank steaks, about 8 ounces each, or 1 large flank steak, 1½ to 2 pounds

Spicy Soy Marinade (page 191)

¼ cup olive oil

Kosher salt and freshly ground black pepper

In a shallow glass or ceramic baking dish, cover the steaks with the marinade. Gently rub it into the meat. Cover and refrigerate for at least 6 hours or up to 8 hours.

Prepare a clean, well-oiled charcoal or gas grill so that the coals or heat element are medium-hot. Or, heat the broiler.

Lift the steaks from the marinade and let the marinade drip into the dish. Brush the steaks with the olive oil and season generously with salt and pepper.

Grill the steaks, turning once, for a total of 12 to 14 minutes for medium-rare meat. Let the steaks rest for about 5 minutes before serving.

Slice the steaks against the grain, and divide among 4 serving plates or arrange on a platter.

Everyone knows that a T-bone steak has a very easy-to-identify bone that is shaped like a "T." Cut from the center section of the short loin between the porterhouse and the club, it's rich, tender, and full of good steak flavor. A T-bone resembles a porterhouse, although it is smaller. **SERVES 4**

T-BONE STEAK

4 T-bone steaks, about 20 ounces each and 1½ inches thick

½ cup olive oil

Kosher salt and freshly ground black pepper

Prepare a clean, well-oiled charcoal or gas grill so that the coals or heat element are medium-hot. Or, heat the broiler.

Brush both sides of the steaks with the olive oil and season liberally with salt and pepper.

Grill the steaks, turning once, for a total of 12 to 14 minutes for rare meat or 16 to 18 minutes for medium-rare. Let the steaks rest for about 10 minutes before serving.

Slice the rested steaks, and divide among 4 plates or arrange on a platter.

Zinfandel Wine

ARGUMENTS OFTEN SURFACE AROUND THE GEOGRAPHICAL LINEAGE OF THIS GRAPE (with scientific evidence to support them), but it is truly the American style of Zinfandel that created its popularity. It has that unique quality of offering jammy blue and red fruit flavors that never have to compete with overpowering tannins. Alcohol can be high and a bit over the top, which can make it difficult with complex dishes. Look for wines from the cooler climates of northern California, notably Sonoma County and regions such as Dry Creek Valley and Russian River Valley that make juicier wines with a livelier acidity.

The recipes in this chapter

are the stuff of memories—or dreams. Even if you have never had Beef Wellington, the very name conjures up images of grand dinner parties, perhaps with a footman behind every chair. On the other hand, both Mom's Meat Loaf and Steak and Kidney Pie are simple fare—the dishes those footmen probably ate at the kitchen table, behind the scenes! All are classics and belong to every generation that loves and appreciates them. I am teaching my own kids how to make some of these dishes and I hope to encourage you to celebrate what was best about days gone by. Never fear: I have made them very accessible to the twenty-first-century home cook.

By now you know that I am less interested in hosting grand dinner parties than I am in welcoming friends and family to my house—usually my kitchen—for informal gatherings that center around good conversation, good music, and good food. All the classic dishes here are perfect for this sort of get-together, and who knows? They may spark some funny or endearing stories of "the first time I tried to make Beef Wellington . . ." or "My grandma loved Steak Diane so much . . ." And that's fun!

Classic dishes call for classic tunes sung by classic crooners:
FRANK SINATRA | RAY CHARLES | HARRY CONNICK, JR. |
SAM COOKE | MICHAEL BUBLE | BRYAN FERRY | ELLA FITZGERALD

STEAK AND BEEF CLASSICS

Prime rib roast makes us think of celebrations, whether it's Christmas dinner, a milestone birthday, or a special dinner party. When I was growing up, my mother cooked it for Christmas Day or New Year's Day—and that was it. We never saw prime rib at home again until the following December. I liked it so much, I nearly always ordered it when I saw it on the menu on those rare occasions when we dined out—and nowadays I still keep a hopeful eye out for it. In my memory, the thick slice of beef covered most of the plate and was nearly always accompanied by a baked potato with sour cream. As a youngster, nothing seemed more grand! I still like prime rib and can't help but think of it as just the thing for an exceptional meal.

Prime ribs of beef are not always prime beef. The name has nothing to do with the USDA grades, although of course some rib roasts are prime. Confusing? Don't worry about it—buy the best roast you can afford, but expect to spend a pretty sum. The roast is cut from the rib section of the forequarter and can be cut so that it has only two ribs or as many as seven ribs, in which case it is large enough for 12 to 14 servings. If you plan to cook a large roast, make sure your oven is big enough!

Rib roasts are juicy and well marbled, with a thick layer of fat over the exterior. They are sold as standing or half standing rib roasts with the short ribs intact. They also are sold as rolled rib roasts, which means the ribs have been removed and the boned meat, including the exterior fat, is rolled and tied. **SERVES 6 TO 8**

PRIME RIB

1 (3-rib) prime beef rib roast, small end with ribs attached (5 to 6 pounds)

2 tablespoons kosher salt

Freshly ground black pepper

¼ cup olive oil

1 yellow onion, coarsely chopped

6 cloves garlic

2 tablespoons grated fresh horseradish

2 tablespoons fresh thyme leaves

½ cup dry red wine

1½ cups beef stock, preferably homemade (page 187)

Position an oven rack at the lowest level of the oven. Preheat the oven to 450°F.

Carefully cut the rib bones from the roast so that the ribs are still attached to each other (you can also ask the butcher to do this for you). Lay the ribs in a roasting pan; they will serve as a rack for the roast. Sprinkle both the ribs and the roast generously with the salt and pepper.

In the bowl of a food processor fitted with the metal blade, process the olive oil, onion, garlic, horseradish, and thyme until a smooth paste forms. Press the paste on all sides of the roast. Put the roast, fat side up, on the ribs in the pan.

Roast for 20 minutes and then reduce the oven temperature to 275°F. Roast for about 1½ hours longer, or until an instant-read thermometer inserted in the thickest part of the meat registers 110°F.

Remove the roast and ribs from the oven, transfer to a platter, and let rest for about 25 minutes, during which time its internal temperature will rise to 135°F for medium-rare meat.

Meanwhile, pour the pan drippings into a glass measuring cup. Scrape or pour off the grease that rises to the surface and reserve the remaining juices.

Set the roasting pan over medium-high heat and add the red wine. Deglaze the pan by scraping the bottom of the pan with a wooden spoon to loosen all the browned bits. When the wine comes to a boil, let it cook for 5 to 8 minutes, until reduced by half. Add the reserved pan juices, any juice that has collected on the platter, and the beef stock. Bring to a boil and cook, stirring often, for 5 to 8 minutes, until reduced again by half.

Slice the roast into pieces defined by where the ribs were—this is easy to determine. Reserve the rib "rack" for another use (I like to make stock with them). Serve with the reduced pan sauce.

Horseradish

FRESH HORSERADISH IS A GNARLY ROOT that is sold in supermarkets from the fall through the spring. Wash the root, peel the tough, outer skin, and trim away any bitter, green spots. Use a grater to shred the white root, avoiding the fibrous core. Peel only what you will use and refrigerate the remaining root wrapped in a kitchen towel.

Once you get into the habit of using fresh horseradish you will prefer its clean, fresh flavor to the horseradish sold in a jar. That said, bottled horseradish is a very good alternative if you can't find fresh. When it comes to prepared horseradish, I like Atomic brand. It is made in small batches and is especially intense and potent—a horseradish lover's dream. You might have to order it online or look for it in specialty stores.

Jarred, or prepared, horseradish is nothing more than shredded horseradish packed in white vinegar or beet juice. When the horseradish is white, it is packed in vinegar; when pink, it is packed in beet juice. Powdered horseradish is also good and can easily be reconstituted with water.

Beef Wellington was the first "fancy" dish I learned to make when I was a line cook at the Strathallan Hotel in Rochester, New York, in 1981. Back then, I was pretty pleased with myself, and to this day I still love the dish. I have heard that this elegant entrée is named for Arthur Wellesley, the first duke of Wellington, who helped defeat Napoleon—and who evidently had a passion for beef, mushrooms, Madeira wine, and pâté, as well as for pastry. Someone—his personal chef? country estate cook?—created a spectacular dish for him using those very ingredients. This may or may not be true, but to this day Beef Wellington is much loved by many.

Although no one knows for sure how the dish came about, suffice it to say that, luckily for us, there is a long history of pastry-wrapped meat dishes in England, Ireland, and France. The dish became the darling of American hostesses in the 1960s and then faded into culinary oblivion, referenced, if at all, with derisive laughter. Happily, it is coming back into style, and none too soon. It's a classic that deserves landmark status.

The pastry holds in the juices so that when the roast is sliced, they mingle with the crispy, browned pastry, pâté, beef, and mushrooms (cooked here into duxelles) for mouthfuls of exploding flavors. I can't think of a better way to spend an afternoon than preparing one of these masterpieces for my friends. Truth be told, with frozen puff pastry available in every supermarket in the land, this is not especially hard to make. Don't roast it until you are ready to serve it, and be prepared for "oohs" and "ahhs." **SERVES 6**

BEEF WELLINGTON

1 center-cut, trimmed beef tenderloin, 2½ pounds

6 tablespoons unsalted butter, softened

1 shallot, minced

½ cup minced cremini mushrooms

2 ounces store-bought pâté de foie gras or other good-quality liver pâté

Kosher salt and freshly ground black pepper

1 sheet puff pastry (from a 17.5-ounce package of frozen puff pastry), thawed

1 large egg yolk, beaten

Red Wine Sauce (page 183)

Preheat the oven to 425°F.

Put the beef in a small roasting pan and spread 2 tablespoons of the butter over the meat. Roast for 10 to 15 minutes, until browned. Remove the meat from the pan and let it cool completely at room temperature. Reserve the pan juices.

In a skillet, heat 2 tablespoons of the butter over medium heat. When melted and hot, sauté the shallot and mushrooms for about 5 minutes, or until the vegetables begin to soften. Remove the skillet from the heat and let the vegetables cool.

In a small bowl, mix together the pâté and remaining 2 tablespoons butter. Season with salt and pepper. Spread the pâté over the beef and then top it with the cooled shallot and mushroom mixture.

Preheat the oven to 450°F. Roll out the sheet of puff pastry so that it measures about 1 inch larger on each side than it was. Put the beef in the center of the pastry rectangle and fold the dough up and over the tenderloin. Seal the edges, making sure the seams are not too thick. If so, press on them to make them thinner. Put the beef Wellington in a 9 by 13-inch flameproof roasting dish, cut a few slits in the top of the dough, and brush with the egg yolk.

Roast for 10 minutes, then reduce the heat to 425°F. Roast for 10 to 15 minutes longer, until the pastry is a rich, golden brown. Remove the Wellington from the pan and set aside to rest for about 10 minutes.

Pour the sauce into the roasting pan with the pan juices and bring to a boil over medium heat. Taste and adjust the seasonings. Transfer to a warm gravy boat.

Slice the Wellington into 6 slices and serve with the red wine sauce.

Cabernet Sauvignon Wine

MORE WINE LOVERS CITE THIS AS THE GRAPE THAT GOT THEM STARTED ("stained their teeth" if you will) than any other. Juicy, rich, and powerful fruit flavors of blackberry, currants, and cassis are at the core of this wine, which is also marked by intensely firm tannins. Cabernets made in America, particularly from California, are noted for their high alcohol content balanced with intense oak flavors hinting of vanilla, cinnamon, and nutmeg. But, as with most grapes, it is in France where Cabernet lovers end up, finding their way to the Bordeaux region. There, the alcohol and oak are kept in check for an emergence of earthier flavors such as roasted coffee beans or fresh-turned soil, both of which harmonize with those bold black fruit flavors.

When Italians cook steak, they go for it in a big way—no surprise considering how much gusto Italians have for all the finer things in life! With the last name of Tramonto, I share the same attitude: "Go big or go home!"

Typically, *bistecca alla fiorentina* is made with a gigantic porterhouse steak—big enough for two—from Italian Chianina or Maremmana cattle; it is generously sprinkled with salt and pepper and brushed with olive oil before grilling over wood or charcoal just until rare. The steak is then served with a drizzle of great olive oil, a squeeze of lemon juice, and a small arugula salad on the side, dressed with the same olive oil and lemon juice. All that is needed to round out the meal is a hearty red wine, usually Chianti, and some grilled crusty bread. **SERVES 4**

STEAK FLORENTINE WITH ARUGULA SALAD

STEAK

2 large cloves garlic, chopped

2 porterhouse steaks, 24 ounces each and 1½ to 1¾ inches thick

Kosher salt and freshly ground black pepper

ARUGULA SALAD

Grated zest and juice of 1 lemon

½ cup extra-virgin olive oil

6 cups arugula

Kosher salt and freshly cracked black pepper

About 2 ounces Parmigiano-Reggiano cheese

TO SERVE

2 lemons, halved

¼ cup extra-virgin olive oil (I use Tuscan olive oil for this dish)

Fleur de sel and freshly cracked black pepper

1 lemon, quartered, for garnish

Salsa Verde (page 181)

To cook the steaks: Rub the garlic over the steaks, including the portion of bone. Season the steaks aggressively with kosher salt and ground pepper and transfer to a glass or rigid plastic container. Cover and refrigerate for at least 1 hour or up to 4 hours to give the flavors time to permeate the meat.

Prepare a clean, well-oiled charcoal or gas grill so that the coals or heat element are medium-hot. Or, heat the broiler.

Grill the steaks, turning once, for a total of 10 minutes for rare meat or about 14 minutes for medium-rare.

Transfer the steaks to a cutting board and let them rest for about 10 minutes before slicing.

To make the arugula salad: In a mixing bowl, whisk together the lemon zest and juice and the olive oil. Add the arugula and toss with the dressing. Season to taste with kosher salt and cracked pepper. Using a vegetable peeler, shave the Parmesan in ribbons over the salad.

Run the knife along the bone of the steaks to carve the meat closest to it. Slice the meat into 1-inch-long slices.

To serve, spread the arugula salad on a large platter and top with the sliced steak. Squeeze the lemon halves over the hot steaks, drizzle with the ¼ cup olive oil, and finish with fleur de sel and cracked black pepper. Garnish the platter with lemon quarters and serve with the salsa verde.

The origins of this dish are a little murky. Some claim it was "invented" in 1950s New York City at the Sherry-Netherland hotel, or perhaps at the Colony restaurant, or maybe the Drake Hotel. Others put its inception in Rio de Janeiro, while far more attribute it to the famed French chef, Escoffier, around the turn of the twentieth century. It's very possible the name comes from the Roman goddess of the hunt, Diana, and the original dish dressed up venison or other game meat. In the final analysis, where it comes from matters less than how it tastes, and this is one incredible dish. It has a special place in my heart because I learned how to make it when I was a sauté cook at the Scotch 'n Sirloin steakhouse in Rochester, New York, in 1979. I still make it today.

I have not altered it much from earlier recipes because it's so good as it is. It is dramatic in its presentation—flamed at the table—and exquisite in its execution. The powerful flavors of Worcestershire sauce and mushrooms do justice to the meat and make this a classic in the best sense of the word. **SERVES 4**

STEAK DIANE

8 center-cut beef tenderloin medallions, each 3 ounces, trimmed and pounded ½ inch thick

Kosher salt and freshly ground black pepper

¼ cup olive oil

1 tablespoon unsalted butter

1 shallot, minced

2 cloves garlic, minced

½ cup thinly sliced cremini mushrooms

¼ cup Veal Jus (page 185)

Juice of 1 lemon

1 teaspoon Worcestershire sauce

2 teaspoons whole-grain mustard

1 tablespoon chopped fresh flat-leaf parsley

1 teaspoon fresh thyme leaves

½ cup heavy cream

1 tablespoon chopped fresh chives

2 tablespoons brandy

Season the medallions generously with salt and pepper.

In a large sauté pan, heat the olive oil over medium heat. When hot, raise the heat to medium-high and sear the medallions for about 2 minutes on each side. Transfer the steaks to a plate.

In the same sauté pan, melt the butter. Sauté the shallot, garlic, and mushrooms for 3 to 4 minutes, until they begin to soften. Add the veal jus, lemon juice, and Worcestershire and season to taste with salt and pepper. Return the steaks to the pan, along with the mustard, parsley, and thyme.

Cook the steaks over medium-high heat, turning once, for 8 to 10 minutes for medium-rare. At this point the steaks will not be cooked as you want them, but will continue to cook when the cream is added.

Add the cream and chives to the skillet and cook just long enough for the cream to heat through. Tilt the pan slightly, holding it above the burner, so that the liquid pools in the front of the pan and pour the brandy over it. With a match, ignite the brandy. The vapors from the brandy will ignite quickly, so take care. Swirl the sauce in the pan, still holding it above the burner, remove the pan from the heat, and let the flames extinguish.

Transfer the medallions to 4 plates and top with the sauce from the pan.

Most food historians agree that Steak au Poivre was conceived in France sometime during the first third of the twentieth century. It traveled well, and by the 1950s and '60s the peppery coated steak was a great favorite in French restaurants in New York, Boston, Chicago, and other cosmopolitan American cities. I am happy to see it popping up again on menus all over the country in fancy French restaurants and bistros. But I mostly like to make it at home when I am expecting guests. Commonly it is served with mashed potatoes or *pommes frites,* although I suspect it would be amazing with the Truffled Mac and Cheese on page 234. **SERVES 4**

STEAK AU POIVRE

¼ cup mixed whole peppercorns (such as black, white, green, Szechuan, and/or Tellicherry)

4 well-marbled boneless New York strip steaks, each 8 to 10 ounces and ¾ to 1 inch thick

Kosher salt

1 teaspoon vegetable oil

1 tablespoon unsalted butter

Au Poivre Sauce (page 174)

Spread the peppercorns on a cutting board or similar surface and using the bottom of a small, heavy skillet, roughly crush them. Take care so they don't fly all over the place: Put the skillet on top of them and press down and back and forth.

Sprinkle both sides of each steak generously with salt and then press the cracked peppercorns into each side to encrust the steaks.

In a large, heavy sauté pan or skillet, heat the oil and butter over high heat. When the butter melts and the oil is hot, sear the steaks for 1½ to 2 minutes, until the bottoms are nice and brown. Turn the meat and sear the other side for about 1 minute. Reduce the heat to medium-high and cook for 12 to 15 minutes for medium-rare. Do not turn the steaks again. Transfer the steaks to a warm platter.

Add the sauce to the pan and bring to a boil over medium-high heat. Cook, scraping the bottom of the pan with a wooden spoon to deglaze. Pour the pan sauce over the steaks and serve.

Syrah Wine

THIS ANCIENT GRAPE VARIETY MAKES LEGENDARY WINES from the Northern Rhone valley, but it is best known by another name—Shiraz—from the opposite corner of the world. In France, the wines from Syrah show light, black fruit flavors with fresh, ground black peppers marked with a cured-meat quality. Australia has capitalized on the broad, food-friendly flavors of this grape under the name Shiraz. In the intense heat of Southeast Australia, the grape makes ink-colored wines with syrupy blackberry and black currant flavors balanced with intense flavors of vanilla (often from American oak barrels).

Filet Oscar is a great favorite with steakhouse aficionados because of the lush, indulgent flavors and top-flight ingredients: filet mignon, crabmeat, asparagus, and béarnaise or hollandaise sauce. When you deconstruct it, it's nothing more than a fancy surf and turf dish, which is fine with me! The now-classic dish was borrowed from another classic: Veal Oscar, which was named for King Oscar II of Sweden (1829–1907). He so popularized the combination of veal, crabmeat, and asparagus that Veal Oscar was served in just about every fancy hotel dining room at the turn of the twentieth century. Man, I love food history. **SERVES 4**

FILET OSCAR

8 thick asparagus spears

4 filet mignons, about 8 ounces each and 2 inches thick

Kosher salt and freshly ground black pepper

8 slices sourdough bread, about ½ inch thick

¼ cup olive oil

2 cups (about ½ pound) loosely packed fresh lump crabmeat

2 tablespoons olive oil

1 tablespoon chopped fresh dill

1 tablespoon chopped fresh flat-leaf parsley

Grated zest and juice of 1 lemon, plus additional zest for garnish

¾ cup Red Wine Sauce (page 183), optional

4 sprigs thyme, for garnish

4 teaspoons extra-virgin olive oil, for garnish

Cracked black pepper, for garnish

1 cup Béarnaise Sauce (page 175), optional

Fill a saucepan or deep skillet about halfway with water and bring to a simmer over medium-high heat. Add the asparagus and blanch for 2 to 3 minutes. Drain and let cool. When cool enough to handle, cut the tips from the spears so that they are about 2 inches long. Set aside. Discard the spears or reserve for another use.

Preheat the oven to 400°F.

Prepare a clean well-oiled charcoal or gas grill so that the coals or heat element are hot. Or, heat the broiler.

Season the filets liberally on both sides with salt and pepper.

Lay the bread on a work surface and using a 3-inch round cookie cutter or upturned glass, stamp out 8 rounds. Transfer the rounds to a baking sheet and brush with olive oil. Bake, turning once, for 5 to 7 minutes. Turn the croutons and brush the flip side with oil. Bake for 3 to 4 minutes longer, or until light golden brown and crisp. Watch them carefully; they brown quickly around the edges. Set aside.

Lower the oven temperature to 350°F.

Lay the asparagus tips in a single layer on one side of a baking pan and spread the crabmeat on the other side. Transfer to the oven and heat for 8 to 10 minutes, until heated through. Cover to keep warm.

Meanwhile, grill the steaks, turning once, for a total of 12 to 14 minutes for rare or 16 to 18 minutes for medium-rare. Let the steaks rest for 5 to 7 minutes.

Stir the asparagus into the warm crabmeat, along with the olive oil, dill, parsley, and lemon zest and juice.

Place a crouton on each of 4 plates. Top each with a grilled filet, and then with another crouton. Top each filet sandwich with the warm asparagus and crab mixture. Spoon the red wine sauce over the tops and garnish each serving with a sprig of thyme, a little lemon zest, a teaspoon of olive oil, and some cracked black pepper. Serve the béarnaise sauce on the side.

Tournedos, sometimes called *petites filets,* are cut from the narrow portion of the beef tenderloin and sliced on the bias—you will probably have to order them from a butcher who knows what he or she is doing. If you prefer, you can substitute thick slices of tenderloin. I cook these with mushrooms, mustard, bacon, and cream, which is a stunning amalgamation of ingredients. I think mustard with beef is one of the best flavor combinations; in fact, it's not off the wall for me to dip pieces of grilled steak in straight mustard. Why not? **SERVES 4**

TOURNEDOS À LA TRAMONTO WITH BACON, MUSHROOMS, AND MUSTARD

CROUTONS

4 slices country-style bread, about ½ inch thick

Olive oil

Salt and freshly ground black pepper

TOURNEDOS

8 tournedos, about 3 ounces each and 1½ to 2 inches thick

8 slices apple-smoked bacon

Salt and freshly ground black pepper

2 tablespoons olive oil

3 tablespoons unsalted butter

1 pound cremini mushrooms, each cut into eighths

2 shallots, finely diced

1 tablespoon chopped garlic

1 cup red wine

1 cup beef stock, preferably homemade (page 187)

½ cup heavy cream

¼ cup coarse-grain mustard

1 tablespoon chopped fresh flat-leaf parsley

To make the croutons: Preheat the oven to 350ºF.

Lay the bread on a cutting board and using a 3-inch round biscuit cutter or upturned glass, stamp out rounds from the center of each slice.

Brush both sides of the croutons with olive oil and season with salt and pepper. Transfer the rounds to a baking sheet. Bake, turning once, for 6 to 8 minutes, until light golden brown. Watch carefully; they brown quickly around the edges.

To cook the tournedos: Season the tournedo liberally with salt and pepper. Wrap each slice of bacon tightly around a tournedos and secure with a toothpick.

In a large skillet, heat the olive oil and 1 tablespoon of the butter over high heat. When the butter melts and the oil is hot, sear the tournedos, turning them in the pan, until golden brown. Cook for 3 to 4 minutes longer for medium-rare meat. Be sure to manipulate the tournedos with tongs and brown the bacon on all sides so that it crisps. Transfer the cooked tournedos to a plate and set aside, covered to keep warm.

Return the skillet to high heat and when the pan drippings are hot, add the mushrooms and cook for 3 to 4 minutes, until golden brown and beginning to release their juices.

Add the shallots and garlic and cook over medium heat for 2 to 3 minutes, until softened.

Add the red wine and bring to a boil over high heat. Reduce the heat slightly and simmer for 3 to 4 minutes, until the liquid reduces by half. Add the stock to the skillet and bring to a boil over high heat. Reduce the heat slightly and simmer for 3 to 4 minutes, until the liquid reduces by half.

Stir in the cream and heat until the cream nearly boils. Immediately reduce the heat so that the cream simmers. Whisk in the mustard and remaining 2 tablespoons butter. Cook, whisking, for about 2 minutes, until the sauce is smooth and well integrated. Season to taste with salt and pepper.

Put a crouton on each of 4 serving plates and top with 2 tournedos (remove the toothpick or twine). Spoon some sauce over each and garnish with parsley.

These are simple kebabs: Nothing more than meat, colorful peppers, onions, and summer squash threaded on skewers, looking very pretty, and tasting even better. The marinade makes the steak sing. Feel free to substitute or add Italian sausage, chicken, or pork. The spirit of a mixed grill makes these even better.

SERVES 6

GRILLED BEEF AND VEGETABLE KEBABS

MARINADE

1 cup olive oil

½ cup honey

½ cup soy sauce

Juice of 1 orange

¼ cup packed brown sugar

3 tablespoons sherry vinegar

1 tablespoon chopped fresh ginger

2 cloves garlic, chopped

1 teaspoon dried red pepper flakes

¾ teaspoon freshly ground black pepper

KEBABS

1 red onion

1 yellow onion

1 green bell pepper, membranes removed and seeded

1 red bell pepper, membranes removed and seeded

1 yellow bell pepper, membranes removed and seeded

1 yellow summer squash

2½ pounds sirloin, strip, or tenderloin steak, about 1 inch thick

Cracked pink peppercorns

Soak 6 long wooden skewers in cold water for 30 to 45 minutes. (If using metal skewers, this is not necessary.)

To make the marinade: In a mixing bowl, whisk together the oil, honey, soy sauce, orange juice, brown sugar, vinegar, ginger, garlic, red pepper flakes, and black pepper.

To make the kebabs: Cut the onions, peppers, and squash into 1½-inch pieces. Cut the steak into 1½- to 2-inch pieces. The idea is to get all the pieces of food approximately the same size. Put the vegetables in one glass, ceramic, or other nonreactive bowl and the meat in another. Divide the marinade evenly between the 2 bowls. Cover both and refrigerate for at least 1 hour or up to 8 hours.

Prepare a clean, well-oiled charcoal or gas grill so that the coals or heat element are medium-hot. Or, heat the broiler.

Lift the vegetables and meat from the bowls and start threading the skewers. Begin with a piece of steak and then alternate the steak with the different vegetables. Once the kebabs are assembled, season them with a sprinkling of the peppercorns.

Grill the kebabs, turning several times, for a total of 8 to 10 minutes. Serve immediately.

The Easy Rules for Kebabs

I LOVE KEBABS FOR OUTDOOR ENTERTAINING. For some reason, serving food threaded on skewers makes a party especially festive and fun. And there is not much cleanup, which is great. There are only a few things to keep in mind when you assemble kebabs:

- You can assemble the skewers ahead of time and lay them on a baking sheet or jelly roll pan. Cover and refrigerate until ready to grill.

- If using wooden or bamboo skewers, be sure to soak them in cool water for at least 20 minutes or up to several hours. This prevents them from scorching on the grill.

- Thread the skewers with pieces of food that are all about the same size.

- Leave a little space between the pieces of food so that heat can surround them and everything cooks evenly.

- Do not overload the skewers.

- If you have enough skewers, thread the food onto two parallel skewers. This stabilizes the food so that it doesn't swivel when you turn the skewers.

Marinade Wisdom

MARINADES ARE GREAT FOR ADDING ANOTHER LAYER OF FLAVOR to meat, poultry, and seafood. While they are no longer necessary to tenderize meat—our meat supply is too good to need much help in that department—the flavors penetrate the meat just enough to leave a hint of bold or more subtle flavors. I usually make extra and keep it in the refrigerator for a quick meal later in the week.

Have fun with marinades but remember that every one should include an acidic ingredient, such as vinegar, lemon or other citrus juice, or yogurt. They also need oil to transfer the flavors to the food.

Once you have finished marinating the raw food, discard the marinade, although if you want to use it as a sauce, boil it for at least 5 minutes to kill any bacteria from the uncooked meat. And be sure to always wash all implements used for the raw food, such as bowls, dishes, utensils, and cutting boards in warm soapy water or run them through the dishwasher.

Steak and kidney pie is traditional pub food that has long been popular in England. When I worked in the United Kingdom back in the 1990s, I had never heard of it, much less tasted it, until I stopped at a pub in the north of England called the Slaughtered Calf in the village of Melton Mowbray in Leicestershire. I was blown off the bar stool with the first forkful. After that, I made a point of trying it as often as I could during my years abroad. I now make it in the cold months when friends come over. It's warm and homey and tastes so good, you don't need much more than a tossed salad for a full meal. If you like kidneys, you will love this. If you are not sure you like kidneys, you will like them here. **SERVES 4 TO 6**

STEAK AND KIDNEY PIE

2 pounds chuck steak,
cut into 1-inch cubes

Kosher salt and freshly
ground black pepper

1 tablespoon olive oil,
plus more if needed

½ pound lamb kidneys, trimmed
and cut into 1-inch cubes

½ teaspoon cayenne

1 tablespoon unsalted butter

2 onions, chopped

3 carrots, roughly chopped

1 clove garlic, chopped

4 cremini mushrooms, thickly sliced

2 tablespoons all-purpose flour

1½ teaspoons chopped fresh thyme

1 teaspoon canned tomato puree

1 bay leaf

1 quart veal jus (page 185) or beef or
chicken stock, preferably homemade
(pages 187–188), or more if needed

1 teaspoon Worcestershire sauce

1½ sheets frozen puff pastry,
thawed (about two-thirds of
a 17.3-ounce package)

1 large egg, beaten

Generously season the beef with salt and black pepper. In a large sauté pan, heat the oil over medium-high heat. When hot, sear the meat, turning the cubes as they cook to insure even browning, for 2 to 3 minutes, until caramelized. Transfer the meat to a Dutch oven or similar large flame-proof casserole dish. Leave the meat drippings in the sauté pan.

Season the kidneys well with salt, black pepper, and the cayenne. Heat the pan drippings over medium heat. When hot, sear the kidneys, turning, for 4 to 6 minutes, until golden brown. Add more oil to the pan if necessary. Transfer to the Dutch oven.

In the same sauté pan, melt the butter over medium-high heat and sauté the onions, carrots, and garlic for 2 to 3 minutes. Add the mushrooms and sauté for 1 to 2 minutes, until the mushrooms begin to release their liquid. Transfer the vegetables to the Dutch oven, along with as much of the pan juices as you can.

Set the Dutch oven over medium heat and stir in the flour so that it coats the ingredients. Cook for 2 to 3 minutes and then stir in the thyme, tomato puree, and bay leaf. Add the stock. There should be enough to barely cover the meat. If not, pour more stock into the pot until the meat is covered. Bring to a simmer over medium-high heat and skim any impurities that rise to the surface.

Simmer the mixture gently, partially covered, for about 1½ hours. Adjust the heat up or down to maintain the simmer and skim the surface several times during cooking. At a gentle simmer, there should be no need to add more liquid. The braising liquid will reduce and thicken somewhat and intensify in flavor.

Check the beef for tenderness; if not fork-tender continue to cook for up to 30 minutes longer. (The livers will be tender; no need to check them.)

Stir in the Worcestershire sauce and season to taste with salt and pepper. Discard the bay leaf. Transfer the beef and kidney filling to a 9-inch pie dish and let cool slightly.

Preheat the oven to 425°F.

Sangiovese Wine

WINES HAVE BEEN MADE FROM SANGIOVESE GRAPES IN TUSCANY FOR CENTURIES and it is the primary grape in Chianti. This grape is so deeply tied to the region that efforts from other countries and regions, which can be very good, aren't taken seriously. A multitude of styles of wines are made within the various subregions of Tuscany, but the wines of Chianti Classico have real versatility with food. "Classico" is added to Chianti to indicate a smaller area of production, and the term also marks a stronger guarantee of quality. Chiantis have red fruit flavor, sometimes dried or fresh, balanced with nutty, cocoa earthiness. The structure is more marked by the sharp acidity, but the longer aged Chianti Riserva can have mouth-drying tannins.

Brush the rim of the pie dish with the beaten egg. On a lightly floured surface, roll out ½ sheet of the puff pastry so that it is ¼ inch thick. Cut a strip of pastry about ¾ inch wide. Lay the strip on the rim of the pie dish, pressing it gently so that it adheres to the egg. The strip of pastry will help the top stay in place. Brush the pastry with egg.

Roll the remaining sheet of puff pastry so that is about ¼ inch thick. It must be larger than the pie dish. If necessary, roll the remaining scraps of the ½ sheet of pastry into the dough to make it large enough.

Carefully drape the pastry over the filling and push down around the side to seal. Crimp the edge with the tines of a fork for a neat finish. Cut a few steam vents in the top and brush completely with the egg. Bake for 30 to 40 minutes, until the crust is golden brown and the filling is bubbling.

Let the pie rest for 8 to 10 minutes before slicing to serve.

When I was a kid, everyone's mother made meat loaf and yet I never understood why my mom's tasted better than the others. My grandma called her meat loaf by its Italian name, *polpettone,* which I think makes it sound almost elegant! When I started making my own meat loaf and added pork (as my mother and grandmother had taught me), I realized that it gave the loaf a lot of moisture and better flavor. When I first made this meat loaf, I called it Ricky's Meat Loaf (Mom called me Ricky), but to be fair to my mother, I have changed the name to be more accurate. **SERVES 6 TO 8**

MOM'S MEAT LOAF

1 tablespoon extra-virgin olive oil

1 red bell pepper, seeded and diced

1 yellow onion, diced

3 cloves garlic, chopped

1 pound ground beef chuck

1 pound ground pork

1 cup grated Parmigiano-Reggiano cheese

2 large eggs, lightly beaten

¾ cup bread crumbs (I like ciabatta crumbs)

2 tablespoons chopped fresh basil

2 tablespoons chopped fresh flat-leaf parsley

1 tablespoon Worcestershire sauce

1 tablespoon balsamic vinegar

1 teaspoon kosher salt

1 teaspoon dried hot red pepper flakes

½ teaspoon freshly ground black pepper

1 cup Pomodoro Sauce (page 177), or high-quality prepared marinara sauce

Heat the olive oil in a medium sauté pan over medium heat. When hot, sauté the pepper, onion, and garlic for 10 to 12 minutes, just until the vegetables begin to soften. Transfer to a plate and set aside to cool to room temperature.

Preheat the oven to 350°F. Lightly oil a baking sheet or an 8 by 5 by 3-inch loaf pan.

In a large bowl, mix together the beef, pork, Parmesan, eggs, and bread crumbs. Add the sautéed vegetables, along with the basil, parsley, Worcestershire, vinegar, salt, hot pepper flakes, and black pepper. Using your hands or a large wooden spoon, work the ingredients just long enough so they are well mixed.

Shape the meat into a free-form loaf on the baking sheet, or place in the loaf pan, patting it into the corners. Spread the sauce evenly over the top.

Bake for 50 to 60 minutes, until an instant-read thermometer registers 160°F when inserted in the thickest part of the loaf.

Let the meat loaf rest for about 5 minutes before cutting into slices to serve.

I cannot deny that a perfectly cooked steak doesn't need much, if any, embellishment; but on the other hand, why not? Another layer of flavor takes the meat to a higher level of excitement. Crispy crusts, seared foie gras, even truffled poached eggs make their mark atop a grilled steak. The experience is more luxurious than ever and exemplifies the expression "Go big or go home!"

I like to go big at home, and so have come up with all manner of toppers, rubs, and butters that infuse the meat with flavor and are just plain fun to use. A flavored butter will take a lowly flank steak to "Wow!" A potent rub will melt into a T-bone so that it is tastier than anyone expects. I hope these toppers, butters, and rubs will inspire you to create your own—they're easy and they're creative. Everyone loves them!

STEAK TOPPERS, RUBS, AND GLAZES

Gorgonzola Crust | Horseradish Crust | Parmesan Crust | Topping
steaks with any of these three full-flavored, crispy crusts is an easy way to give them a little more
punch, a little more excitement, a little more depth, a little more appeal. For a long time, I have liked
how the flavors of a good steak mingle with those of a complex blue cheese such as Gorgonzola,
although you could substitute any good blue in the Gorgonzola crust. The horseradish crust works
beautifully on most cuts of beef or pork. Finally, the Parmesan topping is a crowd pleaser, perfect for
filets, rib eyes, strip steaks, and veal chops.

GORGONZOLA CRUST

MAKES ABOUT 2 CUPS, ENOUGH FOR 4 GOOD-SIZED (12- TO 16-OUNCE) STEAKS

1½ cups panko bread crumbs

½ cup unsalted butter, softened

¼ pound cream cheese, softened

¼ pound crumbled
Gorgonzola cheese

1 teaspoon freshly
squeezed lemon juice

Kosher salt and freshly
ground black pepper

In a mixing bowl, blend together the bread crumbs, butter, cream cheese, Gorgonzola, and lemon juice until well mixed. Season to taste with salt and pepper.

Spread a large rectangle of plastic wrap, about 15 inches long, on the counter. Spoon the butter mixture near one end of the rectangle and, using the plastic wrap, roll the mixture into a log. Tightly twist the ends of the plastic wrap and refrigerate for at least 4 hours or up to 1 week.

Cut ½-inch-thick slices of the log and lay directly on top of just-cooked, hot steaks. Be sure to cover the surface of the meat. The heat from the steak will melt the crust just enough.

Topping a Steak with Crust

HAVING ONE OR MORE OF THESE FLAVORFUL BUTTER ROLLS in the refrigerator can turn an ordinary steak meal into an extraordinary one in a matter of seconds! The crusts dissolve into the meat, hot off the grill or from the broiler, and form a buttery, crispy crust that melts in the mouth. I suggest you cut the slices at least ¼ inch thick and slice enough to cover the meat entirely.

HORSERADISH CRUST

MAKES ABOUT 1½ CUPS, ENOUGH FOR 4 TENDERLOIN STEAKS (FILET MIGNONS) OR 6 SALMON FILLETS

1 cup panko bread crumbs

½ cup prepared horseradish, drained

¼ cup unsalted butter, softened

1 tablespoon Worcestershire sauce

1 teaspoon freshly squeezed lemon juice

Kosher salt and freshly ground black pepper

In a mixing bowl, blend together the bread crumbs, horseradish, butter, Worcestershire sauce, and lemon juice until well mixed. Season to taste with salt and pepper.

Spread a large rectangle of plastic wrap, about 15 inches long, on the counter. Spoon the butter mixture near one end of the rectangle and, using the plastic wrap, roll the mixture into a log. Tightly twist the ends of the plastic wrap and refrigerate for at least 4 hours or up to 1 week.

Cut ½-inch-thick slices of the log and lay directly on top of just-cooked steaks. The heat from the steak will melt the crust just enough.

PARMESAN CRUST

MAKES ABOUT 2 CUPS, ENOUGH FOR 4 GOOD-SIZED (12- TO 16-OUNCE) STEAKS

1 cup grated Parmigiano-Reggiano cheese

½ cup panko bread crumbs

½ cup Garlic Confit (page 181)

¼ cup unsalted butter, softened

1 teaspoon freshly squeezed lemon juice

Kosher salt and freshly ground black pepper

In a mixing bowl, blend together the Parmesan, bread crumbs, garlic confit, butter, and lemon juice until well mixed. Season to taste with salt and pepper.

Spread a large rectangle of plastic wrap, about 15 inches long, on the counter. Spoon the butter mixture near one end of the rectangle and, using the plastic wrap, roll the mixture into a log. Tightly twist the ends of the plastic wrap and refrigerate for at least 4 hours or up to 1 week.

Cut ½-inch-thick slices of the log and lay directly on top of just-cooked steaks. The heat from the steak will melt the crust just enough.

Gorganzola Crust, Horseradish Crust, Parmesan Crust

Maitre d' Butter is just another name for compound butter: a flavored butter used to top meats and to flavor pasta, rice, and potatoes—or just about anything that strikes your fancy. I especially like it on corn on the cob. It moistens and enriches meat, and while you may be hesitant to add butter to a rich cut of meat, a little goes a long way and makes the meal just a little more special. **MAKES ABOUT 2 CUPS, ENOUGH FOR 4 GOOD-SIZED (12- TO 16-OUNCE) STEAKS**

MAITRE D' BUTTER

1 cup unsalted butter, softened

¼ cup white wine

3 shallots, minced

3 cloves garlic, minced

3 tablespoons chopped fresh flat-leaf parsley

2 teaspoons freshly squeezed lemon juice

1 teaspoon Dijon mustard

Kosher salt and freshly ground black pepper

In a mixing bowl, blend the butter with the wine, shallots, garlic, parsley, lemon juice, and mustard. Season to taste with salt and pepper and stir well.

Spread a large rectangle of plastic wrap, about 15 inches long, on the counter. Spoon the butter mixture near one end of the rectangle and, using the plastic wrap, roll the mixture into a log. Tightly twist the ends of the plastic wrap and refrigerate for at least 4 hours or up to 1 week.

Cut ½-inch-thick slices of the log and lay directly on top of just-cooked steaks. The heat from the steak will melt the butter just enough.

If you are fortunate enough to have a local butcher, ask for marrow bones. Otherwise, ask the butcher behind the supermarket meat counter and he or she may be able to get some for you, or you can always order marrow online. The bones are well worth seeking out, as you will know if you've tasted marrow—and if not, you are in for a tasty surprise! As a major-league fan of marrow, I have been known to eat it with a spoon on more than one occasion. Most of the time I spread it on crusty bread with a sprinkle of good salt, or use it to top hot, just-cooked steaks and chops. **SERVES 4**

ROASTED BONE MARROW

8 center-cut beef marrow bones, each about 3 inches long, about 4 pounds in all

Kosher or sea salt and freshly ground black pepper

Specialty salt (such as gray salt, black salt, Hawaiian sea salt, or Murray River pink salt)

Squeeze of freshly squeezed lemon juice

Preheat the oven to 400°F.

Sprinkle the bones generously with kosher salt and pepper. Stand the bones upright in a shallow roasting pan and roast for about 15 minutes, or until the marrow is soft but not oozing from the bones.

Let the bones cool a little and then with a small spoon, scoop the marrow from the bones and transfer to a mixing bowl. Season to taste with specialty salt and pepper and flavor with a squeeze of lemon juice. Serve immediately on top of hot steaks.

Americans have not embraced foie gras to the extent that Europeans have. But once you discover that even a little, such as the two-plus ounces I use here, adds a lushness to dishes that is otherwise elusive to most cooks—whether they cook at home or in a professional kitchen—I'm sure you will be a convert. For more on foie gras, see Blown Away by Foie Gras on page 37. **MAKES ABOUT ¾ CUP, ENOUGH FOR 4 GOOD-SIZED (12- TO 16-OUNCE) STEAKS**

SEARED FOIE GRAS TOPPER

4 portions foie gras, about 2½ ounces each, cut into ½-inch-thick slices

Kosher salt and freshly ground black pepper

Season the foie gras slices generously on both sides with salt and pepper.

Heat a large, dry skillet over high heat until very hot. I recommend using a cast-iron skillet because it gets and stays very hot. Sear the foie gras, turning once, for a total of 2 to 4 minutes, or until browned and heated through. Do not let the slices shrink significantly, as this indicates they are losing too much fat.

Serve on top of hot steaks.

This is a great little accompaniment for pork as well as steak, and is also delicious spread on grilled bread all by itself. The long-cooked onions, boosted with honey and vinegar, cut the meat's fattiness so that the flavor combination is as good as it gets. I like to make this with Vidalia onions for their sweetness and red onions for their color, although you could use all of one or the other. **MAKES ABOUT 1 QUART**

SWEET ONION JAM

2 tablespoons extra-virgin olive oil

2 to 3 Vidalia onions, julienned (about 4 cups)

2 to 3 red onions, julienned (about 4 cups)

½ cup honey

¾ cup red wine

½ cup red wine vinegar

Kosher salt and freshly ground black pepper

In a large saucepan or stockpot, heat the olive oil over medium-high heat. When hot, sauté the onions over medium heat for 20 to 30 minutes, until softened.

Stir in the honey and cook for about 10 minutes, or until the onions start to turn golden brown.

Add the wine and vinegar and cook over medium-high heat for about 15 minutes, or until nearly all the liquid evaporates. Season to taste with salt and pepper and set aside to cool. Use the onions to top hot steaks.

The onions can be cooled and refrigerated in a covered container for up to 3 weeks.

You may have bought a small bottle of black or white truffle oil for another recipe and not found any more use for it—until now! Truffle oil elevates the humble poached egg to luxurious heights. With one bite, you will realize that eggs and truffles are a match made in heaven. I know fresh truffles don't fit into most budgets, but if you can splurge every now and again, you won't be sorry. I like this to top a just-cooked steak, or you could use it in the Lyonnaise Salad on page 60. Use the freshest eggs you can find, preferably those from a farmers' market. **SERVES 4**

TRUFFLE POACHED EGGS

8 cups water

1 tablespoon distilled white vinegar

4 large farmhouse eggs

1 tablespoon white truffle oil

1 teaspoon chopped canned black or white truffles (optional)

Kosher salt and freshly ground black pepper

In a saucepan, bring the water and vinegar to a gentle boil over medium-high heat.

One at a time, break the eggs into a large spoon or small bowl and carefully slip into the poaching liquid. After about 3 minutes, the whites should be cooked through and the yolks still soft. Remove with a slotted spoon and transfer to small plates or the tops of hot steaks.

Drizzle the truffle oil over the eggs and sprinkle with the truffles if using. Season to taste with salt and pepper and serve.

I love this glaze, particularly on pork or meaty fish such as salmon. Brush it over the meat or fish before you cook it and then continue to baste with the glaze during cooking for a sweet, browned crusty finish.

MAKES ABOUT 1 CUP; ENOUGH FOR 4 SALMON STEAKS OR 4 TO 6 PORK CHOPS

MUSTARD GLAZE

½ cup packed light brown sugar

½ cup honey

½ cup whole-grain mustard

2 tablespoons apple cider vinegar

In a mixing bowl, stir together the brown sugar, honey, mustard, and vinegar.

Use right away by brushing over meat or fish before and during cooking. To store, transfer to a tightly lidded container and refrigerate for up to 2 weeks.

Dry Rub for Pork | Herb Dry Rub for Beef | Dry Rub for Chicken | Ginger-Curry Rub for Fish | Rubs are meant to flavor and season meats and fish by enhancing them, but never masking their flavor. They also provide tantalizing accents that can't be achieved any other way. The pork rub is phenomenal for long- and-slow-cooked smoked pork butts, but is equally terrific on pork chops, rubbed on the meat minutes before grilling. The paprika gives the meat a hint of smoky flavor. The herb rub is perfect for steaks destined for the grill, while the chicken rub is delicious on poultry of all kinds. The curry rub is excellent on salmon, tuna, and shrimp and would also be tasty on poultry.

In other words, use these as you think would suit your and your family's tastes. No hard-and-fast rules!

DRY RUB FOR PORK

MAKES ABOUT 1¼ CUPS, ENOUGH FOR 2 PORK TENDERLOINS OR 4 TO 6 PORK CHOPS

½ cup smoked sweet paprika

¼ cup ancho chili powder

2 tablespoons kosher salt

2 tablespoons light brown sugar

2 tablespoons dried thyme

2 tablespoons dried oregano

1 tablespoon dry mustard

1 tablespoon ground cumin

2 teaspoons freshly ground black pepper

1 teaspoon Madras curry powder or other high-quality curry powder

1 teaspoon cayenne

In a mixing bowl, stir together the paprika, chili powder, salt, brown sugar, thyme, oregano, mustard, cumin, black pepper, curry powder, and cayenne.

Use right away or transfer to a tightly lidded container. Store at room temperature in a cool, dry place for up to 2 weeks.

HERB DRY RUB FOR BEEF

MAKES ABOUT 1 CUP, ENOUGH FOR 4 TO 6 (10- TO 12-OUNCE) STEAKS

12 cloves garlic, minced

¼ cup chopped fresh rosemary

¼ cup fresh thyme

¼ cup freshly ground black pepper

2 tablespoons kosher salt

In a mixing bowl, stir together the garlic, rosemary, thyme, pepper, and salt.

Use right away or transfer to a tightly lidded container. Refrigerate for up to 1 week.

DRY RUB FOR CHICKEN

MAKES ABOUT 1 CUP, ENOUGH FOR 1 TO 2 WHOLE CHICKENS

¼ cup packed light brown sugar

¼ cup ancho chili powder or other high-quality chili powder

¼ cup smoked sweet paprika

2 tablespoons ground cumin

2 tablespoons garlic powder

2 tablespoons kosher salt

1 tablespoon freshly ground black pepper

1 teaspoon cayenne

In a mixing bowl, stir together the brown sugar, chili powder, paprika, cumin, garlic powder, salt, black pepper, and cayenne.

Use right away or transfer to a tightly lidded container. Store at room temperature in a cool, dry place for up to 2 weeks.

GINGER-CURRY RUB FOR FISH

MAKES ABOUT ½ CUP, ENOUGH FOR 4 TUNA STEAKS

2 tablespoons minced fresh ginger

2 tablespoons Madras curry powder or other high-quality curry powder

1 tablespoon plus 1 teaspoon kosher salt

1 tablespoon sesame seeds

1 teaspoon dried red pepper flakes

1 teaspoon ground cinnamon

1 teaspoon ground cumin

½ teaspoon ground cloves

In a mixing bowl, stir together the ginger, curry powder, salt, sesame seeds, pepper flakes, cinnamon, cumin, and cloves.

Use right away or transfer to a tightly lidded container. Refrigerate for up to 1 week.

Rub on a Rub

THE RUBS HERE CAN BE LEFT ON THE FOOD for a number of hours or for only a short time. Even 30 minutes before cooking adds great taste, although the longer a rub is on the meat, the more intense the final flavor. It's up to you and how much time you have. While you should use them generously and rub them into the meat or fish with your fingertips, they are not coatings that are just dumped on the food—instead, sprinkle a rub evenly over the food before rubbing it in.

Being a chef, I am all about sauces. They

add depth and interest to a dish and I have never met one I didn't like. But I think a lot of folks think they are scary and difficult. Nothing could be further from reality. Whether you realize it or not, every time you whisk a little wine, stock, lemon juice, or cream into pan juices, you are creating a sauce. When you mix up a vinaigrette, you are making a sauce, although most of us call these thin sauces "dressings." Sure, hollandaise or béarnaise can "break" (curdle) and the first time you reduce a liquid you may not know exactly what to expect, but overall, sauces are easy, and they turn what could be mundane dishes into special ones.

My dad would never put a sauce on a steak. To his mind that was compromising the gift that was the juicy beef. I, on the other hand, have always liked A.1 on my meat and so developed my own version, which I call T:1. I also love a rich, luxurious béarnaise sauce now and again with filet mignon, and a red wine or bordelaise sauce with any grilled steak.

When it comes to fish and seafood, a *sauce ravigote* or a mignonette with chilled mussels, clams, or crabmeat is out of this world. And what beats a tangy cocktail sauce with cold shrimp? Or *gribiche* sauce with fish, instead of the more expected tartar sauce?

Many people have strong opinions about sauces and surely I can be counted among them. There are not many foods that I don't like to enhance with some sort of sauce, be it simple or a little more complex. The French raised the art of saucing food to gastronomic heights and while they did the culinary world a great service, this fact has convinced a lot of novice cooks that sauces are out of their reach. Nonsense! Try the sauces on these pages, and think about how they would taste with your favorite grilled, broiled, sautéed, or roasted foods.

And take a shot at making your own chicken stock or veal jus to have on hand to enrich sauces. (I make large batches and keep them in the freezer, either in small containers or ice cube trays.) But if you haven't time or inclination to make stock, buy some of the very good brands out there and keep a supply so that any time you have the urge for a stock-based sauce, you're good to go!

SAUCES, STOCKS, DRESSINGS, MARINADES, AND SYRUPS

Au Poivre Sauce | Barbecue Sauce | Béarnaise Sauce | Bordelaise Sauce | Cognac Sauce | The sauces included here are used throughout the book, or may only be referenced. I think it's a matter of personal taste how you use them but take my word for it, they all taste great with steak. And that's the point. I want you to enjoy steak when you go to the time, expense, and trouble to cook it and so have offered a sauce for every taste. Of course, you may not want to serve a sauce with your steak, and that's fine, too!

AU POIVRE SAUCE

MAKES 2 CUPS

½ cup brandy

15 whole peppercorns

1 shallot, minced

1 bay leaf

2 cups Veal Jus (page 185)

¾ cup heavy cream

1 lemon slice, ⅛ inch thick

1½ teaspoons sherry vinegar

Combine the brandy, peppercorns, shallot, and bay leaf in a medium saucepan and bring to a boil. Simmer until reduced and almost dry. Add the veal jus and cream and simmer for 15 to 20 minutes.

Remove from the heat and add the lemon slice and sherry vinegar. Let steep for 15 minutes.

Strain and serve immediately or cover and refrigerate for up to 1 week.

BARBECUE SAUCE

MAKES 2 CUPS

3 tablespoons bacon grease

1 yellow onion, chopped

2 jalapeño peppers, minced

2 cloves garlic, minced

2 cups dark brown sugar

2 cups ketchup

1 cup yellow mustard

2 tablespoons Worcestershire sauce

Kosher salt and freshly ground black pepper

In a saucepan, heat the bacon grease and sauté the onion, jalapeño, and garlic for 10 minutes, until softened.

Add the brown sugar, ketchup, mustard, and Worcestershire and stir well to combine. Season to taste with salt and pepper. Cover and simmer for 30 minutes, just until the flavors are melded.

Cover and refrigerate for at least 1 day or for up to 1 week.

BÉARNAISE SAUCE

MAKES ABOUT 2 CUPS

¼ cup white wine

2 tablespoons tarragon vinegar (see Note)

1 tablespoon finely chopped shallot

3 large egg yolks

¾ cup unsalted butter, melted

Juice of ½ lemon

Leaves from 2 sprigs tarragon, chopped

Kosher salt and freshly ground black pepper

In a small saucepan, bring the white wine, vinegar, and shallot to a boil over medium-high heat. Cook at a rapid simmer for 3 to 4 minutes, until the liquid reduces by half. This can be made ahead of time and refrigerated for up to 1 day.

Strain the sauce through a fine-mesh sieve into a bowl. Discard the solids.

In the top of a double boiler set a few inches over water or in a small saucepan or metal bowl set over a larger pan holding a few inches of water, whisk the egg yolks with the vinegar reduction. Bring the water to a boil over medium-high heat and briskly whisk the sauce for 5 to 6 minutes, until the eggs begin to thicken.

In a steady stream, drizzle the melted butter into the sauce, whisking continuously. Once the butter is incorporated and the sauce is smooth, stir in the lemon juice and tarragon. Season to taste with salt and pepper.

Serve immediately, or keep warm over the double boiler filled with simmering water for up to 30 minutes, if necessary.

Note *Tarragon vinegar is easy to find in most supermarkets but if you want to make your own, start with fresh sprigs of tarragon and simmer them in white wine vinegar for about 10 minutes. Let the vinegar cool and then strain it into bottles with tight-fitting lids. Store the vinegar in a cool, dry cupboard for up to 3 months.*

BORDELAISE SAUCE

MAKES ABOUT 1 CUP

3 tablespoons sliced beef marrow

⅔ cup dry red wine

3 shallots, minced

1 teaspoon fresh thyme leaves

Kosher salt and freshly
ground black pepper

⅔ cup Veal Jus (page 185)

3 tablespoons unsalted butter

2 tablespoons chopped
fresh flat-leaf parsley

Fill a small saucepan about halfway with water and bring to a simmer over medium-high heat. Add the marrow and poach for about 5 minutes. Drain and set aside.

In another saucepan, bring the wine, shallots, and thyme to a boil over medium-high heat. Cook for 2 to 3 minutes, until the liquid reduces by half. Season to taste with salt and pepper. Strain through a fine-mesh strainer and discard the solids.

In a small saucepan, bring the veal jus to a simmer over low heat and simmer for about 5 minutes, adjusting the heat up or down to maintain the simmer. Stir in the reduced wine and cook for 2 to 3 minutes longer.

Remove from the heat and whisk the butter into the sauce, a tablespoon at a time, until smooth. Stir in the marrow and parsley, return to medium heat, and cook for 2 to 4 minutes, until the marrow is hot. Serve immediately, or let the sauce cool to room temperature and refrigerate in a lidded container for up to 24 hours. Reheat gently and stir well before using.

COGNAC SAUCE

MAKES ABOUT 1 CUP

1 tablespoon unsalted butter

1 cup sliced fresh mushrooms
(such as shiitake or cremini)

2 cloves garlic, minced

1 tablespoon minced shallot

½ cup Veal Jus (page 185)

3 tablespoons Cognac or brandy

¼ cup heavy cream

2 tablespoons Dijon mustard

½ teaspoon freshly
ground black pepper

In small saucepan, melt the butter and cook the mushrooms, garlic, and shallot for 3 to 4 minutes, until tender.

Stir in veal jus and Cognac. Bring to a boil and reduce the heat. Simmer gently, uncovered, for 5 minutes.

In small bowl, stir together the cream and mustard. Stir into the sauce. Cook and stir until thickened and bubbly. Season with the pepper. Serve immediately, or let the sauce cool to room temperature and refrigerate in a lidded container for up to 24 hours. Reheat gently and stir well before using.

COCKTAIL SAUCE

MAKES ABOUT 2 CUPS

¾ cup prepared chili sauce

¾ cup ketchup

⅓ cup prepared horseradish, drained

Juice of 2 lemons

1 tablespoon sugar

1 teaspoon Tabasco sauce

1 teaspoon Worcestershire sauce

In a mixing bowl, combine all the ingredients and mix well.

Use immediately or cover and refrigerate for up to 1 week.

POMODORO SAUCE

MAKES ABOUT 4 CUPS

2 tablespoons extra-virgin olive oil

2 to 3 cloves garlic, minced

¾ cup white wine

Pinch of crushed red pepper

1½ cans (28 ounces each) whole peeled tomatoes

Kosher salt and freshly ground black pepper

¾ teaspoon sugar

¼ teaspoon chopped fresh basil

In a saucepan, heat 1 tablespoon of the olive oil over low heat. Add the garlic and cook gently for 3 to 4 minutes, until golden brown. Add the wine and crushed red pepper, raise the heat to medium-high, and bring to a brisk simmer. Cook for about 2 minutes, or until the liquid is reduced by half.

Meanwhile, put the tomatoes in a mixing bowl and crush with a fork or potato masher.

Add the tomatoes to the pan and season to taste with salt and pepper. Stir in the sugar. Bring the sauce to a simmer over medium heat and cook, adjusting the heat up or down to maintain the simmer, for 50 to 60 minutes, or until the sauce is slightly thick and fragrant.

Stir the remaining 1 tablespoon olive oil and the basil into the sauce. Taste and add more salt and pepper if needed. Serve immediately, or let the sauce cool to room temperature and refrigerate in a lidded container for up to 24 hours. Reheat gently and stir well before using.

CREOLE RÉMOULADE

MAKES ABOUT 1 QUART

2 cups mayonnaise (I like Hellmann's or Best Foods)

½ cup ketchup

1 rib celery, minced

1 shallot, minced

3 cornichons, chopped

2 tablespoons freshly squeezed lemon juice

1 tablespoon Dijon mustard

1 tablespoon prepared or fresh horseradish

1 tablespoon Worcestershire sauce

1 tablespoon thinly sliced scallion

1 tablespoon chopped fresh flat-leaf parsley

1 tablespoon paprika

1 teaspoon sugar

¼ cup red wine vinegar

¼ cup extra-virgin olive oil

Tabasco

Kosher salt and freshly ground black pepper

In a mixing bowl, combine the mayonnaise, ketchup, celery, shallot, cornichons, lemon juice, mustard, horseradish, Worcestershire, scallion, parsley, paprika, and sugar. Mix on medium speed until well blended. Slowly add the vinegar, and then slowly add the olive oil in a steady stream until the sauce is emulsified and blended well.

Season to taste with Tabasco, salt, and pepper. Refrigerate for 2 hours in an airtight container. Will keep for up to 1 week.

HORSERADISH CREAM

MAKES ABOUT 2 CUPS

1½ cups crème fraîche or good-quality sour cream

½ cup prepared horseradish, drained

2 tablespoons chopped fresh chives

1 tablespoon fresh lemon zest

Kosher salt and freshly ground white pepper

In a mixing bowl, combine the crème fraîche, horseradish, chives, and lemon zest. Season to taste with salt and pepper.

Use immediately or cover and refrigerate for up to 1 week.

MIGNONETTE

MAKES ABOUT ½ CUP, ENOUGH FOR 30 OYSTERS

⅓ cup Champagne vinegar

¼ cup minced shallots

¼ cup chopped fresh chives

3 tablespoons freshly
ground black pepper

In a mixing bowl, combine all the ingredients.

Use immediately or cover and refrigerate for up to 1 week.

MORNAY SAUCE

MAKES ABOUT 3 CUPS

¼ pound Parmigiano-
Reggiano cheese, grated

2 cups fresh or dried
plain bread crumbs

1 tablespoon truffle oil

2 tablespoons unsalted butter

2 tablespoons all-purpose flour

2 cups half-and-half

¼ pound grated Swiss cheese

¼ pound grated sharp
Cheddar cheese

¼ pound grated fontina cheese

2 tablespoons Dijon mustard

Kosher salt and freshly
ground black pepper

Preheat the oven to 375°F.

In a small bowl, stir together the Parmesan, bread crumbs, and truffle oil.
Set aside.

In a heavy saucepan, melt the butter over medium-low heat. Add the flour
and whisk for about 3 minutes, or until smooth. Add the half-and-half
and bring to a simmer, stirring constantly. Cook for about 3 minutes longer,
stirring now and then.

Stir in the cheeses, mustard, and bread crumb mixture and cook, stirring
occasionally, for about 15 minutes, or until the cheeses melt. Season to
taste with salt and pepper. Serve immediately, or let the sauce cool to
room temperature and refrigerate in a lidded container for up to 24 hours.
Reheat gently and stir well before using.

MAPLE-CHILI SAUCE

MAKES ABOUT 1 CUP

¾ cup pure maple syrup

⅓ cup sour cream

⅓ cup mayonnaise

2 tablespoons buttermilk

1 teaspoon paprika

1 teaspoon chili powder

1 teaspoon dry mustard

1 teaspoon chopped fresh chives

Pinch of cayenne

Kosher salt and freshly ground black pepper

In a mixing bowl, stir together the maple syrup, sour cream, mayonnaise, and buttermilk. Add the paprika, chili powder, mustard, chives, and cayenne and stir to mix. Season to taste with salt and pepper.

Use immediately or cover and refrigerate for up to 2 days.

GRILLED RAMP PESTO

MAKES ABOUT 1½ CUPS

6 whole ramps (for more on ramps, see page 211)

1¼ cups extra-virgin olive oil

Kosher salt and freshly ground black pepper

½ cup pine nuts

½ cup fresh flat-leaf parsley leaves

½ cup fresh basil leaves

Prepare a clean, well-oiled charcoal or gas grill so that the coals or heat element are medium-hot. Or, heat an indoor stovetop grill.

Trim the greens from the ramp bulbs and transfer the greens to a shallow bowl. Set the bulbs aside. Add ¼ cup of the oil to the ramp greens, season with salt and pepper, and toss to coat.

Lift the greens from the bowl and grill, turning once, for 4 to 6 minutes, until charred on both sides. Let the greens cool to room temperature and then roughly chop.

In the bowl of a food processor fitted with the metal blade, process the ramp bulbs until coarsely chopped. Add the pine nuts, parsley, and basil and process until smooth. With the processor running, slowly pour the remaining 1 cup olive oil through the feed tube to create a thin paste.

Transfer the pesto to a bowl and fold in the chopped grilled ramps. Use immediately or cover and refrigerate for up to 3 days.

GARLIC CONFIT

MAKES ABOUT 1½ CUPS

12 cloves garlic

1 cup extra-virgin olive oil

In a very small saucepan, cover the garlic cloves with oil. Cook over very low heat for 35 to 45 minutes, until the garlic is very soft. Cool to room temperature. The garlic is ready to use, as is the oil.

Use right away or cover and refrigerate for up to 1 week.

SALSA VERDE

MAKES ABOUT 1 CUP

¼ cup chopped fresh flat-leaf parsley

¼ cup chopped fresh cilantro

¼ cup chopped fresh rosemary

¼ cup chopped drained capers

4 cloves garlic, minced

2 shallots, minced

Grated zest and juice of 1 lemon

1 tablespoon sherry vinegar

1 cup extra-virgin olive oil

Kosher salt and freshly
ground black pepper

In a bowl, toss together the parsley, cilantro, rosemary, capers, garlic, shallots, lemon zest and juice, and vinegar. Drizzle the olive oil over the mixture and toss gently. Season to taste with salt and pepper and let the sauce sit for about 20 minutes before serving.

JARED'S BEER MUSTARD

MAKES ABOUT 3 CUPS

12 ounces (1½ cups) flat
dark beer (see Note)

2 cups dry mustard

1 cup packed dark brown sugar

2 tablespoons apple cider vinegar

2 teaspoons salt

½ teaspoon ground turmeric

In a large saucepan, whisk together all the ingredients. Cook over medium-high heat until boiling. Remove from the heat and cool to room temperature.

Use immediately or cover and refrigerate for up to 3 weeks.

Note *If you don't already have flat beer, pour the beer in a small bowl, cover loosely, and let stand at room temperature for about 8 hours or overnight. Believe me, by then the beer will have lost all its effervescence!*

RED CHILI OIL

MAKES ABOUT 2 CUPS

1 cup canola oil

1 cup olive oil

2 cloves garlic, sliced

2 ounces Calabrian chiles, chopped

2 tablespoons crushed
hot red pepper flakes

Kosher salt and cracked black pepper

In a saucepan, bring the canola oil, olive oil, garlic, chiles, and pepper flakes to a simmer over low heat. Simmer for about 20 minutes. Cool slightly.

Transfer to a blender and pulse 3 to 4 times to break up the ingredients. Do not overblend. Season to taste with salt and pepper and pulse once more.

Strain the oil through a sieve lined with cheesecloth that has been set over a bowl for at least 6 hours or overnight. Transfer to a glass container.

Use immediately or cover and refrigerate for up to 1 week.

RED WINE SAUCE

MAKES ½ CUP, 4 SERVINGS

3 tablespoons unsalted
butter, cut into pieces

2 medium shallots, minced

½ cup dry red wine

½ cup Veal Jus (page 185)

1 tablespoon balsamic vinegar

1 teaspoon Dijon mustard

1 teaspoon minced fresh thyme leaves

Kosher salt and freshly
ground black pepper

Melt 1 tablespoon of the butter in a medium saucepan over medium heat. Add the shallots and cook over low heat, stirring frequently, until translucent.

Raise the heat to high, add the wine and veal jus, and bring to a boil. Simmer until the liquid is reduced by half.

Add the vinegar and mustard and cook until the sauce has the consistency you like. It should be thick enough to coat the back of a spoon.

Remove from the heat and stir in the remaining 2 tablespoons butter. This will help thicken the sauce a little more and give it a nice glossy appearance. Add the thyme and season with salt and pepper to taste. Serve immediately, or let the sauce cool to room temperature and refrigerate in a lidded container for up to 24 hours. Reheat gently and stir well before using.

SAUCE RAVIGOTE

MAKES 1 CUP

1 large hard-cooked egg

½ cup extra-virgin olive oil

3 tablespoons white wine vinegar

½ cup finely chopped yellow onion

2 teaspoons drained capers, rinsed

1 teaspoon Dijon mustard

1 teaspoon finely chopped
fresh flat-leaf parsley

1 teaspoon finely chopped
fresh chervil

1 teaspoon finely chopped
fresh chives

Kosher salt and freshly
ground black pepper

Peel and halve the egg. Using the back of a spoon, force the egg halves through a medium-mesh sieve into a bowl.

Whisk in the olive oil and vinegar. Stir in the onion, capers, mustard, parsley, chervil, and chives. Season to taste with salt and pepper.

Transfer to a lidded container and refrigerate for up to 1 week.

T:1 SAUCE

MAKES ABOUT 1½ CUPS

1 cup ketchup

¼ cup water

¼ cup dried shiitake mushrooms

¼ cup Worcestershire sauce

¼ cup freshly squeezed lemon juice

¼ cup distilled white vinegar

½ cup coarsely chopped yellow onion

1 large clove garlic, minced

3 tablespoons soy sauce

2 tablespoons dark brown sugar

1 tablespoon dry mustard

In a saucepan, combine the ketchup, water, mushrooms, Worcestershire, lemon juice, and vinegar. Whisk well and then stir in the onion, garlic, soy sauce, brown sugar, and mustard.

Bring to a simmer over medium heat and cook for about 45 minutes, or until the sauce reaches a pourable, thick consistency.

Strain the sauce through a fine-mesh sieve into a bowl and discard the solids. Set the sauce aside to cool.

Use immediately or cover and refrigerate for up to 1 week.

VEAL JUS

MAKES ABOUT 2 QUARTS

10 pounds meaty veal bones

About 8 quarts water

1 pound carrots, roughly chopped

1 pound onions, roughly chopped

4 large leeks, trimmed
and roughly chopped

4 sprigs fresh thyme

4 large sprigs flat-leaf parsley

1 bay leaf

1 tablespoon black peppercorns

1 tablespoon tomato paste

Preheat the oven to 450°F. Lightly oil 2 large shallow roasting pans.

In one of the prepared pans, arrange the bones in a single layer. Roast for 30 to 45 minutes, until golden brown.

Transfer the bones and any meat attached to them to a 14-quart stock-pot and cover with the water. You can do this in 2 pots if you don't have a large one. Scrape any browned bits from the bottom of the roasting pan into the pot, too. Avoid the fat. Bring to a simmer over medium-high heat. Skim any foam and impurities that rise to the surface. Reduce the heat to medium-low, partially cover, and simmer for 6 to 8 hours or longer. Adjust the heat up or down to maintain a gentle simmer.

Meanwhile, spread the carrots, onions, and leeks in the second roasting pan and roast for 20 to 30 minutes, until lightly browned. Cool the vegetables, cover, and refrigerate until needed.

During the last 2 hours of simmering, add the roasted vegetables to the stock, along with the thyme, parsley, bay leaf, peppercorns, and tomato paste, and stir well.

Cool the stock in a sink filled with cold water and ice cubes. When cool, skim the fat off the surface. Strain through a fine-mesh sieve into 2 smaller pots. Bring to a simmer over medium-high heat and simmer for about 1 hour, or until reduced to 2 quarts.

Let the stock cool to room temperature and then refrigerate, uncovered, until cold. Cover and refrigerate for up to 1 week, or freeze for up to 3 months.

MUSHROOM JUS

MAKES ABOUT 2 CUPS

2 tablespoons unsalted butter

2 tablespoons minced shallots

1 tablespoon minced garlic

2 cups sliced shiitake mushrooms

Kosher salt and freshly ground black pepper

2 cups Veal Jus (page 185), demi-glace, or reduced chicken stock (page 188)

In a medium-sized saucepan, melt the butter over medium heat. Sauté the shallots and garlic for 3 to 4 minutes, until softened.

Add the mushrooms and sauté for about 3 minutes, or until the mushrooms begin to exude their liquid. Season to taste with salt and pepper.

Add the veal jus, raise the heat to medium-high, and bring to a simmer. Cook for 5 to 6 minutes, or until the sauce comes together. Serve immediately or cover and refrigerate for up to 3 days.

BEEF STOCK

MAKES ABOUT 8 CUPS

1 pound meaty beef bones

2 tablespoons vegetable oil

1 cup chopped onions

½ cup chopped carrots

½ cup chopped celery

2 tablespoons tomato paste

1 tablespoon chopped
fresh thyme leaves

1 tablespoon black peppercorns

2 bay leaves

½ cup dry red or dry white
wine, optional

10 cups water

Rinse the beef bones well under cold water to remove any blood. Set aside.

Heat the oil in a large saucepan over low heat. Add the onions, carrots, and celery to the pan and cook, stirring occasionally, for about 5 minutes, or until the vegetables soften but are not colored. Stir in the tomato paste, thyme, peppercorns, and bay leaves.

If using the wine, add it now and stir to dissolve the tomato paste. Add the bones and water. Bring to a simmer over medium heat. Carefully skim off any fat and froth that float to the surface of the liquid. Reduce the heat to low and continue to simmer slowly for 2 to 3 hours, or until somewhat reduced and flavorful.

Strain the stock through a chinois or fine-mesh sieve into a large bowl. Discard the bones and vegetables. Cool the stock in a large bowl or sink filled with cold water and ice cubes. Cover and refrigerate until chilled, and then remove the layer of congealed fat from the surface.

Transfer to covered storage containers and refrigerate for up to 3 days or freeze for up to 3 months.

CHICKEN STOCK

MAKES 5 QUARTS

2 gallons cold water

4 pounds chicken carcasses, including necks and backs

1 large onion, quartered

4 carrots, peeled and cut in half

4 ribs celery, cut in half

1 leek, white part only, cut lengthwise in half

10 sprigs thyme

10 sprigs parsley with stems

2 bay leaves

8 to 10 peppercorns

2 cloves garlic, peeled

Combine the water, chicken, onion, carrots, celery, leek, thyme, parsley, bay leaves, peppercorns, and garlic in a 12-quart stockpot over high heat. Cook until bubbles begin to break through the surface of the liquid. Decrease the heat to medium-low so that the stock maintains a low, gentle simmer and simmer, uncovered, for 6 to 8 hours. Skim the scum from the stock with a spoon or fine-mesh strainer every 10 to 15 minutes for the first hour of cooking and twice each hour for the next 2 hours.

Strain the stock through a fine-mesh strainer into another large stockpot or heatproof container. Discard the solids. Cool the stock in a large bowl or sink filled with cold water and ice cubes. Refrigerate overnight.

Remove the solidified fat from the surface of the liquid. Refrigerate the stock in a container with a lid for up to 1 week; or pour into ice cube trays and store in the freezer for up to 3 months.

SIMPLE SYRUP

MAKES ABOUT 2 CUPS

2 cups sugar

2 cups water

In a medium saucepan, combine the sugar and water and stir over medium heat until the sugar dissolves. Raise the heat to high and bring to a boil. As soon as the syrup boils, remove the pan from the heat and set aside to cool.

Use immediately or transfer to a container with a tight-fitting lid and refrigerate for up to 1 week.

RÉMOULADE

MAKES ABOUT 3 CUPS

2 cups mayonnaise

1 tablespoon whole-grain mustard

1 tablespoon freshly squeezed lemon juice

1 tablespoon chopped fresh flat-leaf parsley

1 tablespoon thinly sliced scallion

1 shallot, minced

1 rib celery, minced

1 teaspoon prepared horseradish (I like the Atomic brand)

3 cornichons, chopped

Kosher salt and freshly ground black pepper

In a mixing bowl, stir together the mayonnaise, mustard, lemon juice, parsley, scallion, shallot, celery, horseradish, and cornichons. Season to taste with salt and pepper. Cover and refrigerate for 30 minutes or up 24 hours.

HORSERADISH SPREAD

MAKES ABOUT 1 CUP

½ cup mayonnaise (I like Hellmann's or Best Foods)

3 tablespoons prepared horseradish

1 tablespoon sour cream

1 tablespoon whole-grain mustard

In a mixing bowl, stir together all the ingredients.

Use immediately or cover and refrigerate for up to 3 days.

CLASSIC TARTAR SAUCE

MAKES ABOUT 2 CUPS

1 cup mayonnaise

¼ cup minced sweet pickle

2 tablespoons minced shallot

2 tablespoons drained capers

2 tablespoons Dijon mustard

2 tablespoons chopped
fresh flat-leaf parsley

2 tablespoons minced scallion

1 hard-cooked egg forced through
a coarse sieve or chopped

1 teaspoon freshly
squeezed lemon juice

1 teaspoon extra-virgin olive oil

½ teaspoon chopped fresh tarragon

½ teaspoon cayenne

In a small bowl, stir together all the ingredients until well mixed. Cover and refrigerate for 30 minutes, or up to 24 hours.

TRAMONTO'S HOUSE DRESSING

MAKES ABOUT 2 CUPS

¼ cup red wine vinegar

¼ cup Champagne vinegar

1 tablespoon water

1 teaspoon sugar

1 teaspoon dry mustard

1 teaspoon Dijon mustard

1 teaspoon minced garlic

1½ cups extra-virgin olive oil

1 tablespoon chopped fresh basil

Pinch of chopped fresh
or dried oregano

Pinch of crushed red pepper flakes

Kosher salt and freshly
ground black pepper

In the jar of a blender, combine the wine vinegar, Champagne vinegar, water, sugar, dry mustard, Dijon mustard, and garlic. Process until blended.

With the motor running, add the oil in a drizzle through the lid until the dressing emulsifies.

Pour the dressing into a lidded glass jar and stir in the basil, oregano, and red pepper flakes. Season to taste with salt and pepper. Cover the jar and shake gently to mix.

Use immediately or cover and refrigerate for up to 1 week. Stir or gently shake the dressing before using.

BALSAMIC MARINADE

MAKES ABOUT 3½ CUPS, ENOUGH FOR 4 TO 6 (12- TO 16-OUNCE) STEAKS

¾ cup balsamic vinegar

2 teaspoons grated orange zest

¼ cup freshly squeezed orange juice

2 cloves garlic, minced

1 shallot, minced

1 tablespoon chopped fresh thyme

2½ cups olive oil

Kosher salt and freshly
ground black pepper

In a glass, ceramic, or other nonreactive mixing bowl, stir together the vinegar, orange zest and juice, garlic, shallot, and thyme. Whisk in the olive oil until it comes together. Season to taste with salt and pepper.

Use immediately or cover and refrigerate for up to 3 days.

SPICY SOY MARINADE

MAKES ABOUT 2½ CUPS, ENOUGH FOR 2 TO 4 (12- TO 16-OUNCE) STEAKS

1 cup olive oil

½ cup chopped fresh cilantro

⅓ cup soy sauce

¼ cup red wine vinegar

2 tablespoons freshly
squeezed lemon juice

1½ tablespoons Worcestershire sauce

1 tablespoon Dijon mustard

2 cloves garlic, minced

2 jalapeño peppers, coarsely chopped

½ teaspoon freshly
ground black pepper

In a glass, ceramic, or other non-reactive bowl or container, mix all the ingredients. Use immediately or cover and refrigerate for up to 2 days.

SHERRY VINAIGRETTE

MAKES ABOUT ½ CUP

¼ cup extra-virgin olive oil

2 tablespoons sherry vinegar

1 tablespoon freshly
squeezed orange juice

1 tablespoon minced shallot

1 tablespoon torn fresh basil leaves

1½ teaspoons honey

1 teaspoon Dijon mustard

Salt and freshly ground black pepper

In a large bowl, whisk together the oil, vinegar, orange juice, shallot, basil, honey, and mustard. Season to taste with salt and pepper. Use immediately or cover and refrigerate for up to 3 days.

GRIBICHE SAUCE

MAKES ABOUT 1 CUP

3 large hard-cooked eggs

1 large egg yolk

1½ teaspoons Dijon mustard

½ cup vegetable oil (such
as grapeseed or canola)

2 tablespoons brine from
a jar of cornichons

1 teaspoon minced shallot

1 teaspoon chopped fresh
flat-leaf parsley

1 teaspoon finely chopped cornichon

Freshly squeezed lemon juice

Kosher salt and freshly
ground black pepper

Peel the hard-cooked eggs and separate the yolks from the whites. Set the whites aside.

In the bowl of a food processor fitted with the metal blade, pulse the cooked egg yolks, the raw egg yolk, and the mustard just until blended. With the motor running, slowly add the oil through the feed tube to make a sauce with the consistency of mayonnaise. Add the brine and pulse to thin the sauce a little.

Transfer the sauce to a bowl and, with a rubber spatula, fold in the shallot, parsley, and cornichon.

Chop the reserved egg whites and fold into the sauce. Season to taste with lemon juice and salt and pepper.

Use immediately or cover and refrigerate for up to 3 days.

RICK'S SOY SAUCE

MAKES ABOUT 5 CUPS

1½ cups water

1 (5-inch) piece konbu
(dried seaweed)

1 quart soy sauce

1 tablespoon bonito flakes
(dried fish flakes)

In a large saucepan, bring the water and konbu to a simmer over medium heat. Discard the konbu. Raise the heat and bring the water to a rolling boil.

In a separate saucepan, bring the soy sauce to a boil over medium-high heat.

Add the boiling soy sauce to the water and adjust the heat so that the liquid simmers. Simmer for 3 to 5 minutes.

Remove from the heat and stir in the bonito flakes. Let the flakes settle to the bottom of the pan. After about 7 minutes, strain through a *chinoise* or fine-mesh sieve. Discard the solids. Use immediately or cover and store in a cool, dry cupboard for up to 3 weeks.

LEMON AIOLI

MAKES ABOUT 1½ CUPS

1 cup homemade or high-quality,
store-bought mayonnaise

¼ cup sour cream

1 tablespoon grated lemon zest

2 tablespoons freshly
squeezed lemon juice

1 tablespoon chopped
fresh flat-leaf parsley

1 teaspoon minced garlic

Kosher salt and freshly
ground black pepper

In a mixing bowl, whisk together the mayonnaise, sour cream, lemon zest and juice, parsley, and garlic. Season to taste with salt and pepper.

Use immediately or cover and refrigerate for up to 5 days.

You don't have to buy a steak to have a great meat dish; you don't even have to buy beef. There are plenty of times you'll feel like dialing back a little and cooking another type of meat, such as pork, lamb, or veal. Or you may want to cook a killer chicken dish or grill a duck breast. The recipes in this chapter will allow you to do all this and more.

The more you know about the various cuts of meat and poultry and the more you experiment with cooking them, the happier you will be. A few of the recipes here are old favorites, such as shepherd's pie and fried chicken. Others are a little more modern, such as the stuffed leg of lamb with a pesto made from ramps, or the grilled duck with lemongrass, turnips, and prunes. I have always liked liver and onions and so included a wonderful recipe for this old standby. And because I have a fondness for braised dishes, I couldn't leave out the braised pork shanks, perfect for a cold night or wintry Sunday afternoon. Ditto for ribs—I could no more write a book that included recipes for grilled meats and not include ribs than I could walk through a farmers' market and come away empty-handed. I am not hard-wired to be so constrained!

This is a chapter about meats and poultry other than steaks and beef classics, and so in the spirit of "anything goes," I suggest the smooth, sweet tones of great jazz:
JOHN COLTRANE | CHARLIE PARKER | CHICK COREA | NANCY WILSON
WYNTON MARSALIS | HERBIE HANCOCK | AND MORE

OTHER MEAT AND POULTRY

This is a pork lover's dream come true. The kids love it and yet it's a little bit fancy and so works well for guests. I am a major fan of pork and the sausage stuffing here doubles the impact. Make sure the grill is very hot before putting the chops on the clean, well-oiled grilling grid. Have I mentioned that I liked sausage and pork chops in the same dish? **SERVES 4**

GRILLED PORK CHOPS WITH MUSHROOM-SAUSAGE STUFFING

About ½ pound day-old Italian bread, ciabatta, or sourdough bread, torn into chunks or cut into cubes

½ cup plus 6 tablespoons olive oil

Kosher salt and freshly ground black pepper

1 yellow onion, chopped

2 cloves garlic, minced

1 pound sweet Italian sausage, casings removed

1 teaspoon chopped fresh sage

1 teaspoon chopped fresh marjoram or oregano

¾ pound cremini mushrooms, sliced

1 cup grated Parmigiano-Reggiano cheese

½ cup chopped fresh flat-leaf parsley

1½ cups chicken stock, preferably homemade (page 188)

4 boneless pork loin chops, 6 to 8 ounces each and about 1 inch thick

Preheat the oven to 350°F.

In a large bowl, toss the bread chunks with ½ cup of the olive oil and salt and pepper to taste. Spread on a baking sheet and toast in the oven, shaking the pan several times to insure even browning, for 5 to 6 minutes, until lightly browned. Let the bread cool for about 10 minutes, then transfer to a large bowl.

In a large skillet, heat 2 tablespoons of the oil over medium heat. When hot, sauté the onion and garlic for about 3 minutes, or until the onion softens. Take care so the garlic does not burn. If it appears to be scorching, lower the heat.

Add the sausage, sage, and marjoram and cook, stirring with a wooden spoon to break up the sausage meat, for about 10 minutes, or until the sausage is cooked through. Transfer to the bowl with the bread and set aside.

Add 2 tablespoons of the oil to the skillet and heat over medium heat. When hot, add the mushrooms and cook, uncovered, for about 5 minutes, or until the mushrooms give off their juices, the juices evaporate, and the mushrooms begin to brown.

Transfer the mushrooms to the mixing bowl. Add the Parmesan and parsley and mix well. Slowly add the stock, stirring to mix, and season to taste with salt and pepper. Cover the bowl and refrigerate until chilled. The stuffing can be made and refrigerated up to 2 days in advance.

Meanwhile, prepare a clean, well-oiled charcoal or gas grill so that the charcoal is medium-hot or the heating elements are hot.

Using a sharp knife, cut pockets into the chops by slicing horizontally into the thickest side, working the knife through the meat nearly to the other side. Wiggle the knife in the meat to make the pockets.

Using your fingers or a spoon, stuff the pockets with the sausage mixture until overflowing. Tie the chops like a package with kitchen twine to hold the stuffing in place. Rub both sides of the chops with the remaining 2 tablespoons olive oil and season well with salt and pepper.

Grill the pork chops, turning once with tongs, for a total 10 to 15 minutes, until browned and cooked through. If you are not sure the meat is done, insert an instant-read thermometer into the stuffing; it should read 165°F. Remove the string, let the chops rest for about 5 minutes, and serve.

PORK CUTS

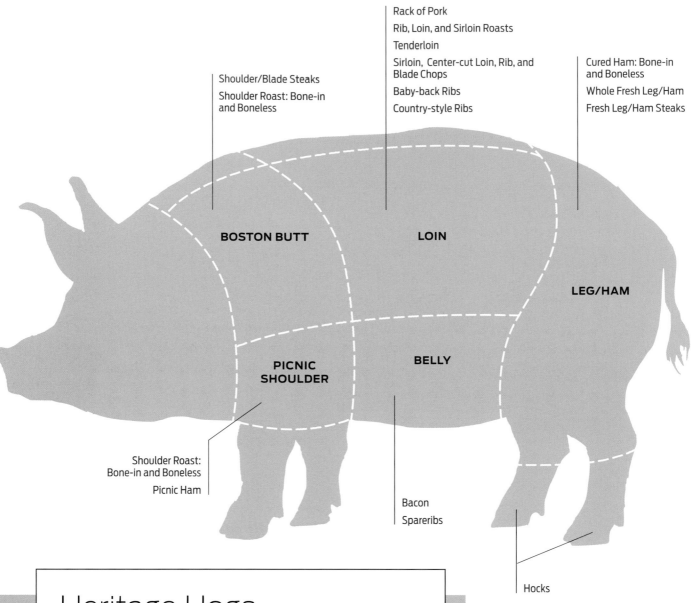

Shoulder/Blade Steaks
Shoulder Roast: Bone-in and Boneless

Rack of Pork
Rib, Loin, and Sirloin Roasts
Tenderloin
Sirloin, Center-cut Loin, Rib, and Blade Chops
Baby-back Ribs
Country-style Ribs

Cured Ham: Bone-in and Boneless
Whole Fresh Leg/Ham
Fresh Leg/Ham Steaks

BOSTON BUTT

LOIN

LEG/HAM

PICNIC SHOULDER

BELLY

Shoulder Roast: Bone-in and Boneless
Picnic Ham

Bacon
Spareribs

Hocks

Heritage Hogs

AS A CHEF, I am pleased that heritage breeds of animals are catching the imagination of small farmers and consumers. As an animal lover, I am thrilled to know that these beasts are raised humanely. The meat tastes great: rich, full, and flavorful—the way I expect meat tasted in more agrarian times. Although they are still rare, hogs such as Large Black, Gloustershire, Mulefoot, and Tamworth are being bred in ever in-creasing numbers. Try them if you see them; you won't be disappointed!

I love ribs; during the summer we cook them all the time for great, messy outdoor meals. My family never misses dinner when they know ribs will be on the menu and more often than not, a few friends show up, too! I always make lots. Chicago does not have a regional barbecue tradition, so I have developed one of my own and decided to dub it "Chicago-style" because, well … why not? I combine the yellow mustard of Carolina barbecue sauce with the smokiness of Memphis sauces for outstanding ribs. The trick is to cook the ribs low and slow for the silken, moist texture you want. Serve with the cornbread on page 226 and the Shell Bean Ragout on page 249. While you could use spareribs here, I like St. Louis ribs, which are shorter and meatier, but that's just me. **SERVES 4**

CHICAGO-STYLE BARBECUED SMOKED RIBS

4 slabs St. Louis–cut pork ribs, each with 12 or 13 ribs

Dry Rub for Pork (page 172)

1 to 1½ cups Barbecue Sauce (page 174)

Rub the ribs generously on both sides with the dry rub. Transfer to a large pan and refrigerate, uncovered, for at least 8 hours and up to 12 hours. By doing this you will form what is called a "pellicle" on the meat. This will help the smoke adhere to the meat.

Prepare and preheat the smoker according the manufacturer's instructions. I suggest using applewood or cherry wood. If using a gas or charcoal grill for smoking, prepare the grill so that the heating elements are low or the charcoal dies down. Top them with soaked applewood or cherry wood chips.

Put the slabs of ribs on the shelf of the smoker or on the grill rack, cover, and smoke at 225°F for about 5 hours, or until they are juicy and smoky. If using a gas or charcoal grill, add more chips to the fire about once every hour. Do not let the heat of the smoker rise above 250°F or go below 200°F.

After about 4 hours, start basting the ribs generously with as much of the barbecue sauce as needed every 15 minutes. You might use it all. This will help form a nice crust on the ribs.

Serve the ribs with the remaining sauce.

Pinot Noir Wine

THE PINOT NOIR GRAPE VARIES DRAMATICALLY DEPENDING ON WHERE IT IS GROWN. Flavors of the wine range from dried red cherry and cola-like spice to dried rose petal, which makes it difficult to veer from a known label. No matter where it is grown, it is very difficult in the vineyard, a characteristic that raises the price to the consumer. The Burgundy region of France is where the greatest pinot noirs are made, but with high expectations and price tags, disappointment is sometimes found in the glass (often from drinking the wines too young). Aging isn't as much of a factor for wine produced in other parts of the world. The Willamette Valley of Oregon has consistent quality and a devout fan base, but the Central Otago region of New Zealand is also making some of the most mouthwatering versions of this wine.

Grenache Wine

A GRAPE THAT IS UNDER THE RADAR OF MOST WINE LOVERS, Grenache is the main player in some of the most popular French export wines. Côte du Rhone is certainly the lightest version that features this grape, marked by meaty flavors opposite stewed black fruit flavors. Châteauneuf-du-Pape marks the other side of the spectrum; layers and layers of plums, bacon, white pepper, and tobacco make this wine highly sought after (and quite expensive). Grenache wine is also made in limited amounts, with much success, in South Australia, Southeastern Spain, and the Pacific Northwest of America.

You may never have made your own sausage, but if you're game to try, here's an easy, tasty recipe. Buy at least 5 feet of casings, because you will need more than you expect and may find some holes. It's super cheap and sold by most butchers. Of course, you can also buy it online. Indeed, the Internet is a beautiful thing, and with a little searching you can also discover more than you need to know about sausage making—and then some! You will need a sausage-making attachment on your standing mixer to make the link sausages, or you can simply form the meat mixture into patties. And don't forget, leftover sausage meat freezes beautifully. Don't have time to make sausage? That's cool; I've been there. Buy the best you can find from a butcher and serve them with the cabbage and mustard. Don't forget the Guinness stout, dark beer, or red ale.

SERVES 6 TO 8

HOUSEMADE GARLIC SAUSAGE WITH BRAISED RED CABBAGE AND BEER MUSTARD

5 feet medium hog casings (see Note)

3½ pounds lean pork butt, cubed

½ pound pork fat, cubed

½ cup dry white wine

4 teaspoons finely minced garlic

1 tablespoon kosher salt

1 tablespoon freshly ground black pepper

2 teaspoons sugar

1 scant teaspoon chopped fresh thyme

Braised Red Cabbage with Green Apples (page 238)

Jared's Beer Mustard (page 182)

Prepare the casings by attaching one end of them to your sink faucet. Run lukewarm water through them for about 2 minutes. Set aside.

Through the fine disk of a meat grinder, grind the pork butt and pork fat. (If you don't have a grinder, ask the butcher to do this for you.)

Transfer the ground meat to a bowl and mix in the wine, garlic, salt, pepper, sugar, and thyme. Using your hands, mix well so that all the ingredients are well integrated.

Using a sausage stuffer, stuff the meat into the sausage casings and twist into 4-inch links. Or simply form the meat into 4- or 5-ounce patties.

Prepare a clean, well-oiled charcoal or gas grill so that the coals or heat element are medium-hot. Or, heat the broiler.

Grill the sausage, turning, 10 to 12 minutes for the links or 5 to 7 minutes for the patties, until an instant-read thermometer inserted in the centers registers 155ºF.

Spoon the warm cabbage onto a large platter and top with the sausage. Spoon a healthy amount of mustard over the sausages and serve.

Note *Sausage casings and all manner of sausage-making equipment are available through The Sausage Maker of Buffalo, New York. Their website is at www.sausagemaker.com Browse the site. It's a lot of fun to see what's out there.*

I love to cook everything—particularly braised dishes—and pork shanks are a regular part of my inventory, especially in the fall. I think of braising shanks as a rite of passage that hits the spot in October and early November when the weather in Chicago turns chilly: Rake the leaves, service the furnace, stack the firewood, and braise the pork shanks! Like so many braised dishes, this one only gets better if you make it ahead of time and so it's a good one-pot meal to make over the weekend and eat for several days. I often make extra, so we can have pulled pork sandwiches or shredded pork tossed with pasta later. Use your imagination and you won't be disappointed. **SERVES 4**

BRAISED PORK SHANKS WITH LENTILS

PORK SHANKS

4 fresh (not smoked) pork hind shanks, about 1 pound each

Kosher salt and freshly ground black pepper

½ cup olive oil

2 ripe Roma tomatoes, seeded and cut into large dice

1 carrot, peeled and cut into large dice

1 yellow onion, cut into large dice

1 rib celery, cut into large dice

2 cloves garlic, sliced

1 sprig rosemary

3 sprigs thyme

2 cups white wine

4 cups Veal Jus (page 185) or chicken stock, preferably homemade (page 188)

To prepare the pork shanks: Season the shanks generously with salt and pepper and refrigerate for at least 3 hours or preferably up to 8 hours.

Preheat the oven to 300°F.

Heat a Dutch oven or similar pot over medium-high heat and add the olive oil. When hot, sear the pork shanks for 6 to 8 minutes on each side, or until evenly golden brown. Remove the shanks and set aside.

Add the tomatoes, carrot, onion, celery, garlic, rosemary, and thyme to the pot and sauté for 3 to 4 minutes, until the vegetables begin to soften. Add the wine, bring to a rapid simmer, and stir with a wooden spoon to scrape up any browned bits from the bottom of the pan.

Add the stock and pork shanks and bring to a boil. Cover the pot, transfer to the oven, and cook for 2 to 3 hours, until the meat is fork-tender. Remove from the oven and let the shanks cool in the liquid to room temperature. The shanks can be prepared to this point, cooled, and refrigerated in the liquid for up to 48 hours.

LENTILS

⅓ cup olive oil

2 shallots, minced

1 red bell pepper, seeded
and finely diced

1 yellow bell pepper, seeded
and finely diced

1 jalapeño pepper, seeded
and finely diced

1 clove garlic, minced

1 tablespoon chopped
fresh thyme leaves

Kosher salt and freshly
ground black pepper

2 cups dried green lentils

6 cups chicken stock, preferably
homemade (page 188)

Grated zest of 1 orange

1 tablespoon fresh rosemary leaves

To make the lentils: In a saucepan, heat the olive oil over medium heat. When hot, add the shallots, red and yellow peppers, jalapeño, garlic, and thyme and season to taste with salt and pepper. Cook gently, stirring, for 8 to 10 minutes, until the shallots are translucent and the peppers soften.

Add the lentils and chicken stock and bring to a simmer over medium-high heat. Cover and cook for 30 to 35 minutes, until the lentils are tender.

To serve, reheat the shanks and braising liquid. Put the lentils in a shallow serving bowl, similar to a pasta bowl, and top with the pork shanks. Spoon the braising liquid and the vegetables still in the pan over the shanks.

In a small bowl, mix together the orange zest and rosemary. Sprinkle the mixture over the pork shanks and serve.

Merlot Wine

THE MERLOT GRAPE IS USED A BIT MORE FOR BLENDING AS OF LATE, but less than 10 years ago, it was probably one of the most asked-for red wines. As if it was a brand in itself, merlot was extremely popular, regardless of who actually made the wine. This prompted wine makers to plant more vines and produce as much as possible. Quality began to suffer, and the wine-drinking masses became more educated about the variety out there in the wine world— the bubble burst. But now this classic grape variety is making something of comeback. France still produces a lot, but quality is up and quantity is down in South America and in California. When done well, soft red plum flavors and black cherry are often supported by just enough tannin and smoky oak.

This is the perfect meal for a cool fall day, when summer is fading to memory and the cold winter is just around the corner. It's a flexible dish, meant to be assembled according to the availability of the game and your budget. I really like a variety of flavors and textures on a plate and this fits the bill. Serve it with the Barbecue Sauce on page 174 or Jared's Beer Mustard on page 182. Jared used to work with me and believe me, the mustard is great! **SERVES 4**

MIXED GRILL OF GAME WITH SMOKED WILD BOAR SAUSAGE, VENISON, AND QUAIL

8 medallions of venison, about 2 ounces each (see Note)

4 semi-boneless quail (see Note)

1 red onion, sliced into ¼-inch-thick rounds

Olive oil, for brushing

Kosher salt and freshly ground black pepper

4 smoked wild boar sausages, 4 to 6 ounces each (see Note)

2 tablespoons aged balsamic vinegar

Cavalo Nero (page 253)

Shell Bean Ragout (page 249)

Prepare a clean, well-oiled charcoal or gas grill so that the coals or heat element are medium-hot. Or, heat the broiler.

Brush the venison, quail, and onion slices with olive oil and season generously with salt and pepper.

Lay the quail on a cool side of the grill, skin side down, cover, and grill for about 5 minutes. Turn the birds and grill for 5 minutes longer, or until cooked through. Transfer to a plate.

Prick the sausages a few times with the tip of a small, sharp knife or with a fork and grill, turning several times, for a total of 10 to 12 minutes, or until cooked through. Transfer to a plate.

Grill the onion slices, turning once, for a total of 5 to 7 minutes, until charred on both sides. Transfer to a bowl. Add the vinegar, toss, and cover with plastic wrap until ready to serve.

Grill the venison, turning once, for a total 5 to 7 minutes for medium-rare. Transfer to a plate.

Arrange the cavalo nero and ragout on a large platter, top with the grilled meats and onions, and serve.

Note *Semi-boneless quail is available at www.vermontquail.com. Boar sausage and venison are available from Broken Arrow Ranch at www.broke narrowranch.com.*

LAMB CUTS

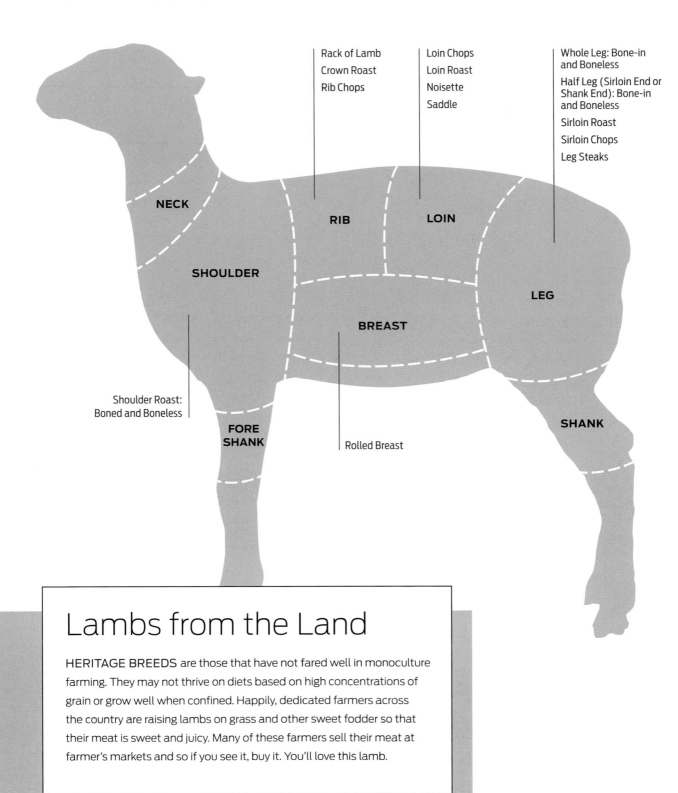

Rack of Lamb
Crown Roast
Rib Chops

Loin Chops
Loin Roast
Noisette
Saddle

Whole Leg: Bone-in and Boneless

Half Leg (Sirloin End or Shank End): Bone-in and Boneless

Sirloin Roast

Sirloin Chops

Leg Steaks

NECK

RIB

LOIN

SHOULDER

LEG

BREAST

Shoulder Roast:
Boned and Boneless

FORE
SHANK

SHANK

Rolled Breast

Lambs from the Land

HERITAGE BREEDS are those that have not fared well in monoculture farming. They may not thrive on diets based on high concentrations of grain or grow well when confined. Happily, dedicated farmers across the country are raising lambs on grass and other sweet fodder so that their meat is sweet and juicy. Many of these farmers sell their meat at farmer's markets and so if you see it, buy it. You'll love this lamb.

If you don't have a great lamb stew in your repertoire, you are now in luck. We love this when the nights get longer and colder, because there's nothing more comforting than sitting down to a pot of stew. Even better with some creamed spinach (page 239) and celery root gratin (page 245)—or perhaps just a green salad, crusty bread, and some buttered egg noodles. The word *navarin* means nothing more exotic than a "ragout," or "stew." The name most likely comes from the French word *navet,* which means "turnip." I think you'll agree that the addition of turnips and parsnips to this dish make it sing *en Français*! **SERVES 6 TO 8**

NAVARIN OF LAMB

3 pounds boneless lamb shank steak, cut from the shank end of the leg, fat trimmed, cut into ¾-inch cubes

Kosher salt and freshly ground black pepper

¼ cup unsalted butter

2 tablespoons olive oil

8 cipollini onions, cut into wedges

4 small baby turnips, peeled and diced

3 small parsnips, peeled and diced

3 carrots, peeled and diced

3 ribs celery, diced

4 cloves garlic, crushed

¼ cup all-purpose flour

2 tablespoons tomato paste

2 teaspoons Dijon mustard

3 small Yukon Gold potatoes, peeled and diced

6 cups beef or chicken stock, preferably homemade (page 187)

1 bouquet garni of thyme, parsley, and bay leaf (see Note)

1 pound slender fresh green beans or haricots verts, ends trimmed

¼ cup chopped fresh flat-leaf parsley

Season the meat generously with salt and pepper.

In a large pot or Dutch oven, heat the butter and oil over medium-high heat. Add the meat and cook, stirring, for 6 to 8 minutes, until nicely browned. Lift the meat from the pan with a slotted spoon and set aside. You might have to do this in batches.

In the same pan, sauté the onions over medium heat for 6 to 8 minutes, until golden. Add the turnips, parsnips, carrots, celery, and garlic and cook gently for 2 to 3 minutes, until they begin to soften. Stir in the flour and then the tomato paste and mustard.

Return the meat to the pot, add the potatoes and stock, and mix thoroughly. Drop in the bouquet garni. Cover and bring to a boil over medium-high heat. Reduce the heat and simmer, covered, for about 1 hour. Adjust the heat up or down to maintain the simmer. Alternatively, cook the stew in a 300°F oven for 45 minutes to 1 hour.

Add the green beans and cook for 20 to 30 minutes longer, or until the beans are cooked through, the meat is tender, and the sauce coats the back of a wooden spoon. Discard the bouquet garni. Season to taste with salt and pepper, sprinkle with the parsley, and serve.

Note *To make a bouquet garni, lay a large square of cheesecloth on a work surface and put a small bunch (3 or 4 sprigs) of thyme and another of parsley in the center. Add a bay leaf. Gather the corners together to make a bundle. Tie the bundle closed with kitchen twine.*

It wasn't until I moved to England to work at Stapleford Park, a hotel about 90 miles from London, that I tasted shepherd's pie—and decided it was my kind of food! Mrs. Assam, our next-door neighbor and former lead housekeeper for the estate that now was the hotel, invited me to a welcome dinner and served the pie. Shepherd's pie is an example of a working-class dish that can soar to great heights when well made. Some folks make it with ground beef, which works just fine, but I like ground lamb and so urge you to ask the butcher to get some for you. **SERVES 4**

SHEPHERD'S PIE

2 pounds Yukon Gold potatoes, peeled

1 cup whole milk

6 tablespoons unsalted butter

Kosher salt and freshly ground black pepper

1 yellow onion, chopped

1½ pounds ground lamb

3 cloves garlic, minced

1 teaspoon tomato paste

1½ teaspoons Worcestershire sauce

1½ teaspoons red wine vinegar

1¼ cups Veal Jus (page 185), or chicken stock, preferably homemade (page 188)

2 tablespoons chopped fresh thyme leaves

1 tablespoon grated Cheddar cheese

1 tablespoon grated Parmigiano-Reggiano cheese

In a saucepan, cover the potatoes with cold water and bring to a boil over medium-high heat. Reduce the heat and simmer rapidly for about 20 minutes, or until the potatoes are fork-tender. Drain.

In another saucepan, heat the milk and 3 tablespoons of the butter over medium heat until the butter melts. Remove from the heat.

Pass the drained potatoes through the medium disk of a food mill into a bowl. Stir in the milk mixture and season to taste with salt and pepper. Set aside.

In a medium sauté pan, melt the remaining 3 tablespoons butter over medium heat. Sauté the onion for 2 to 3 minutes, until translucent. Add the lamb and garlic and cook, stirring well, until mixed. Increase the heat to medium-high and cook, stirring and turning, until the meat browns. Pour off the fat in the pan and discard.

Stir the tomato paste into the lamb mixture and cook for about 2 minutes. Add the Worcestershire and vinegar. With a wooden spoon, scrape any brown bits sticking to the bottom of the pan. Add the veal jus and thyme and mix well.

Preheat the broiler.

Transfer the meat to a shallow casserole that is about 13 by 9 inches, or large enough to hold the meat comfortably. Spread the potatoes over the meat with a spatula. Scatter both cheeses over the potatoes.

Brown the pie under the broiler, about 4 inches from the heat source, just until the cheese melts and the potatoes turn light golden brown around the edge.

I have heard that the word *Chicago* originated from the Potawatomi word *checagou* or *checaguar,* which means "wild onions," and while there are other theories, I like this one as much as any. Evidently the land near Lake Michigan where our city now stands was home to acres and acres of wild leeks, also known as ramps. The early spring vegetable is like a cross between a scallion and a leek, with a wisp of garlic as well as mild onion flavor. We can still find ramps in rural areas around Chicago—and they grow along the nation's eastern corridor as well. Like asparagus and morel mushrooms, ramps are welcome harbingers of spring and so I could not resist pairing them with lamb, another springtime food. **SERVES 6**

STUFFED LEG OF LAMB WITH GRILLED RAMP PESTO

1½ cups fresh flat-leaf parsley leaves

3 cloves garlic

1 tablespoon finely chopped fresh chives

1 boneless leg of lamb, about 2½ pounds

Kosher salt and freshly ground black pepper

2 tablespoons olive oil

Grilled Ramp Pesto (page 180)

2 tablespoons finely chopped fresh mint leaves

Preheat the oven to 350°F.

Finely chop the parsley and garlic together and transfer to a small bowl. Add the chives and stir to mix.

Spread the lamb open on a work surface, flat side down, and season liberally with salt and pepper. Spread the herb mixture evenly over the lamb and then fold in half. Tie the lamb at 1-inch intervals with kitchen twine and pat dry with paper towels. Transfer to a small roasting pan and rub with the oil. Sprinkle with more salt and pepper.

Roast the lamb for 40 to 50 minutes, until an instant-read thermometer inserted about 2 inches on the diagonal into the meat registers 130° to 135°F for medium-rare. Test the meat in several places, as different parts of meat cook at different rates. Transfer to a plate and let the meat rest for 20 minutes.

Cut off and discard the twine and slice the lamb against the grain. Put on serving plates and top with the pesto and mint.

Most kids hate liver, but when I was a boy, we had liver and onions two or three times a month and both my dad and I were in heaven. My mother was not as fond of it as we were, but she was game and made it just for us. Thanks, Mom! Be sure to use high-quality calf's liver and show the love by taking care to cook it carefully—calf's liver is not suitable for a slapdash kitchen style. I have also made the onions to spoon over sirloin steak and believe me, it's out of this world! Try it, even if you forget about the liver. **SERVES 4**

CALF'S LIVER AND ONIONS

½ cup olive oil

2 large onions, cut into
¼-inch-thick slices

¼ pound pancetta, thinly sliced

1 cup sugar

1 cup red wine vinegar

1 cup dry red wine

2 cups quick-mix flour (such as
Wondra) or all-purpose flour

Kosher salt and freshly
ground black pepper

1 pound calf's livers, cut into
½-inch-thick slices

¼ cup balsamic vinegar

2 tablespoons chopped
fresh flat-leaf parsley

Wonders of Wondra

WONDRA QUICK-MIX FLOUR is easy to spot in the supermarket because it's the flour packaged in a cylindrical container, somewhat similar to an oatmeal container. I like using it for coating liver and other food because it's very finely ground and so forms a crispy crust when cooked. It also dissolves more quickly and thoroughly in gravies and sauces.

Preheat the oven to 400°F. Line a baking sheet or jelly roll pan with parchment or waxed paper.

In a large skillet, heat ¼ cup of the olive oil over medium heat. When hot, decrease the heat to low and sauté the onions for about 25 minutes, or until caramelized. Transfer to a bowl and set aside.

Lay the pancetta on the prepared baking sheet. Bake for about 15 minutes, or until crisp. Do not turn the pancetta as it cooks. Transfer to paper towels to drain. Set aside.

In a large saucepan, combine the sugar, wine vinegar, and wine and bring to a boil over high heat. Decrease the heat to medium-high and simmer for about 15 minutes, or until the sauce reduces by half and has a nice syrupy consistency. Adjust the heat up or down to maintain a rapid simmer. Transfer the wine sauce to a bowl, cover, and set aside.

Season the flour with salt and pepper and spread in a shallow dish. Dredge the livers in the flour, coating on all sides.

In a clean skillet, heat the remaining ¼ cup olive oil over medium-high heat. When hot, cook the livers, turning once but otherwise not disturbing them, for a total of about 8 minutes, or until mahogany brown on both sides. Only turn once and do not press down on the livers. This method insures livers with a creamy center and a crispy crust. Transfer to a platter.

Pour the balsamic vinegar into the skillet and add the onions. Bring to a simmer over medium-high heat and cook for about 3 minutes, or until the onions are well coated with the vinegar and begin to glaze. Return the liver to the skillet, cook for about 1 minute, and sprinkle with the parsley.

Transfer the livers and onions to a platter, top with the pancetta, and drizzle with the red wine sauce.

Dirty Martini

STARTING WITH THE GLASS, everything must be as cold as possible for a Dirty Martini to be perfect. If your freezer doesn't have room for martini glasses, fill the glasses with ice and few splashes of water while you construct the drink.

Decide on whether you prefer vodka or gin and then pour 2½ ounces (5 tablespoons) of the white liquor into a cocktail shaker. The "dirty" part generally comes from olive juice, but experimenting with other briny flavors is fun. Try caper juice, pickle juice, or a combination of these two with olive juice. The amount of juice depends on preference, but ½ ounce (1 tablespoon) is a good place to start. Add the juice to the shaker.

Dry vermouth is typically negated when you make a dirty martini because the briny flavor is what is desired, more than the sweetness of the vermouth, but adding ¼ ounce (½ tablespoon) vermouth adds a lot of complexity to the drink. Add some ice to the shaker, cover, and shake vigorously. It should be shaken so hard that when the drink is strained into the chilled martini glass a thin layer of ice shards tops the drink. Garnish with a skewer of olives.

I developed this dish one day after a trip to the farmers' market when the *cavalo nero* was plentiful and gorgeous and found that braising it and serving it with veal chops made a perfect fall meal. This would also be tasty with pork chops. When I cook veal chops, I never cook them past medium-done, and prefer them to be medium-rare so that they are juicy and succulent. **SERVES 4**

ROASTED DOUBLE-CUT VEAL CHOPS WITH BRAISED CAVALO NERO, LEMON, AND OLIVE OIL

2 lemons

6 cloves garlic, minced

Kosher salt

2 tablespoons chopped fresh rosemary

2 tablespoons chopped fresh thyme

6 tablespoons extra-virgin olive oil

Freshly ground black pepper

4 frenched veal rib chops, each 14 to 16 ounces and about 1½ inches thick

1 cup dry white wine

1 cup chicken stock, preferably homemade (page 188)

2 tablespoons unsalted butter, cut into pieces

1 tablespoon chopped fresh flat-leaf parsley

Cavalo Nero (page 253)

1 cup Red Wine Sauce (page 183)

Zest one of the lemons and set the zest aside. Juice the 2 lemons and set the juice aside.

On a cutting board, mash the garlic with a pinch of salt. Transfer to a small bowl and stir in the rosemary and thyme. Stir in 3 tablespoons of olive oil and season with pepper.

Pat the veal chops dry with paper towels and rub the garlic paste all over. You can prepare the chops up to this point 24 hours ahead of time, cover, and refrigerate.

Preheat the oven to 375°F.

In a large skillet, heat 2 tablespoons of the olive oil over medium-high heat until hot but not smoking. Sear the chops, turning once, for a total of 6 minutes, or until golden brown. You will have to do this in batches. Transfer the chops to a shallow roasting pan. Do not wash the skillet.

Roast the chops for 20 to 25 minutes, until an instant-read thermometer inserted horizontally into the chops registers 135° to 140°F for medium-rare.

Meanwhile, in the same skillet, bring the lemon juice and wine to a boil over high heat and, with a wooden spoon, scrape up the browned bits sticking to the pan. Boil for about 5 minutes, or until reduced to about ¼ cup. Add the stock and boil for about 5 minutes longer, or until the sauce reduces to about ¾ cup.

Remove the chops from the roasting pan. Pour any pan drippings into the wine sauce. Bring to a boil and add the butter, a piece at a time, stirring it into the sauce until incorporated. Do not add another piece until the one before is incorporated. Season to taste with salt and pepper.

In a small bowl, mix together the lemon zest and parsley.

Divide the *cavalo nero* among 4 serving plates. Top each serving with a veal chop and spoon the sauce over each. Drizzle the chops with the remaining 1 tablespoon olive oil, sprinkle with the lemon and parsley mixture, and serve.

This technique, which mimics oven roasting on an outdoor grill, provides crispy-skinned chicken with juicy meat. If you love roasted chicken, try it—you won't be disappointed. It's one of my very favorite ways to cook chicken and very few people can resist the crispy, brown skin and moist, tender meat. I learned to value a perfectly roasted chicken from my friend Julia Child, who believed it was something every home cook should be able to accomplish. If you are not comfortable halving the chickens yourself, ask the butcher to do it for you. Make sure the grill is nice and clean and the grilling grid is well oiled to prevent sticking. I think the squash salad is just the thing here. **SERVES 4**

GRILLED CHICKEN WITH ROASTED SQUASH SALAD

2 free-range chickens, 3½ to 4 pounds each, halved

2 tablespoons olive oil

2 cloves garlic, minced

4 teaspoons Dijon mustard

¼ cup chipotle chili powder

Kosher salt and freshly ground black pepper

Roasted Squash Salad (page 250)

1 lemon, cut into 4 wedges

Rub the chicken halves all over with the olive oil, garlic, and mustard.

In a small bowl, mix together the chili powder and about a tablespoon each of salt and pepper and rub all over the chickens. Push some beneath the skin, being careful not to tear the skin. Refrigerate the chickens for about 1 hour or up to 24 hours.

Prepare a clean, well-oiled charcoal or gas grill so that the coals or heat element are medium-hot. Arrange the heating elements or charcoal for indirect grilling.

Put the chickens, skin sides down, on the unheated side of the cooking grate. Cover the grill and cook, turning once, for 15 to 20 minutes, until the meat is cooked through, the skin is crisp and well browned, and an instant-read thermometer inserted in the thickest part of a thigh reads 165°F. Watch carefully and move the chickens back and forth between the hot and cooler parts of the grill, first to crisp the chicken skin and then to cook the birds a little more slowly for a while. Use your judgment for this. This is simply a technique to prevent the birds from charring on the outside. Let the chickens rest for 5 to 10 minutes on a cutting board.

Put the squash salad on a large platter and place the chicken halves next to it. Garnish the platter with salt and pepper and lemon wedges.

When summer tomatoes are at their best, we make this at least once a week. It's an easy at-home dish and has become a Tramonto family favorite. Top-notch ingredients are key for the salad. The key for the chicken is to get it on and off the grill quickly. Don't let it overcook and don't let it rest once it's done. Make sure everything is ready when the chicken is, because the last thing you want is dry poultry in this glorious summer meal. **SERVES 4**

GRILLED CHICKEN PAILLARDS WITH PANZANELLA

¼ cup freshly squeezed lemon juice

¼ cup extra-virgin olive oil

1 clove garlic, minced

1 teaspoon chopped
fresh thyme leaves

Freshly ground black pepper

4 boneless, skinless, chicken breasts,
6 to 8 ounces each, pounded thin

Kosher salt

Panzanella Salad (page 54)

In a wide, shallow mixing bowl, whisk together the lemon juice, olive oil, garlic, and thyme and season to taste with black pepper. Add the chicken and turn to coat. Cover and refrigerate for at least 30 minutes or up to 24 hours.

Prepare a clean, well-oiled charcoal or gas grill so that the coals or heat element are medium-hot. Or, heat the broiler.

Lift the chicken from the marinade and let any excess drip back into the bowl. Season the chicken well with salt and pepper. Grill the chicken, turning once, for a total 4 to 6 minutes, until golden brown and cooked through. Serve the chicken on a platter topped with the panzanella.

Bloody Mary Bar

THE IDEA OF A BLOODY MARY BAR is to offer tomato juice, vodka, seasonings, and a wealth of garnishes, from lemon and lime wedges, olives, celery, pickles, blanched asparagus, cubes of cheese, and slices of ham or sausage. The garnishes add to the "food factor" of the cocktail. My Bloody Mary bar takes the variety one step further in that Bloody Mary aficionados can choose among hot, sweet, or briny seasonings, or modifiers. The bar consists of tomato juice and vodka, along with squirt bottles or small pitchers of the three different modifiers (see below) and as many garnishes as you can dream up. Each modifier can stand on its own with vodka and tomato juice, but mixing them in various combinations should be encouraged.

I know very few people go to the trouble of juicing their own tomatoes and certainly canned tomato juice is excellent, but if you have a juicer and a bumper crop of tomatoes, try it. Incredible!

BLOODY MARY
SERVES 1

1½ ounces (3 tablespoons) vodka

1 ounce (2 tablespoons) desired modifier (see below)

2 to 3 ounces (4 to 6 tablespoons) tomato juice, fresh if possible

Lemon wedge

Garnishes as desired

In a tall glass, stir together the vodka and modifier. Add ice to the glass to fill and then pour in the tomato juice. Squeeze in the lemon wedge, stir, and adjust with modifiers to taste. Then garnish away!

THE MODIFIERS

Each of these measurements can be changed to fit personal tastes—they are meant to be intense because they will be mixed with tomato juice and vodka. Use water (or beer) to thin to the desired consistency.

HOT

¼ cup Worcestershire sauce

2 tablespoons hot pepper sauce

2 teaspoons red pepper flakes

2 teaspoons horseradish

1 teaspoon celery salt

1 teaspoon cayenne

BRINY

¼ cup Worcestershire sauce

¼ cup olive juice (from a bottle of olives)

¼ cup pickle juice (from a jar of pickles)

2 teaspoons drained chopped capers

1 teaspoon celery salt

1 teaspoon freshly ground black pepper

SWEET

½ cup ketchup

¼ cup Worcestershire sauce

3 tablespoons Simple Syrup (page 191)

2 teaspoons freshly ground white pepper

1 teaspoon celery salt

Although I didn't grow up in the South, I have always loved fried chicken. My mother cooked it at home, and I even thought it a great treat when we bought dinner at KFC (or Kentucky Fried Chicken, as it was called then). Nowadays when I travel I seek out local fried chicken eateries, which is a lot of fun, not to mention awesomely delicious. I've enjoyed great fried chicken at places like Price's Chicken Coop in Charlotte, North Carolina, Jestine's Kitchen in Charleston, South Carolina, and Paula Deen's restaurant, The Lady and Sons, in Savannah, Georgia. In Chicago, I also like the fried chicken at Table 52, Art Smith's Southern-style restaurant. I have wanted to share my recipe for fried chicken for the longest time, but it didn't really fit into my previous books, which featured Italian food, bistro cooking, and recipes for fine dining. Fried chicken is perfect in this book. Invite your friends over for a fried chicken party; they will love it. **SERVES 4**

FRIED CHICKEN

3 cups buttermilk

2 tablespoons olive oil

1 teaspoon kosher salt

1 large organic or free-range chicken, about 4 pounds, cut into 8 pieces

Vegetable oil, for frying

2 cups self-rising flour

½ teaspoon sweet paprika

⅓ teaspoon garlic powder

¼ teaspoon freshly ground black pepper

¼ teaspoon cayenne

In a large bowl, stir together the buttermilk, olive oil, and salt. Add the chicken pieces, turning several times to make sure they are well coated with the mixture. Cover and refrigerate for about 2 hours.

Pour enough vegetable oil into a large, deep skillet for a depth of 2 inches. Heat over medium-high heat until a deep-fat fryer thermometer registers 360°F. Meanwhile, in a mixing bowl, whisk together the flour, paprika, garlic powder, black pepper, and cayenne.

Lift the chicken pieces from the buttermilk, shake off any excess, and then roll the chicken pieces in the flour to coat. Shake off any excess flour and let the chicken sit for about 10 minutes. Beginning with the dark meat (legs and thighs), cook the chicken in the hot oil for 15 to 20 minutes, until it's golden brown and cooked through. Adjust the heat up or down to maintain the temperature of the oil so that it bubbles around the chicken pieces steadily. Lift the chicken from the oil with a large slotted spoon, spider, or tongs. Set aside to drain on paper towels.

Let the oil regain its temperature and then cook the breasts and wings for 15 to 20 minutes, until golden brown and cooked through. Adjust the heat up or down to maintain the temperature of the oil so that it bubbles around the chicken pieces steadily. Lift the chicken from the oil with a large slotted spoon, spider, or tongs. Set aside to drain on paper towels for about 5 minutes. Serve the fried chicken on a platter.

I simply love duck, and find it surprising how few people cook it. Don't be afraid of it—embrace it! It is easy to grill and tastes rich, luxuriant, and just plain wonderful. Duck pairs very well with sweet vegetables and stone fruits such as plums and peaches, which explains why I rely on turnips and prunes here. You probably will have to buy frozen duck, although you may find it fresh at a farmers' market. Frozen duck is fine, as long as it is of good quality. Be sure to score the fatty skin so that the fat will drain during grilling. **SERVES 4**

GRILLED LEMONGRASS DUCK WITH TURNIPS AND PRUNES

2 stalks lemongrass, coarsely chopped

¼ cup sake

¼ cup olive oil

1 tablespoon minced fresh ginger

2 scallions, trimmed and coarsely chopped

1 large clove garlic, minced

4 dried star anise, crushed

Coarsely ground black pepper

4 boneless, skin-on duck breast halves

Kosher salt

Turnips with Cinnamon Prunes (page 248)

In the bowl of a food processor fitted with the metal blade, puree the lemongrass stalks until smooth.

In a small bowl, whisk together the lemongrass, sake, olive oil, ginger, scallions, garlic, star anise, and 2 teaspoons pepper.

Trim the duck breasts of any tough connective tissues and using a small, sharp knife, score the skin in a diamond pattern. Lay the duck breasts in a shallow glass or ceramic or other nonreactive dish and pour the marinade over them. Turn several times to coat. Cover and refrigerate for at least 6 hours or up to 12 hours.

Prepare a clean, well-oiled charcoal or gas grill so that the coals or heat element are medium-hot. Or, heat the broiler.

Lift the duck breasts from the marinade and wipe off any excess marinade with a paper towel. Season well with salt and pepper. Grill, skin side up, for about 5 minutes. Turn and grill for 3 to 4 minutes longer for medium-rare. The breasts should be a deep, mahogany brown and the skin crispy. Let the duck breasts rest for about 5 minutes. Slice the meat into thin slices.

Divide the turnips and prunes among 4 serving plates and top with the sliced duck.

I could easily sit down

to a meal of side dishes because I am so crazy about them. I loaded the menu at Tramonto's Steak and Seafood restaurant with so many that we had vegetarian customers who were extremely happy with our broad selection. I have included some steak-house classics, like creamed spinach, steak fries, and twice-baked potatoes, as well as some that may not be as familiar, such as Turnips with Cinnamon Prunes and a cheesy, bacon-y cornbread.

I pay close attention to the seasons when I create side dishes and so suggest you serve the Braised Red Cabbage with Green Apples in the fall and winter and the Shell Bean Ragout at the height of the summer.

Any and all of these taste delicious with steak. Most are great accompaniments to the pork, veal, lamb, and poultry in Chapter 10 as well. None is difficult and I urge you to mix and match them so that the side dishes at your next party will be as spectacular as the main event. Why not? These are dishes that beg for a creative flourish as well as a simple touch.

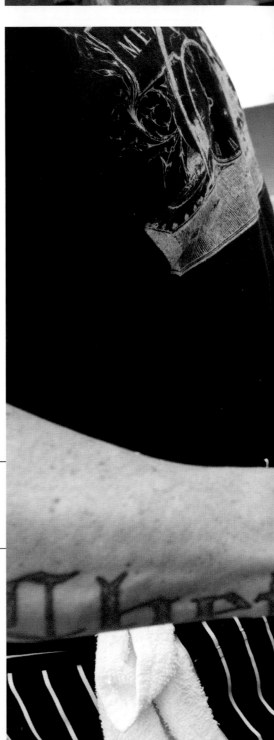

I think of gospel music when I make side dishes. The inspirational words and soaring notes encourage endless creativity. Who do I like? Everyone! THE BLIND BROTHERS OF ALABAMA | THE HARLEM GOSPEL CHOIR | KIRK FRANKLIN | YOLANDA ADAMS | OF COURSE ELVIS PRESLEY

HE WHO IS FAITHFUL IN WHAT IS LEAST IS FAITHFUL ALSO IN MUCH; AND HE WHO IS UNJUST IN WHAT IS LEAST IS UNJUST ALSO IN MUCH. — LUKE 16:10

SIDE DISHES

I like to surprise my friends with savory bread puddings; most people expect bread pudding to be sweet and so this is a conversation starter. Essentially it is just another form of bread stuffing or dressing and is therefore a great way to use leftover brioche or any good, rustic bread. Have fun with the ingredients—you can add sausage or bacon to the pudding or use different herbs and other kinds of mushrooms. Let your imagination run wild! **SERVES 12**

BREAD PUDDING WITH GRUYÈRE AND SHIITAKE MUSHROOMS

6 tablespoons unsalted butter

1 pound shiitake mushroom caps, thinly sliced

2 large leeks, white and some green parts, trimmed and chopped (about 2 cups)

1 tablespoon minced garlic

1 tablespoon chopped thyme leaves

Kosher salt and freshly ground black pepper

¼ cup white wine

12 slices brioche bread, about ½ inch thick, torn into rough 1-inch pieces

1 cup grated Gruyère cheese

1 cup grated Parmigiano-Reggiano cheese

3 cups half-and-half

2 tablespoons sherry, Madeira, brandy, or Cognac

5 large eggs

Butter an 8-inch square baking pan with 3 tablespoons of the butter.

In a large sauté pan, melt the remaining 3 tablespoons of the butter over medium-high heat. When melted, add the mushrooms and leeks and sauté for 2 to 3 minutes, until softened. Stir in the garlic and thyme and season to taste with salt and pepper.

Add the wine and stir with a wooden spoon, scraping up the browned bits from the bottom of the pan. Cook over medium heat for 2 to 3 minutes, until nearly all the liquid evaporates.

Transfer to a large mixing bowl, add the bread, ½ cup of Gruyère, and ½ cup of Parmesan, and toss well. Transfer to the prepared baking pan.

In a small bowl, stir the half-and-half with the sherry. Add the eggs and whisk well. Season with salt and pepper and pour over the bread. With the back of a spoon or spatula, press gently on the bread to insure that it is completely submerged. Cover with plastic wrap and refrigerate for at least 2 hours or up to 6 hours.

Preheat the oven to 350ºF.

Top the bread pudding with the remaining ½ cup Gruyère and ½ cup Parmesan, spreading the cheese evenly. Cover loosely with foil and bake for about 1 hour. Remove the foil and bake for 20 minutes longer, or until the pudding is golden brown. Let the pudding cool for a few minutes before cutting into 2-inch squares for serving.

Every time I bake this cornbread I think of my friend Chef Emeril Lagasse and the great meals I have had at Emeril's New Orleans, where the cornbread is out of this world. Every time I serve it, my guests are just happy I did! It's an easy recipe that works best if served hot, right from the oven, which is how they have been doing it in the South for generations. I like to use Anson Mills cornmeal, which is processed in South Carolina the old-fashioned way, but this would be good with any brand of cornmeal. **SERVES 6**

CORNBREAD WITH BACON AND MONTEREY JACK

6 slices bacon

1¼ cups coarse-ground yellow cornmeal

¾ cup all-purpose flour

½ cup sugar

2 teaspoons baking powder

1 teaspoon baking soda

2 large eggs

1½ cups buttermilk

1 cup grated Monterey Jack or Colby Jack cheese

1 tablespoon chopped chives, for garnish

Preheat the oven to 350°F.

Lay the bacon slices in a shallow baking pan and bake for 9 to 10 minutes, until they begin to crisp. Do not turn during cooking. Drain the bacon on paper towels. Reserve the rendered bacon fat; you should have about ¼ cup. When the bacon is cool, break or chop into small pieces.

Increase the oven temperature to 375°F. Pour the bacon fat into a 10-inch cast-iron skillet and put the skillet in the oven while it preheats.

In a mixing bowl, whisk together the cornmeal, flour, sugar, baking powder, and baking soda.

In another bowl, whisk together the eggs and buttermilk. Pour into the dry ingredients and stir well until mixed. Cover with plastic wrap and let sit at room temperature for 15 to 20 minutes.

Fold the grated cheese and chopped bacon into the cornbread batter.

Carefully remove the hot skillet from the oven and pour in the batter; it should sizzle. Return the skillet to the oven and bake for 25 to 30 minutes, until the top is nicely browned and a toothpick inserted into the center comes out clean. Cut into wedges and serve garnished with chives.

This recipe puts the steakhouse stamp on traditional mashed potatoes. I make it with Atomic horseradish, which packs a potent punch and to my mind does the job! You might prefer a milder horseradish, which is just fine, too. The marriage of horseradish and meat is a classic one, although don't hesitate to serve these alongside fish steaks such as salmon and tuna. You could also turn these potatoes into garlic mashers by tossing a handful of minced roasted garlic cloves into the potatoes in place of the horseradish. Make it your own! **SERVES 4 TO 6**

HORSERADISH POTATO PURÉE

8 medium Yukon Gold
potatoes, peeled

Kosher salt

2 cups half-and-half

½ cup unsalted butter

½ cup drained prepared horseradish

Freshly ground black pepper

1 tablespoon chopped
fresh flat-leaf parsley

Preheat the oven to 350°F.

In a large saucepan, cover the potatoes with water. Add salt to the water and bring to a boil over medium-high heat. Cook at a brisk simmer for about 30 minutes, or until fork-tender. Drain the potatoes and spread on a baking sheet.

Place the potatoes in the oven for 6 to 7 minutes to remove excess moisture so that they can absorb more flavor.

Meanwhile, in another saucepan, heat the half-and-half and butter over low heat until the butter melts. Remove from the heat, cover, and set aside.

Force the potatoes through the medium disk of a food mill or a ricer into a bowl. Stir in the hot cream and the horseradish. Season with salt and pepper and garnish with the parsley. Serve right away.

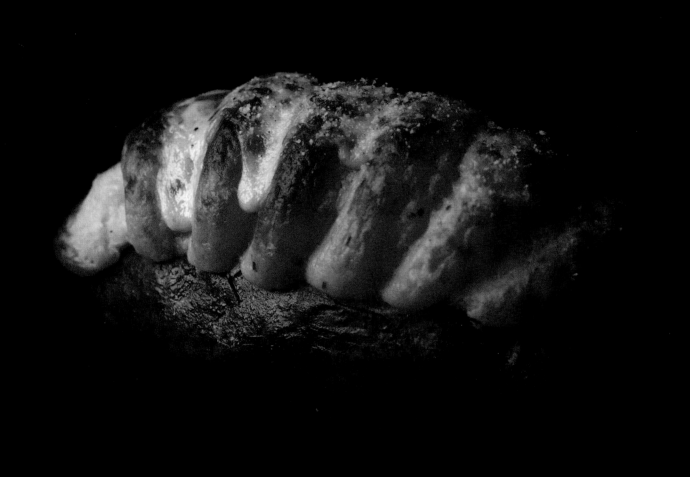

I have always found these to be crowd pleasers, whether I am making dinner for a group of friends or for Eileen and our three boys. The potatoes are terrific alongside grilled steak or any other meat, and they can be prepared up to a day ahead of time and refrigerated before the second baking. I like Irish Cheddar with them, but any other Cheddar would be delicious, or even feta or goat cheese. Have fun with it! **SERVES 4**

TWICE-BAKED POTATOES WITH IRISH CHEDDAR

4 large russet potatoes

2 teaspoons olive oil

¾ cup half-and-half

½ cup sour cream, plus additional for serving

1½ cups shredded Irish Cheddar cheese or your favorite Cheddar

¼ cup thinly sliced scallions

2 tablespoons unsalted butter, melted

Kosher salt and freshly ground black pepper

¼ cup grated Parmigiano-Reggiano cheese

1 tablespoon chopped chives

Preheat the oven to 400°F.

Scrub the potatoes under cold, running water, pat dry, and rub with the olive oil. Pierce several times with a fork and arrange on a baking sheet. Bake for about 1 hour, or until fork-tender. The potatoes may need a little more time, depending on their size. Remove the potatoes from the oven and reduce the oven temperature to 375°F.

Let the potatoes cool until just cool enough to handle. Cut them lengthwise in half, taking care to keep the skins intact. Scoop the flesh from the skins and reserve the shells.

Force the potato flesh through the medium disk of a food mill or a ricer into a bowl. Add the half-and-half, sour cream, 1 cup of the Cheddar, the scallions, and melted butter and mix gently. Season to taste with salt and pepper.

Spoon or pipe the potato mixture into the empty potato skin shells. Top with the remaining ½ cup Cheddar and the Parmesan. Place the potatoes on a baking sheet. (At this point, the potatoes can be loosely covered and refrigerated for up to 24 hours.)

Bake the potatoes for 35 to 40 minutes, until the tops are golden brown. Top each potato half with a tablespoon of sour cream and sprinkle with chives. Serve immediately.

When you read the name of this recipe you might think *I will have to try it next Thanksgiving*. While that's a great idea, I suggest you try the recipe ASAP! Don't wait for the holidays to indulge in incredible, healthful sweet potatoes. Look for them at farmers' markets in the early fall and cook them up as soon as you can for the sweetest, most delicious side dish imaginable. I like pecans with sweet potatoes, as both are American foods, but you could use any sort of spiced nuts. **SERVES 4**

MAPLE–SWEET POTATO MASH WITH SPICED PECANS

3 large sweet potatoes

½ cup unsalted butter

¼ cup heavy cream

¼ cup pure maple syrup

Kosher salt and freshly ground black pepper

½ cup chopped Spiced Pecans (page 52)

Preheat the oven to 375°F. Line a baking sheet with parchment paper or aluminum foil.

Pierce the potatoes in a few places with a fork and place on the baking sheet. Bake for about 1 hour, or until fork-tender. The potatoes may need a little more time, depending on their size.

Let the potatoes cool until just cool enough to handle. Cut them in half and scoop the flesh from the skin; discard the skin. Force the potato flesh through the medium disk of a food mill or a ricer into a bowl.

In a small saucepan, heat the butter and cream over medium heat, stirring now and then until the butter melts. You could also do this in the microwave in a microwave-safe dish.

Stir the cream mixture and the maple syrup into the potatoes and season to taste with salt and pepper. Transfer to a serving bowl and top with the pecans. Serve right away. The potatoes, without the pecans, can also be refrigerated in a lidded container for up to 2 days. Heat gently before topping with the pecans and serving.

Another recipe for fries? Absolutely! There's a reason potatoes fried in duck fat are the current rage with many restaurant chefs: They taste amazingly good. It's a bit of an undertaking to do this at home, partly because you might have to search for the duck fat online if your local gourmet store does not carry it, but your friends will be very happy you went to the trouble. Of course, you can follow this recipe using canola or peanut oil, too. But whatever you do, go for it! **SERVES 4**

DUCK-FAT STEAK FRIES

2 pounds Kennebec or russet potatoes

3 pounds duck fat

Kosher salt and freshly ground black pepper

Scrub the potatoes thoroughly under cold water. Using a large chef's knife, square off the rounded sides of the potatoes to create rectangular cubes. Cut into ½-inch-thick fries, each 3 to 4 inches long. As they are cut, transfer the fries to a large bowl filled about halfway with cold water.

Hold the bowl under cool running water for about 20 minutes, blocking the potatoes with your hand so that they don't wash over the top of the bowl. (Cover the bowl with a damp dishtowel to keep the potatoes inside it if you get tired of standing at the sink.) By this time, the fries will be rinsed of excess starch, won't oxidize, and will fry better. Drain well and pat dry with paper towels. They should be as dry as possible.

Meanwhile, in a deep-fat fryer or large, heavy pot, heat the duck fat over medium-high heat to a temperature of 325°F. I recommend using a thermometer rather than other tests to determine if the oil is hot enough—such as seeing if a pinch of flour or droplets of water sizzle in the hot oil—because you want the oil to be the correct temperature for the potatoes to be their very best.

Fry the potatoes for about 6 minutes, or until lightly browned. Remove with a slotted spoon and drain on a paper towel–lined plate. Do not crowd the pan; fry the potatoes in batches if necessary. Let the fries cool to room temperature.

Increase the heat and let the duck fat reach a temperature of 375°F.

Fry the potatoes again in the hot fat for 3 to 4 minutes, until crisp, golden brown, and irresistible! Drain the fries on fresh paper towels and then toss with salt and pepper in a bowl. Serve hot.

Like so many Americans, I fondly recall macaroni and cheese as a favorite childhood dish. I still like it—who doesn't?—and have always made it for the kids. To kick it up a little for the adults in any crowd, I find truffle oil turns the ordinary into the extraordinary, and it's a perfect accompaniment to grilled steak. If you happen to have some fresh truffles lying around, chop them up and add them to the casserole. On the other hand, you could leave out the truffle oil (and truffles) and enjoy a terrific mac and cheese without them! **SERVES 4**

TRUFFLED MAC AND CHEESE

1 cup bread crumbs

½ cup grated Parmigiano-Reggiano cheese

3 tablespoons white truffle oil

2 tablespoons unsalted butter

2 tablespoons all-purpose flour

2 cups half-and-half

¼ pound Swiss cheese, grated

¼ pound sharp Cheddar cheese, grated

¼ pound fontina cheese, grated

1 teaspoon Dijon mustard

Kosher salt and freshly ground black pepper

½ pound elbow macaroni

Preheat the oven to 375ºF. Butter a 1-quart baking dish or casserole.

In a small mixing bowl, toss the bread crumbs and Parmesan with 1 tablespoon of the truffle oil. Set aside.

In a large, heavy saucepan, melt the butter over medium heat. Whisk in the flour and cook, whisking continuously, for about 3 minutes, or until smooth and blended. Whisk in the half-and-half and bring to a simmer. Cook for about 3 minutes longer.

Stir the Swiss, Cheddar, and fontina cheeses and the mustard into the cream mixture until the cheeses melt. Remove from the heat and stir in the remaining 2 tablespoons truffle oil. Season to taste with salt and pepper.

Meanwhile, cook the macaroni according to the package instructions or for about 7 minutes, until al dente. Drain the pasta, add to the cheese sauce, and mix well. Transfer the macaroni and cheese to the prepared baking dish. (You can make the casserole up to this point, cover, and refrigerate for up to 24 hours.)

Top the macaroni and cheese evenly with the bread crumb mixture. Bake for 25 to 30 minutes, until the topping turns golden brown. Serve immediately.

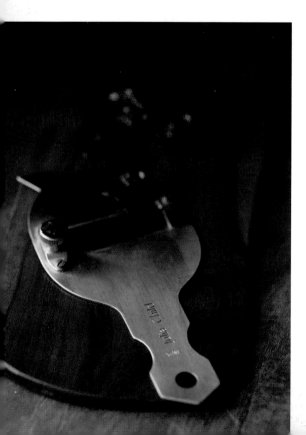

It's just not true that restaurants are the only place for truly spectacular onion rings. You can make them at home by using a malted waffle batter to coat the raw onions. The restaurant industry standard flour for the batter is Carbon's Golden Malted Pancake & Waffle Flour, which is sold through the website www.goldenmalted.com and is also available in some shops. You may have seen onion rings stacked on small poles in restaurants, which makes an appetizing presentation. The poles are sold in most cookware stores and you might want to invest in them for your next party—the onion rings will be even more of a hit! I like to dip them in a chili sauce that is just crazy good. The sauce also brightens up sandwiches: Try it on your favorite fish sandwiches or the soft-shell crab sandwich on page 88. **SERVES 4**

WAFFLE-BATTERED ONION RINGS WITH MAPLE-CHILI SAUCE

Canola or other vegetable oil, for deep-frying

¾ cup water

2 large eggs

5 tablespoons unsalted butter, melted

2 cups malted waffle flour (I use Carbon's Golden Malted flour)

2 yellow onions, cut into ½-inch-thick slices

Kosher salt and freshly ground black pepper

Maple-Chili Sauce (page 180)

Fill a deep-fat fryer or large, heavy pot halfway with canola oil. Heat to a temperature of 350°F.

Meanwhile, in a mixing bowl, whisk together the water, eggs, and melted butter. Add the flour and stir well to break up any clumps.

Using one hand, dip the onion slices in the batter, then gently drop into the hot oil and fry for 2 to 3 minutes, until golden brown and crunchy. Do this in 3 to 4 batches so that you don't overcrowd the fryer, letting the oil regain its temperature between batches.

Lift the onions from the oil with a slotted spoon and drain on a paper towel–lined plate. Season to taste with salt and pepper. Serve immediately with a bowl of the Maple-Chili Sauce for dipping.

This is a dish that practically screams "fall!" I like it with pork chops, sausage, or any braised lamb or beef. The cabbage bleeds as it cooks, so the final dish is bright red and pretty. Tart Granny Smith apples are a perfect match to the slightly acidic mustard and caraway seeds. I have also substituted pears for the apples with wonderful results. **SERVES 4**

BRAISED RED CABBAGE WITH GREEN APPLES

2 tablespoons duck fat
or unsalted butter

1 yellow onion, thinly sliced

1 head red cabbage, quartered,
cored, and thinly sliced

¾ cup dry red wine

½ cup apple cider vinegar

1 large tart green apple (such
as Granny Smith), peeled,
cored, and coarsely grated

½ cup packed light brown sugar

2 tablespoons caraway seeds

2 tablespoons yellow mustard seeds

Kosher salt and freshly
ground black pepper

4 to 5 slices cooked bacon,
chopped (optional)

In a large sauté pan, melt the duck fat over medium-high heat. Add the onion and sauté for about 5 minutes, or until softened. Add the cabbage and toss for 2 to 3 minutes, until it begins to wilt.

Add the wine, vinegar, apple, brown sugar, caraway seeds, and mustard seeds and stir well to combine. Season to taste with salt and pepper.

Cut a circle of parchment paper to fit over the food in the pan. Cut a small vent in the center of the paper and set it directly on the cabbage. Reduce the heat to medium and simmer for about 45 minutes, or until the cabbage is soft. Adjust the seasoning with salt and pepper and serve hot, garnished with the bacon.

Creamed spinach has been served in steakhouses since the days when New York's Delmonico's ruled the restaurant trade and has always been a great favorite. But talk about super-charged! This is not your ordinary creamed spinach—it is so much better, made with tender baby spinach, clotted cream, and freshly grated nutmeg. If you already love creamed spinach, you will be thrilled; if you are not a fan yet, you will be! **SERVES 4**

RICK'S STEAKHOUSE CREAMED SPINACH

2 pounds fresh baby spinach

2 tablespoons unsalted butter

½ cup chopped shallots

1 teaspoon minced garlic

½ cup clotted cream or crème fraîche

¼ teaspoon freshly grated nutmeg

Kosher salt and freshly
ground black pepper

2 tablespoons grated
Parmigiano-Reggiano cheese

In a large pot, bring about 2 gallons of water to a boil over high heat. Add the spinach and cook for about 2 minutes, just to wilt. Drain in a colander and use a spoon to press on the spinach to extract as much moisture as possible. Chop the drained spinach finely.

In a large sauté pan, melt the butter over medium heat. Add the shallots and garlic and sauté for about 2 minutes, or until the shallots soften.

Add the spinach and cook, stirring, just until its liquid is released. Stir in the cream and nutmeg and season to taste with salt and pepper. Bring to a simmer and cook for about 5 minutes, or until the cream reduces by about half. Stir in the Parmesan and cook for about 1 minute longer. Serve right away.

We eat a lot of broccoli rabe at our house, and whether it's grilled, sautéed, steamed, or stir-fried, we love it. In this recipe I put it directly on the grill, although you may want to put it in a vegetable-grilling basket. Either way, the smokiness imbues the already pleasingly bitter green with another layer of flavor and depth. I love this with beef especially, and nothing could be simpler. If you have not already made the garlic confit, use any garlic-infused oil. **SERVES 4**

GRILLED BROCCOLI RABE

1 pound broccoli rabe, trimmed

4 tablespoons oil from Garlic Confit (page 181)

1 teaspoon dried red pepper flakes

Kosher salt and freshly ground black pepper

In a saucepan filled about halfway with boiling, salted water, blanch the broccoli rabe for about 1 minute, or just until the rabe begins to wilt. Drain well and transfer to a bowl.

Add 3 tablespoons of the oil and the pepper flakes to the broccoli rabe, toss well, and season to taste with salt and pepper. Set aside for at least 15 minutes or up to 30 minutes to marinate.

Prepare a charcoal or gas grill so that the coals or heat element are medium-hot.

Grill the stalks of rabe for about 2 minutes on each side. This will let you get some char and smoke on the broccoli rabe. Transfer to a plate, drizzle with the remaining 1 tablespoon garlic oil, and serve immediately.

Roasting the beets on top of a bed of salt keeps them from burning and draws out their moisture, which makes them super easy to peel. This is one of my signature dishes at the steakhouse and I rarely cook beets any other way. Since this method is so easy and efficient, I suggest you try it. I like the beets with just about anything but particularly with fish. **SERVES 4**

ROASTED BEETS WITH CHARRED FENNEL AND ORANGE

3 cups kosher salt, plus more for seasoning

8 red baby beets, trimmed but not peeled

8 yellow baby beets, trimmed but not peeled

8 candy-striped baby beets, trimmed but not peeled

½ cup extra-virgin olive oil

Freshly ground black pepper

2 fennel bulbs

2 oranges

Preheat the oven to 350ºF. Spread the salt over the bottom of a shallow roasting pan or sheet pan.

In a large bowl, combine the beets, 3 tablespoons of the olive oil, 1 tablespoon salt, and 1 teaspoon pepper.

Lay 3 or 4 large sheets of aluminum foil on the work surface and divide the beets among them. Wrap the beets in the foil and set the packets on the salt.

Roast for 45 to 50 minutes, until the beets are tender. Let the beets cool in the foil for about 45 minutes, which will make them easier to peel.

Peel each beet and cut in half. (You can prepare the beets to this point and refrigerate for up to 2 days.)

Preheat the oven to 375ºF.

Trim the fronds from the fennel bulbs, core them if needed, and cut the bulbs into 8 equal segments. Cut the oranges into 8 segments; do not peel. Place the fennel and orange segments in two separate bowls and toss with the remaining olive oil. Season to taste with salt and pepper.

Spread the fennel in a shallow baking pan and roast for 20 to 30 minutes, until beginning to soften and lightly browned. Add the orange segments, toss, and roast for about 5 minutes longer. Add the peeled beet halves. Continue to roast for about 10 minutes, or until the fennel is tender and the beets are very hot. Serve immediately.

Sautéed mushrooms are a universal side for steak or veal, regardless of the type. I find this dish is all about the fresh thyme and lemon, and you can play around with the mushrooms a little, using those that are available on any given day at the farmers' market or grocery store. **SERVES 4**

SAUTÉ OF WILD MUSHROOMS WITH GARLIC CONFIT

¼ cup extra-virgin olive oil

2 pounds assorted wild mushrooms (such as chanterelles, hen of the woods, or Trumpet Royales), thickly sliced

Kosher salt and freshly ground black pepper

1 shallot, minced

4 cloves Garlic Confit (page 181), chopped into a paste

2 tablespoons unsalted butter

2 tablespoons fresh thyme leaves

1 tablespoon chopped fresh flat-leaf parsley

Juice of 1 lemon

In a large, heavy-bottomed sauté pan, heat the olive oil over high heat. When very hot—almost smoking—add the mushrooms and season with salt and pepper. Do not shake the pan but let the mushrooms cook for about 2 minutes to develop a nice, brown crust.

Add the shallot, garlic paste, butter, and thyme and cook, stirring, for 2 to 3 minutes longer, until the mushrooms are tender. Do not overcook. Add the parsley and lemon juice and serve right away.

The humble celery root is arguably the most underutilized vegetable in the world, which is a shame as its earthy flavor makes it a natural with roasts, braises, and steaks. Use the truffles with this or not; either way your friends will love it—and probably will ask you what it is. If you want to substitute rutabaga for the celery root, the gratin will be top-notch, too. **SERVES 4**

TRUFFLED CELERY ROOT GRATIN

1 cup chicken stock, preferably homemade (page 188)

2 cups heavy cream

2 large celery roots, about 1½ pounds each, trimmed, peeled, and cut lengthwise into quarters

2 tablespoons white truffle oil

Kosher salt and freshly ground black pepper

1 cup finely shredded Gruyère cheese

1 tablespoon chopped chives

Preheat the oven to 350°F.

In a large pot, bring the stock and cream to a simmer over medium heat. Add the celery root quarters, cover, and cook for 20 to 30 minutes, turning the celery root several times in the liquid. Remove the pot from the heat and using a slotted spoon or tongs, transfer the celery root to a cutting board and let cool slightly.

Bring the liquid in the pot to a boil and cook for 10 to 15 minutes so that it thickens a little.

When the celery root is cool enough to handle, cut into ¼-inch-thick slices. Layer the slices in a 9-inch square baking dish, overlapping them slightly.

Whisk the truffle oil into the reduced cooking liquid and season to taste with salt and pepper. Pour the hot liquid over the celery root to cover completely. Sprinkle the cheese evenly over the casserole. Bake for 35 to 40 minutes, until the casserole bubbles and the cheese melts. Garnish with chives and serve hot.

When it comes to steak, these Brussels sprouts are one of the best accompaniments around. Since a lot of folks aren't sure how to cook the sprouts, here's an easy, quick recipe that can be dressed up with a buttery, rich béarnaise sauce—or not. The key to great Brussels sprouts is to blanch them first until al dente and then cook them as instructed in a recipe. For these, the fat from pancetta adds incredible flavor. Of course, you can substitute bacon for the pancetta or, if need be, use just a little reserved bacon fat from another dish. But don't neglect the fat—a little goes a long way! **SERVES 4**

PAN-ROASTED BRUSSELS SPROUTS

Kosher salt

1 pound Brussels sprouts, each halved

2 tablespoons extra-virgin olive oil

¼ pound thickly sliced pancetta, cut into ¼-inch dice

4 large shallots, quartered

Freshly ground black pepper

Béarnaise Sauce (page 175), optional

In a large pot, bring about 6 quarts of water and 2 tablespoons of salt to a boil over medium-high heat. Add the Brussels sprouts and when the water returns to the boil, cook for about 5 minutes. Using a slotted spoon, remove the sprouts from the pot and immediately plunge in a large bowl filled with ice and water.

Meanwhile, in a medium skillet, heat the olive oil over medium heat. When hot, sauté the pancetta for 8 to 10 minutes, until it is slightly crisp and the fat is rendered.

Stir in the shallots, season with salt and pepper, and cook for about 10 minutes, or until golden brown. Add the Brussels sprouts and continue cooking, stirring occasionally, for 8 to 10 minutes, until the Brussels sprouts have a nice golden brown color.

Divide the Brussels sprouts among 4 serving plates and serve, topped with warm béarnaise sauce.

These sweet-tasting turnips and prunes pair well with the Grilled Lemongrass Duck on page 221, as well as with just about any poultry or pork dish. I have, at times, substituted plums or another stone fruit for the prunes with excellent results. Fresh fruit does not require soaking. **SERVES 4**

TURNIPS WITH CINNAMON PRUNES

1 cup pitted prunes (about ¼ pound)

2 cups strong, brewed black tea (such as Earl Grey)

1 cinnamon stick

Coarsely chopped zest of ½ orange

6 tablespoons unsalted butter

3 pounds baby turnips, peeled and cut into ½-inch wedges

Kosher salt and freshly ground pepper

1 onion, finely chopped

1 large clove garlic, minced

1 cup chicken stock, preferably homemade (page 188)

3 tablespoons soy sauce

1 large sprig thyme

In a small saucepan, cover the prunes with the tea. Add the cinnamon stick and orange zest and bring to a simmer over medium-high heat. As soon as the tea simmers, remove the pan from the heat and let stand for about 1 hour, or until the prunes plump up in the cooling liquid. Drain, discarding the tea, cinnamon stick, and orange zest. Set the prunes aside.

In a large skillet, melt 4 tablespoons of the butter over medium-high heat. Add the turnips and season to taste with salt and pepper. Cook, stirring, for about 2 minutes, or just until heated through.

Add enough water to cover the turnips by 1 inch and bring to a boil. Reduce the heat and simmer for 10 to 12 minutes, until tender. Drain the turnips.

In the same or another skillet, melt the remaining 2 tablespoons butter over medium-high heat. Add the onion and cook for about 5 minutes, or until softened. Stir in the garlic and cook for about 1 minute, or until fragrant.

Add the prunes, turnips, stock, soy sauce, and thyme. Stir and season to taste with salt and pepper. Bring to a simmer over medium-low heat. Cook, stirring, for 5 to 7 minutes, until the vegetables are tender and the liquid has reduced and starts to glaze the turnips. Discard the thyme sprig and serve immediately.

While the season lasts, I encourage you to cook with fresh shell beans, often found at farmers' markets. These are any legume that is shelled to find the small beans or peas nestled inside, including fava, lima, cranberry, and pinto beans—to name only a few. Most of the year they are sold dried, which are good, too, but they are exceptional when cooked fresh. You will be amazed by the difference. The bacon adds rich flavor and the jalapeño just a little heat. I find this ragout is best if made a few hours ahead of time, or even a day before it's served, and it's good served hot or cold. **SERVES 4 TO 6**

SHELL BEAN RAGOUT

¼ cup extra-virgin olive oil

1 (½-pound) slab bacon,
cut into 2 or 3 chunks

1 onion, diced

1 jalapeño pepper, seeded and diced

2 cloves garlic, minced

1 bunch fresh thyme, leaves only

1 bunch fresh sage, leaves torn

1 bay leaf

Kosher salt and freshly
ground black pepper

2 pounds any variety fresh
shell beans, shelled

In a large pot, heat the olive oil over medium heat. Add the bacon and cook for 8 to 10 minutes, until lightly brown. Add the onion and jalapeño and sauté until translucent. Add the garlic, thyme, sage, and bay leaf and season to taste with salt and pepper.

Add the beans, stir to coat them in the fat, and pour in just enough water to cover. Bring to a simmer over medium-high heat and simmer for 30 to 45 minutes, or until the beans are tender but not too mushy. Add more water if needed and adjust the heat up or down to maintain the simmer.

Remove and discard the bacon and bay leaf. Serve the beans right away, or cover and refrigerate for up to 1 day. The beans are best if allowed to sit for a day. If you do this, be sure to leave the bacon in the pot with the beans until you reheat them.

As delicious as this is with the grilled chicken on page 217, it's also great with other meats and full-bodied fish — or on its own. The pomegranate juice and seeds mingle with the vinegar and olive oil to make a vinaigrette that gallantly stands up to the roasted winter squash. **SERVES 4**

ROASTED SQUASH SALAD

1 butternut or other winter squash, about 2 pounds

2 tablespoons extra-virgin olive oil

Kosher salt and freshly ground black pepper

2 tablespoons champagne vinegar

1½ tablespoons pumpkin seed oil

2 teaspoons pomegranate molasses

1½ teaspoons fresh lemon juice

4 ounces arugula (about 8 lightly packed cups)

½ cup toasted pumpkin seeds (pepitos), coarsely chopped, see Note, page 82

½ cup fresh pomegranate seeds

Preheat the oven to 450°F.

Peel the squash, remove the seeds, and cut the squash into ½-inch cubes. You will have 4½ to 5 cups of squash. Transfer to a large bowl and toss with the olive oil and a liberal amount of salt and pepper.

Spread the squash on a rimmed baking sheet and roast for about 15 minutes. Use a wide spatula to turn the squash and roast for 15 minutes longer, or until the edges of the cubes turn brown. Remove from the oven and let the squash cool at room temperature.

In a large, shallow serving bowl, whisk together the vinegar, pumpkin seed oil, pomegranate molasses, and lemon juice. Season to taste with salt and pepper.

Add the squash, arugula, pumpkin seeds, and pomegranate seeds, toss to coat, and serve.

While these tomatoes require a little time and attention, the effort is well worth it. The seasoned olive oil bathes the tomatoes as they stew so that the end result is irresistibly rich and flavorful. What is better than tomatoes and good, fruity olive oil? It's all here. **MAKES 2 TO 2½ CUPS**

STEWED TOMATOES

2½ pounds Roma tomatoes
(8 to 10 tomatoes)

5 tablespoons extra-virgin olive oil

1½ cloves garlic, sliced

3 sprigs rosemary

2½ sprigs thyme

Pinch of crushed red pepper flakes

Kosher salt

8 fresh basil leaves

In a large pot filled about halfway with boiling water set over medium-high heat, blanch the tomatoes for about 7 seconds. With a slotted spoon, lift the tomatoes from the water and set aside to cool (do not shock them in cold water).

When cool enough to handle, slip the skins off the tomatoes and halve lengthwise. Hold them over a plate and gently squeeze out the seeds and juice. Discard the juice and seeds and reserve the tomatoes.

In a sauté pan, heat 4 tablespoons of the olive oil, the garlic, rosemary, thyme, and red pepper flakes over medium heat. When very warm, remove from the heat and let stand for at least 10 minutes to give the garlic and herbs time to steep in the oil and flavor it.

Meanwhile, in a large saucepan, heat the remaining 1 tablespoon olive oil over medium heat. When hot, add the tomatoes and salt. Cook, stirring, for 10 to 15 minutes, until the tomatoes start to break down and become very dry.

Strain the herb-infused olive oil through a fine-mesh sieve or *chinoise* into the tomatoes. Discard the solids. Cook the tomatoes and olive oil, stirring occasionally, for 4 to 7 minutes, until the sauce has emulsified. The tomatoes will have a sheen from the oil and will turn a bright reddish-orange. At this point, the sauce will taste very fresh. Stir in the basil and season to taste with salt.

I made this on Ming Tsai's PBS television show, *Simply Ming,* and he went crazy for it, which to be honest, did not surprise me as I love it too. I learned to make it from my Italian grandmother who was a terrific cook. I serve it alongside or spooned over grilled meats and poultry. It's a cross between a zesty condiment and a side dish, and will keep for a month in the refrigerator—an added benefit. **MAKES ABOUT 6 CUPS OR 3 PINT JARS; ABOUT 12 SERVINGS**

PICKLED EGGPLANT

3 pounds eggplant, peeled, sliced lengthwise, and cut into julienne strips

2½ tablespoons kosher salt

4 cups Champagne vinegar

4 cups water

4 cloves garlic, sliced

1½ tablespoons dried oregano

¼ cup fresh oregano leaves

1 tablespoon dried red pepper flakes

Grated zest of 2 lemons

Extra-virgin olive oil, for packing the eggplant

In a mixing bowl, toss the eggplant with the salt. Transfer to a colander and set the colander over a bowl to catch the draining liquid. Weight the eggplant with another bowl holding a few cans of soup and set aside at room temperature to drain for 24 hours.

In a large saucepan, bring the vinegar and water to a boil over high heat. Add the drained eggplant and return to the boil. Immediately drain the eggplant in a colander, discarding the vinegar. Spread the eggplant on clean dishtowels to dry for 2 to 3 hours.

Pack the strips tightly into sterilized jars, layering them with the garlic, dried and fresh oregano, red pepper flakes, and zest. Tamp the eggplant gently into the jars. Pour enough olive oil over the eggplant to cover, pouring slowly so that it gets all the way to the bottom. Cover tightly and refrigerate for at least 1 week and up to 1 month.

How to Sterilize Jars and Lids

BEGIN WITH CLEAN JARS that you have washed in hot, soapy water and rinsed well or that you have run through the dishwasher (some even have "sterilize" cycles that can substitute for submerging the jars in boiling water, although I usually do both). Submerge the jars in a large pot filled with boiling water and let boil for about 5 minutes. Let the jars sit in the hot water, off the heat, until you are ready to fill them.

Canning lids are flat with a rubber ring around the inside. Sterilize them, too, in a pan of boiling water for about 5 minutes. Lift them out with tongs or a lid-lifting tool (which is magnetized to grip the lids). The lids are only good for one-time use, although the screw-on rings used to hold the lids in place can be used repeatedly.

Sometimes called Tuscan kale, *cavalo nero* is a member of the same family as cabbage, kale, and broccoli and is recognized by its tall stalks and narrow green leaves. I have listed Swiss chard as a substitute for the *cavalo nero,* but I hope you will make every effort to find the real thing. Nothing is as good for this preparation, which is a little hot, a little bitter, and extremely tasty. In this dish, I mix it with hominy, which is nothing more exotic than dried corn kernels that have been soaked in an alkali solution to remove their outer skins and then are boiled for hours. When you buy hominy—which is sold in in cans—the kernels look a little like soft, puffy corn kernels and add the gentle flavor of corn to the greens. **SERVES 4**

CAVALO NERO

2 bunches *cavalo nero* or Swiss chard, stemmed and cleaned

⅓ cup extra-virgin olive oil

½ sprig rosemary, 2 to 3 inches long

1 dried red chili d'arbol

1 yellow onion, thinly sliced

2 garlic cloves, thinly sliced

Kosher salt

1 (29-ounce) can hominy, drained and rinsed

Freshly ground black pepper

In a large pot filled about halfway with salted boiling water, blanch the *cavalo nero* for about 2 minutes. Drain and let cool. When cool, squeeze the excess water from it with your hands.

In a large saucepan, heat the oil over medium-high heat. When hot, add the rosemary and chili and let sizzle in the oil for about 1 minute. Add the onion and garlic and season with salt. Reduce the heat to medium-low and cook gently for about 10 minutes, or until the onion is soft and starting to color slightly.

Add the *cavalo nero* and stir to mix well. Season with more salt and cook the greens slowly over low heat, stirring often, for about 25 minutes, until they turn a dark, almost black color and become slightly crispy at the edges.

Add the hominy, stir well, and cook for 5 to 10 minutes longer, until heated through. Season to taste with salt and pepper and serve.

I have never claimed to be a

pastry chef. I have worked for many years with the great Gale Gand, one of the country's best pastry chefs, and so have never had to learn that end of the business. This does not mean I don't appreciate a good dessert after a satisfying meal. Far from it! But I have learned that all I need is a handful of reliable recipes and every party will end on a sweet, high note.

If you learn how to make a good pie crust, you can make nearly any kind of pie. If you learn how to make vanilla ice cream, you can whip up any flavor. I have taken a cue from great dessert cooks such as Richard Sax, Maida Heatter, and Julia Child who counseled their readers to keep it simple and keep it seasonal and you will never go wrong. On that note, I have mastered a simple brûlée and a mind-blowing chocolate pudding, as well as a number of ice cream desserts. There's a chocolate cake on these pages and seductive bread pudding. Need more? I don't think so! If I can do it, so can you.

We like to end the meal with positive Christian energy and so, for some great rock, load up the iPod with music by:

SARAH KELLY | ANGELO AND VERONICA | HILLSONG | MERCYME
| TRENT AND KEISHA CORY | CASTING CROWNS | AVALON

DESSERTS

Even if they insist they "couldn't eat another bite," your friends will happily dig into one of these sundaes. I call the banana split "vertical" because it's served in a tall ice cream sundae glass, with banana slices waving happily from the top of the glass. I have provided recipes for both the banana and peanut butter ice cream, but of course you could make just one and buy a high-quality ice cream for the other. Or buy all the ice cream. Bananas, peanuts, chocolate, strawberries: Doesn't get much better, my friends! **SERVES 4**

VERTICAL BANANA SPLITS

BANANA ICE CREAM

3 extremely ripe bananas

2 cups half-and-half

6 large egg yolks

½ cup sugar

½ teaspoon pure vanilla extract

¼ teaspoon salt

PEANUT BUTTER ICE CREAM

1 cup heavy cream

1¾ cups half-and-half

1¼ cups sugar

1 cup large egg yolks (14 eggs)

1 cup creamy peanut butter (about 8 ounces)

CHOCOLATE SAUCE

1 pound semisweet chocolate, coarsely chopped

2 tablespoons light corn syrup

About ½ cup water

CANDIED PEANUTS

1 cup unsalted peeled blanched peanuts (see Note)

½ cup sugar

2 tablespoons water

¼ teaspoon salt

SUNDAE

2 bananas, split vertically

2 tablespoons sugar

1 pint strawberries, hulled and quartered

About 12 fresh mint leaves

Whipped cream, for serving

To make the banana ice cream: In the bowl of a food processor fitted with the metal blade, puree the bananas until very smooth. You could also do this in a blender.

In a small saucepan, heat the half-and-half over medium-high heat until briskly simmering.

In a mixing bowl, whisk the egg yolks and sugar together until smooth and the color is uniform. Slowly add about half of the hot half-and-half mixture to the egg yolks, whisking constantly. This will temper the eggs so that they don't curdle. Return to the saucepan, reduce the heat to low, and stir constantly for 5 to 6 minutes, until the custard thickens and coats the back of a wooden spoon.

Strain the custard through a fine-mesh sieve into a bowl. Stir in the pureed bananas, vanilla extract, and salt. Let the mixture cool to room temperature. Cover and refrigerate for at least 3 hours or until very cold.

Freeze the banana mixture in an ice cream machine following the manufacturer's instructions. When done, transfer the ice cream to a freezer container and freeze for at least 4 hours.

To make the peanut butter ice cream: In a small saucepan, heat the cream and half-and-half over medium-high heat until briskly simmering.

In a mixing bowl, whisk the sugar and egg yolks together until smooth and the color is uniform. Slowly add about half of the hot cream mixture to the egg yolks, whisking constantly. Return to the saucepan, reduce the heat to low, and stir constantly for 5 to 6 minutes, until the custard thickens and coats the back of a wooden spoon.

Strain the custard through a fine-mesh sieve over the peanut butter in a large bowl. Stir well until the peanut butter is well incorporated and the mixture is smooth. Let cool to room temperature. Cover and refrigerate for at least 3 hours or until very cold.

Freeze the peanut butter mixture in an ice cream machine following the manufacturer's instructions. When done, transfer the ice cream to a freezer container and freeze for at least 4 hours.

To make the chocolate sauce: In the top of a double boiler or a metal bowl set over a pot of barely simmering water, melt the chocolate.

Keep the heat on low because even a small amount of steam or a droplet of water can cause the chocolate to seize or stiffen, ruining it.

Off the heat, whisk the corn syrup and water into the melted chocolate until completely mixed. Add more or less water for the desired consistency.

To make the candied peanuts: Preheat the oven to 350°F. Spread the peanuts on a baking sheet and toast in the oven for 7 to 10 minutes, until lightly browned. Stir once or twice during toasting. Let the peanuts cool.

In a large sauté pan or Dutch oven, heat the sugar, water, and salt over medium-high heat until large bubbles form. Add the toasted peanuts and stir constantly with a wooden spoon for 2 to 3 minutes, until the sugar crystallizes. Reduce the heat to medium-low and continue stirring until the sugar caramelizes (turns golden brown). Spread the peanuts on a baking sheet and cool to room temperature. Transfer to a cutting board and chop into halves or coarse pieces.

To assemble the sundaes: Cut the bananas into slices, arrange on a baking sheet, and sprinkle with the sugar. Caramelize the sugar with a butane torch or under a hot broiler. Let the bananas cool.

In each of 4 chilled sundae glasses, layer the ingredients: Put a few strawberries and a mint leaf in the bottom of each one and then a spoonful of whipped cream. Top with a scoop of banana ice cream and a scoop of peanut butter ice cream. Add some more strawberries and mint and top these with chocolate sauce and peanuts. Finally, add the bananas, inserted vertically into the sundae. Top with a dollop of whipped cream and some more mint leaves and serve.

Note *If you cannot find peanuts that are already blanched and peeled, blanch raw unsalted peanuts. In a pot of boiling water set over medium-high heat, blanch the peanuts for about 1 minute. Drain and spread the peanuts on a kitchen towel to dry. Use the towel to rub the peanuts and remove the skins.*

The Ins and Outs of Homemade Ice Cream

A FEW OF MY RECIPES HERE INCLUDE HOMEMADE ICE CREAM, and it's possible this could make you throw up your hands with frustration. What? He expects me to make the ice cream?! Is he out of his mind?

I understand how you feel and of course any number of the premium ice creams available in every supermarket in the land will be more-than-adequate substitutes, but if you are in the mood, churn your own and get ready for a heady experience. Plus, your friends will be amazed that you went to the trouble—and your kids will think you a hero.

I make ice cream from a custard base, which is a little more complicated than the plain cream and sugar ice creams, also called Philadelphia ice cream. The custard gives the finished dish amazing body, creaminess, and full flavor.

It's important to have a reliable ice cream machine. These are not hard to find and don't cost a fortune. I like the sort with a liquid-gel canister that must be frozen (usually for about 24 hours) before you begin. They are easy to use and turn out exemplary ice cream.

When you make ice cream, have everything cold, cold, cold. This means the ingredients, the bowls, and the utensils. Make sure there is room in the refrigerator for chilling the mixture before you freeze it, and that there is room in the freezer for the ice cream to firm up. Follow recipes carefully—don't arbitrarily reduce the amount of sugar or decide to use half-and-half instead of heavy cream. Too little sugar makes the ice cream grainy; the fat from the cream gives it its smoothness and richness.

I doubt you will make ice cream every time you make one of the desserts in the book, but if you try a few times, you will become a convert. Homemade really does taste best!

While cherry pie is traditional in February around the time of George Washington's birthday, I cannot lie: I think of it as the most summery of summertime desserts. Here in Chicagoland we get fresh cherries from Door County, Wisconsin, and so making this is nearly a rite of passage as July pushes into August. The recipe here is for a double crust pie—which is magnificent. It is important to brush egg wash on the edge of both the top and bottom crusts so that when crimped together they hug each other during baking. At times I forget all about the bottom crust and make this with a top crust only, sort of like a cobbler—which is appropriate for a non-pastry chef like me! Either way, it's spectacular. Ditto for using fresh, frozen, or canned berries. **SERVES 8**

CHERRY PIE

PIE DOUGH

3 cups all-purpose flour

½ teaspoon salt

1 cup vegetable shortening (such as Crisco), cut or broken into pieces

⅓ to ½ cup ice water

CHERRY FILLING

1 cup sugar

¼ cup instant clear gel powder (see Note)

4 cups fresh, thawed frozen, or drained canned sour cherries, pitted, juice reserved

1 tablespoon freshly squeezed lemon juice

1 tablespoon unsalted butter

1 teaspoon almond extract (optional)

1 large egg, beaten, for egg wash

To make the dough: In the bowl of a food processor fitted with the metal blade, combine the flour and salt and pulse 2 or 3 times, until mixed. Add the shortening and pulse until the mixture resembles small peas. Slowly add the water through the feed tube, pulsing until the dough comes together.

Turn the dough out onto a lightly floured surface and gather into a ball. Do not handle the dough more than necessary or it will toughen. Wrap the dough in plastic wrap and refrigerate for at least 30 minutes.

To make the filling: In a small bowl, stir together the sugar and gel.

In a large saucepan, mix the reserved cherry juice with the lemon juice (if using fresh cherries, combine 2 tablespoons water with the lemon juice). Add the sugar mixture and whisk until dissolved. Set the pan over medium-high heat and whisk constantly until the mixture comes to a boil. Boil, whisking continuously, for about 5 minutes, until the sauce thickens.

Off the heat, whisk in the butter and almond extract. When the butter is totally incorporated, stir in the cherries. Set aside to cool to room temperature.

Preheat the oven to 425°F. Position an oven rack in the center of the oven.

Cut the pie dough in half. On a lightly floured surface, roll one half into a circle about 11 inches in diameter. Fit the dough into a 9-inch pie plate, draping the excess over the side of the plate. Spoon the cherry filling into the pie shell.

Roll the remaining dough into a circle about 10 inches in diameter.

With a small brush, brush the egg wash over the exposed portions of the dough around the rim of the pie plate. Brush the edge of the 10-inch round and carefully invert over the filling so that the edges of the dough rounds meet. Crimp the dough with your fingers or a fork. Brush the remaining egg wash over the top and cut a few steam vents into the top.

Put the pie on a baking sheet and bake for 15 minutes. Reduce the temperature to 350°F and bake for 40 to 60 minutes longer, until the crust is golden brown. Let the pie cool on a wire rack and serve.

Note *Instant clear gel powder is a processed starch that has been pre-cooked so that it swells and thickens instantly without cooking. It is flavorless and colorless and products made with it are smooth, plump, and have no starchy taste. If you cannot find it in the supermarket or specialty shop, you can order it online (see page 280).*

I have asked for this, or a banana cream pie, for my birthday since I was a kid; my wife Eileen obliges these days. It's rich, sweet, and indulgent, kissed by luxuriant coconut, and I do nothing but smile broadly when I see birthday candles on top of the pie rather than a more traditional cake. When I serve this after a steak dinner, my guests melt with happiness. So do I! **SERVES 8**

COCONUT CREAM PIE

PIE DOUGH

1½ cups all-purpose flour

¼ teaspoon salt

½ cup vegetable shortening (such as Crisco), cut or broken into pieces

2 to 4 tablespoons ice water

COCONUT FILLING

4 large egg yolks

½ cup plus 2 tablespoons sugar

¼ cup cornstarch

1 cup whole milk

½ (13.5-ounce) can coconut milk

1 tablespoon unsalted butter

½ teaspoon pure vanilla extract

½ cup plus 2 tablespoons heavy cream, whipped to soft peaks, plus more for garnish

½ cup shredded coconut, plus more for garnish

To make the dough: In the bowl of a food processor fitted with the metal blade, combine the flour and salt and pulse 2 or 3 times, until mixed. Add the shortening and pulse until the mixture resembles small peas. Slowly add the water through the feed tube, pulsing until the dough comes together.

Turn the dough out onto a lightly floured surface and gather into a ball. Do not handle the dough more than necessary or it will toughen. Wrap the dough in plastic and refrigerate for at least 30 minutes.

To make the filling: In a large bowl, whisk together the egg yolks, sugar, and cornstarch until pale yellow in color.

In a medium saucepan, heat the whole milk and coconut milk over medium-high heat until it simmers briskly but is not boiling. Pour about half of the milk mixture into the yolk mixture and whisk until combined. This tempers the yolks so that they do not curdle. Return the milk and yolk mixture to the saucepan and cook over medium-low heat, whisking constantly, for 7 to 10 minutes, until boiling.

Off the heat, whisk in the butter and vanilla until incorporated. Let cool to room temperature. Transfer to a bowl and fold in the whipped cream and shredded coconut. Refrigerate for about 30 minutes.

Preheat the oven to 350ºF.

On a lightly floured surface, roll the dough into a circle about 11 inches in diameter. Fit the dough into a 9-inch pie plate, draping the excess over the side of the plate. Pierce the bottom of the dough with a fork and then line it with parchment paper. Weight the paper with pie weights, dried beans, or rice and bake for about 15 minutes. Remove the parchment paper and weights. Continue baking the pie shell for about 10 minutes, or until lightly golden brown. Let cool.

To assemble the pie: Put the coconut cream in the pie shell. Top with a little extra whipped cream and shredded coconut.

Anything with the flavor of citrus is satisfying after a rich, filling steak dinner and anyone who knows me knows how much I appreciate that particular flavor. These little crème brûlées are elegant and impressive and yet very easy to make ahead of time. The tang of key limes gives them just enough of a jolt.

I have always been a fan of the flavor of key limes, but if you can't find them, use the more common limes. This recipe demonstrates what I learned from Gale Gand, who has been my culinary partner for years and who is one of the best pastry chefs in the business. **SERVES 6**

KEY LIME BRÛLÉES

Preheat the oven to 300°F.

In a saucepan over medium heat, heat the heavy cream, granulated sugar, zest, and vanilla bean for about 5 minutes, or until small bubbles appear around the edges of the pan. Set aside to steep for 10 minutes. Remove and discard the vanilla bean or reserve it for another use.

In a mixing bowl, whisk the egg yolks and then slowly add the warm cream mixture, whisking constantly so that the eggs do not curdle. Stir in the lime juice.

Divide the custard among six 6-ounce ramekins or custard cups. Place the ramekins in a roasting pan large enough to hold them easily. Pour enough warm water into the pan to come to a depth of about 1 inch. Bake for 25 to 30 minutes, until the custards are set in the middle.

Remove the ramekins from the roasting pan and let cool to room temperature. Refrigerate until chilled, at least 2 hours.

Blot any extra moisture from the tops of the custards with a paper towel. Sprinkle the raw sugar evenly over the custards. Caramelize the tops with a butane blowtorch or under a hot broiler. Take care that the sugar does not burn. Let the brûlées sit for a few minutes before serving topped with a few raspberries.

How to Split a Vanilla Bean

LAY THE BEAN ON A CUTTING BOARD and draw the dull side of a paring knife over the bean's husk to flatten it. With the sharp side of the knife, cut the bean along one side and open it. Scrape the seeds from the husk and use according to the recipe. The bean will infuse sugar with lovely vanilla flavor if you bury it in a canister of granulated sugar. The sugar is wonderful sprinkled on berries or used to sweeten cream—or any other way you can imagine!

I am most drawn to simple, old-fashioned desserts and chocolate pudding falls squarely into that category. I make mine with both dark and milk chocolate to boost the pure chocolatyness of it, and then garnish it with grated white chocolate. To bring out all this chocolate glory, I finish the old-time dessert with a modern touch: a sprinkle of artisanal salt. Wow! Amazing chocolate flavor and a rare treat for the chocoholic in all of us! **SERVES 6**

KILLER CHOCOLATE PUDDING

2½ ounces bittersweet or semisweet chocolate, coarsely chopped

2½ ounces milk chocolate, coarsely chopped

3 large egg yolks

¼ cup sugar

2 cups heavy cream

¼ teaspoon kosher salt

Whipped cream, for serving

2½ ounces white chocolate, coarsely grated

Black salt, fleur de sel, or another artisanal salt, for sprinkling

In a microwave-safe dish or large measuring cup, microwave the chopped bittersweet and milk chocolates on medium power for about 30 seconds. Remove the container from the microwave and stir. Microwave for 30 seconds longer, or until the chocolate looks shiny and wet. At this point, you should be able to stir the chocolate into a liquid pool. The chocolate will not melt completely in the microwave but needs to be stirred. Do not microwave it for longer than 30 seconds at a time.

In a heatproof (not metal) mixing bowl, whisk the egg yolks with the sugar.

In a saucepan, combine the cream and kosher salt and cook over medium heat until nearly boiling. Pour half of the hot cream into the eggs and whisk together. This tempers the eggs so that they do not curdle. Return the cream and egg mixture to the saucepan and stir the custard over low heat for 3 to 5 minutes, or until smooth and a thermometer registers 160°F. Take care that the custard does not scorch on the bottom of the pan.

Strain the custard through a fine-mesh sieve over the melted chocolate and whisk together until thoroughly combined. Let cool. Cover and refrigerate until very cold, at least 2 hours.

To serve, spoon the pudding into small bowls or plates and serve topped with whipped cream and garnished with white chocolate and a sprinkling of artisanal salt.

Salt with Chocolate; Salt with Nearly Everything

THE NUMBER OF SPECIALTY SALTS AVAILABLE TODAY IS ASTOUNDING, and wonderful. While these are rarely used to season food as it cooks, they are great for finishing a dish. They also are amazing when carefully paired with chocolate and you will find that many of the best chocolatiers offer elegant truffles topped with a few grains of salt. Play with different salts and you'll be just as pleased as I am by how different they taste from each other and how just a little sprinkle perks up a dish at the last minute. To learn more about specialty salts or order a few, go to www.salttraders.com or www.saltworks.us.

SALT GLOSSARY

AUSTRALIAN MURRAY RIVER SALT: Apricot-colored, flaky salt from the Murray River's underground brine deposits. It has a mild flavor and the flakes melt easily into hot food taken from the oven, grill, or pan.

CYPRUS BLACK SALT: This salt is made from Mediterranean flake salt mixed with activated charcoal. The color is great and the flavor distinct and mild.

FLEUR DE SEL: From France's Brittany coast, the salt is ivory colored and imparts the pure flavor of the sea.

HAWAIIAN RED SALT: This salt is enriched and colored by the naturally occurring red clay of the islands, which adds iron. The salt has great flavor and color.

KOSHER SALT: Made from granular salt that is pressed into flakes. Contains no additives.

MALDON SALT: A natural sea salt made by the Maldon Crystal Salt Company in Great Britain. Many find this to taste of the sea and have a distinctive, pleasing saltiness, so less is needed.

PINK PERUVIAN MOUNTAIN SALT: Mined high in the Andes Mountains in naturally-fed salt ponds, the salt is pale pink with a pleasant but strong flavor.

Just about everyone likes warm, comforting bread pudding and this one is just about perfect on a chilly fall evening or cold winter's night. While it's a homey dessert, the rum flavor and rum sauce turn it into a dessert fit for guests. If you make the effort to buy brioche, the pudding will be super rich, although it's always tasty with challah, French bread, or country-style white bread. Try them all and decide which is your favorite. **SERVES 8**

RUM BREAD PUDDING

BREAD PUDDING

16 cups lightly packed cubes of brioche or challah bread (2 standard-sized loaves)

1½ cups granulated sugar

3 large eggs

1 quart half-and-half

2 tablespoons pure vanilla extract

1½ teaspoons ground cinnamon

1 teaspoon grated orange zest

⅛ teaspoon salt

1 cup golden raisins

1 cup pecans, toasted and chopped

RUM SAUCE

1 cup unsalted butter, softened

1½ cups granulated sugar

⅓ cup confectioners' sugar

2 large eggs

½ cup dark spiced rum

To make the bread pudding: Preheat the oven to 350°F. Spray a 9 by 13-inch baking dish with vegetable oil spray.

Spread the bread on ungreased baking sheets and bake, turning once or twice, for 5 to 7 minutes, until firm but barely colored. Let the bread cool and transfer to a large mixing bowl.

In the bowl of a standing mixer fitted with the paddle attachment and set on medium-high speed, beat the sugar and eggs for about 5 minutes, or until pale yellow. Reduce the speed to low and slowly add the half-and-half, vanilla, cinnamon, zest, and salt.

Pour the custard over the bread, add the raisins and pecans, and fold together until well mixed. Transfer to the prepared baking dish, pressing down on the bread so the custard moistens every piece evenly. Set aside to soak for about 15 minutes.

Bake the pudding for 40 to 55 minutes, until a toothpick inserted in the bread comes out clean. Cool slightly before serving.

To make the rum sauce: In the top of a double boiler or a metal bowl, blend the butter with the granulated and confectioners' sugars with a rubber spatula until smooth. Set the double boiler or bowl over a pot of simmering water and cook, whisking, for about 20 minutes, or until the mixture is smooth and lightly colored. Adjust the heat up or down to maintain a simmer and add more water to the bottom pot if necessary.

In a small bowl, whisk the eggs. Pour about ½ cup of the butter mixture into the eggs, whisking, to temper the eggs. Pour the eggs back into the pan and whisk over the simmering water for about 5 minutes, or until the sauce thickens.

Remove from the heat and stir in the rum. Keep the sauce warm over simmering water until ready to serve.

Cut the pudding into pieces and serve with the rum sauce.

This will please those who love lemon tarts and those who adore lemon meringue pie—it's a blending of both and of course can also be made with lime juice instead of lemon juice. This is one of the first desserts I ever learned to make. I was a young line cook at the Strathallan Hotel in my hometown of Rochester, New York, and Gale Gand was just starting her impressive career as a pastry chef. When I was asked to help out with desserts, Gale showed me how to make this. I have never stopped relying on it as a refreshing dessert that meets the mark after dinner. My mom was excited when she learned I could make one of her very favorite desserts! **SERVES 8**

LEMON MERINGUE TART

TART DOUGH

2½ cups cake flour

⅓ cup sugar

1 cup unsalted butter, cubed and chilled

4 large egg yolks

3 tablespoons sour cream

LEMON FILLING

1 cup freshly squeezed lemon juice

2 cups sugar

8 large egg yolks

2 large eggs

1 cup unsalted butter, cubed and chilled

MERINGUE

4 large egg whites

½ teaspoon cream of tartar

Pinch of salt

½ cup sugar

Grated lemon zest, for garnish

To make the dough: In the bowl of a food processor fitted with the metal blade, pulse the flour, sugar, and butter until the mixture resembles small peas.

Add the egg yolks and sour cream and pulse just until the dough comes together in a mass. Turn the dough out onto a lightly floured surface, gather into a ball, and wrap in plastic. Refrigerate for at least 1 hour or up to 3 hours.

On a lightly floured surface, roll the dough into a circle about 11 inches in diameter. Transfer the dough to an 11-inch tart pan with a removable bottom, draping the excess over the side of the pan. Gently lift the edge of the dough and press it into the bottom and fluted part of the tart pan, creating somewhat of a 90-degree angle. With a rolling pin, roll over the edge of the tart mold to cut off the excess dough. Chill the tart shell for 30 minutes.

Preheat the oven to 350°F.

Line the chilled pastry with parchment paper. Weight the paper with pie weights, dried beans, or rice and bake for about 15 minutes, rotating once. Remove the parchment paper and weights. Continue baking the pie shell for about 10 minutes, or until lightly golden brown. Let cool. Carefully remove the tart pan edge from the crust, leaving the crust on the removable bottom.

Meanwhile, to make the filling: In the top of a double boiler or a metal bowl set over a pot of simmering water, whisk together the lemon juice, sugar, egg yolks, and eggs over medium heat. Whisk until the mixture thickens and reaches a temperature of 160°F.

Strain the lemon curd through a fine-mesh sieve into a bowl. While it is still hot, whisk in the butter. Set aside to cool.

To make the meringue: In a clean, dry bowl of an electric mixer fitted with the whisk attachment and set on low speed, mix the egg whites and cream of tartar until blended. Add the salt. Increase the speed to medium and whip the whites until foamy. Begin adding the sugar a little at a

time, whisking until the meringue reaches stiff peaks. This will take 5 to 7 minutes.

To assemble the pie: With the tart shell on the baking sheet, gently spoon the lemon curd into it. Spread the meringue over the curd so that it covers it completely. Make a few swirls in the meringue.

Bake for 3 to 5 minutes, watching closely, until the meringue turns golden brown. If you have a butane torch, you can finish browning the meringue with it once it's taken from the oven. Serve garnished with lemon zest.

What makes this not so traditional is the inclusion of a strawberry soup and the use of biscuits instead of cake. While the key to this super dessert is fresh, juicy strawberries, best in June and July in the Midwest where I live, it's also delicious with frozen berries, which tend to be very good when packed without syrup. I think of it as the quintessential Fourth of July dessert. You may not realize this, but the strawberry soup freezes really well so you can make shortcake later in the year. **SERVES 8**

NOT-YOUR-TRADITIONAL STRAWBERRY SHORTCAKE

STRAWBERRY SOUP

1 pint fresh strawberries, hulled or 8 ounces thawed frozen strawberries

½ cup granulated sugar

2 tablespoons water

BISCUITS

¾ cup all-purpose flour

¼ cup cake flour

1½ tablespoons granulated sugar

2 teaspoons baking powder

⅛ teaspoon salt

¼ cup unsalted butter, cubed and chilled

½ teaspoon freshly grated ginger

½ cup plus 2 tablespoons heavy cream, plus more for brushing

2 tablespoons raw sugar

1 pint fresh strawberries, hulled and quartered, for serving

Whipped cream, for serving

To make the soup: In a medium saucepan, mix the strawberries sugar, and water and cook over low heat for 30 to 45 minutes, until the liquid develops a syrupy consistency. Do not stir the berries more than once or twice during cooking or the soup will be cloudy.

Strain the strawberries through a fine-mesh sieve into a bowl; do not push down on the berries to extract more juice. Discard the solids and let the liquid cool.

To make the biscuits: Preheat the oven to 350°F.

In the bowl of a food processor fitted with the metal blade, combine the all-purpose and cake flours, granulated sugar, baking powder, and salt and pulse 2 or 3 times, until mixed. Add the butter and ginger and pulse 2 or 3 times to mix. With the motor running, add the cream through the feed tube and process just until the dough comes together.

Turn the biscuit dough out onto a lightly floured work surface and knead it a few times to make a cohesive ball. Do not overwork the dough or it will toughen. Roll the dough into a round that is ½ to 1 inch thick. Cut rounds from the dough using a 3-inch biscuit cutter or an upturned drinking glass. Gather the scraps, roll out again, and cut out more biscuits. You should have 8 biscuits.

Arrange the biscuits on a baking sheet lined with parchment paper, leaving a little space between them. Brush the tops of the biscuits with cream and sprinkle with raw sugar. Bake, rotating the baking sheet once, for about 15 minutes, or until the biscuits are golden brown. Let the biscuits cool on wire racks.

To serve: In a mixing bowl, pour the cooled strawberry soup over the quartered fresh berries.

Cut the biscuits in half and put a bottom half on each of 8 serving plates. Spoon the berries and soup over the biscuits and top with a dollop of whipped cream. Put the top halves of the biscuits on the whipped cream at a slight angle. Serve right away.

The flavor combination of chocolate and cherries is one of my all-time favorites. Think chocolate-covered cherries and you'll get what I mean. This intense chocolate-cherry ice cream cake is a surefire winner for a crowd and will clearly make lots of friends! I explain how to make cherry ice cream, but you could buy it, too. **SERVES 12**

TRIPLE CHOCOLATE CAKE WITH CHERRY ICE CREAM

CHERRY ICE CREAM

8 ounces frozen sour cherries, thawed, reserving any liquid

2 cups half-and-half

6 large egg yolks

½ cup sugar

½ teaspoon pure vanilla extract

CHOCOLATE CAKE

3 cups sugar

2¼ cups all-purpose flour

1 cup plus 2 tablespoons unsweetened cocoa powder

2½ teaspoons baking powder

2½ teaspoons baking soda

1½ teaspoons salt

5 large eggs

1½ cups whole milk

¾ cup vegetable oil

1 tablespoon pure vanilla extract

1½ cups hot water

CHOCOLATE MOUSSE

1 pound plus 1 ounce bittersweet or semisweet chocolate, coarsely chopped

1 cup heavy cream

10 large egg whites

¼ cup sugar

5 large egg yolks

CHOCOLATE GANACHE

12 ounces bittersweet or semisweet chocolate, coarsely chopped

1¾ cups sour cream, at room temperature

To make the ice cream: Chop one-fourth of the cherries and set aside to use as garnish. In a saucepan, cook the remaining cherries and reserved liquid over low heat for about 30 minutes, until reduced to a syrupy consistency. Let cool to room temperature. Puree in a blender until smooth.

In another saucepan, heat the half-and-half over medium-high heat until briskly simmering.

In a mixing bowl, whisk the egg yolks and sugar together until smooth and the color is uniform. Slowly add about half of the hot half-and-half mixture to the egg yolks, whisking constantly. This will temper the eggs so that they don't curdle. Return to the saucepan, reduce the heat to low, and stir constantly for 5 to 6 minutes, until the custard thickens and coats the back of a wooden spoon.

Strain through a fine-mesh sieve into a bowl. Stir in the cherry puree and vanilla extract. Let the mixture cool to room temperature. Cover and refrigerate until very cold, at least 3 hours.

Freeze the cherry mixture in an ice cream machine following the manufacturer's instructions. When done, transfer the ice cream to a freezer container and freeze for at least 4 hours.

To make the cake: Preheat the oven to 350°F. Butter and flour three 8-inch round nonstick cake pans. Tap out any excess flour. In the bowl of a standing mixer set on low speed, mix together the sugar, flour, cocoa powder, baking powder, baking soda, and salt. In a mixing bowl, whisk together the eggs, milk, oil, and vanilla extract.

Add the liquid ingredients to the dry ingredients and mix on low to medium speed until well mixed. Scrape the sides and bottom of the bowl to make sure all is incorporated. With the mixer running, slowly add the hot water and beat until incorporated.

Divide the cake batter among the 3 prepared pans and smooth the surfaces. Bake for 15 to 20 minutes, rotating the pans once, until a toothpick inserted in the centers comes out clean. Let the pans cool on wire racks for about 10 minutes. Turn the cake layers out onto the wire racks to cool completely.

To make the mousse: Put the chocolate in a large glass or ceramic bowl (not metal). In a saucepan, heat the cream over medium-high heat until boiling and then pour over the chocolate, whisking until the chocolate melts and the mixture is smooth.

In the bowl of a standing mixer fitted with the whisk attachment, whisk the egg whites and sugar on low speed until foamy. Increase the speed to high and whisk to stiff peaks. This will take 5 to 7 minutes.

Add the egg yolks to the melted chocolate mixture and whisk well. Fold about a third of the egg whites into the chocolate mixture and when blended, fold in the remaining whites. Refrigerate until needed or up to 2 days.

To make the ganache: In the top of a double boiler or a metal bowl set over a pot of barely simmering water, melt the chocolate. Keep the heat on low because even a small amount of steam or a droplet of water can cause the chocolate to seize or stiffen, ruining it.

Stir the room-temperature sour cream into the chocolate and mix together. If the sour cream is too cool, it will cause the chocolate to stiffen. If necessary, keep the ganache over the warm water with the heat off until needed.

To assemble: Place one cake layer on the serving platter. Spread an even layer of the mousse over the cake. Place another layer over the mousse and then top with the third cake layer. There will be a little extra mousse, but you can serve it alongside the cake.

Refrigerate for 15 minutes to chill. Frost the top and sides of the cake with the ganache. Serve garnished with the reserved chopped cherries and the cherry ice cream.

A still-warm fruit cobbler with a scoop of melty vanilla ice cream is a dessert fit for the angels. When summer's peaches and blueberries are ripe and plentiful in the farmers' market, I make this cobbler a lot, particularly if we're planning to entertain a bunch of friends. The dough is pressed into small pieces that form a cobbled topping, but for a more finished look, roll the dough into a larger piece and lay it over the fruit. I use this same recipe for rhubarb and strawberry cobblers in the spring and apple and pear in the fall. Always a winner! Always delicious! **SERVES 8**

PEACH AND BLUEBERRY COBBLER WITH VANILLA ICE CREAM

VANILLA ICE CREAM

2 cups half-and-half

1 vanilla bean, split lengthwise, or ½ teaspoon pure vanilla extract

3 large egg yolks

1 cup granulated sugar

½ teaspoon pure vanilla extract

¼ teaspoon salt

FILLING

4 pounds ripe peaches (about 12)

¼ cup all-purpose flour

¼ cup packed light brown sugar

¼ cup honey

½ cup water

1½ tablespoons freshly squeezed lemon juice

2 tablespoons unsalted butter

1 pint blueberries

TOPPING

2 cups minus 2 tablespoons all-purpose flour, sifted

2¾ teaspoons baking powder

¼ teaspoon salt

6 tablespoons unsalted butter, cut into ½-inch pieces and chilled

⅔ cup whole milk

¼ cup heavy cream

¼ cup coarse raw sugar

To make the ice cream: In a small saucepan, heat the half-and-half with the vanilla bean, if using, over medium-high heat until briskly simmering.

In a mixing bowl, whisk the egg yolks and granulated sugar together until smooth and the color is uniform. Slowly add about half of the hot half-and-half mixture to the egg yolks, whisking constantly. This will temper the eggs so that they don't curdle. Return to the saucepan, reduce the heat to low, and stir constantly for 5 to 6 minutes, until the custard thickens and coats the back of a wooden spoon.

Strain the custard through a fine-mesh sieve into a bowl. Remove and discard the vanilla bean or reserve it for another use. Stir the salt and the vanilla extract, if using, into the custard. Let the mixture cool to room temperature. Cover and refrigerate until very cold, at least 3 hours.

Freeze the mixture in an ice cream machine following the manufacturer's instructions. When done, transfer the ice cream to a freezer container and freeze for at least 4 hours.

To make the filling: Fill a large saucepan about half full of water and bring to a boil over medium-high heat. Drop the peaches into the boiling water and simmer for about 30 seconds. Lift from the water with a slotted spoon and immediately submerge in a bowl filled with ice and water. Peel the skins from the peaches. Halve the peaches and discard the skin and pits. Cut the peaches into quarters and drain on a towel.

In a large saucepan, mix together the flour, brown sugar, and honey. Add the water and whisk until smooth. Cook over medium heat, scraping down the sides of the pan, for 2 to 3 minutes, until the mixture thickens. Reduce the heat to medium-low and cook for about 1 minute longer, stirring. Add one-third of the peaches and cook for 1 minute. Off the heat, stir in the lemon juice and butter. Stir gently until the butter is fully incorporated.

In a shallow, 3-quart baking dish or casserole, arrange the remaining peaches and the blueberries so that the fruit covers the bottom of the dish. Pour the cooked peaches over the raw fruit.

To make the cobble topping: Preheat the oven to 450°F.

In the bowl of a food processor fitted with the metal blade, combine the flour, baking powder, and salt and pulse 2 or 3 times to mix. Add the butter and pulse several times, until the mixture resembles small peas. Add the milk through the feed tube and pulse 2 more times just to mix.

Turn the dough out onto a lightly floured surface and knead lightly just until it sticks together.

Break 1-inch pieces of dough from the mass, flatten them, and arrange over the fruit, leaving about ½ inch between each piece. During baking, the pieces will expand a little and form a cobbled effect. Brush the dough with the cream and sprinkle with the raw sugar.

Bake the cobbler for 20 minutes, rotating the dish 180 degrees once, until the topping is golden brown and the filling is bubbling. Serve hot with scoops of vanilla ice cream.

This is as rich and opulent as any good cheesecake should be, but the pumpkin flavor surprises a lot of people. Pumpkin cheesecake? Yet it's precisely the flavor that makes this the ideal dessert when you entertain friends in the fall. Everyone loves it. *Pepitas* are pumpkin seeds found in specialty markets, often in the bulk food section. If you prefer, substitute pine nuts or almonds, using the same method to candy them. **SERVES 12**

PUMPKIN CHEESECAKE WITH AMARETTI CRUST AND CANDIED PEPITAS

AMARETTI CRUST

1¼ cups graham cracker crumbs (from about 18 whole graham crackers)

¼ cup Amaretti cookie crumbs (from about 10 cookies), plus more for garnish

¼ cup granulated sugar

⅓ cup unsalted butter, melted

PUMPKIN FILLING

1½ pounds cream cheese, softened

1 cup granulated sugar

¼ cup packed light brown sugar

2 large eggs

1¾ cups canned unflavored pumpkin

½ cup plus 2 tablespoons evaporated milk

2 tablespoons cornstarch

1¼ teaspoons ground cinnamon

1 teaspoon pure vanilla extract

½ teaspoon ground nutmeg

¼ teaspoon ground allspice

Whipped cream, for serving

Candied Pepitas (page 278), for serving

Preheat the oven to 350°F.

To make the crust: In a mixing bowl, stir together the graham cracker crumbs, Amaretti crumbs, sugar, and butter. Mix well using your fingers. Press the mixture into the bottom of a 10-inch springform pan. Set the springform pan on a baking sheet and bake for 6 to 8 minutes, until the crust is firm and set. Remove the crust from the oven and reduce the temperature to 300°F.

Meanwhile, to make the filling: In the bowl of a standing mixer fitted with the paddle attachment and set on medium speed, blend the cream cheese until smooth. Add the granulated and brown sugars and continue mixing, scraping the sides of the bowl, for 2 to 3 minutes, until smooth. With the mixer on medium-low speed, slowly add the eggs, pumpkin, milk, cornstarch, cinnamon, vanilla extract, and allspice, scraping down the sides after each addition.

Spoon the filling into the springform pan and smooth the top with a rubber spatula. Bake on the baking sheet for 60 to 70 minutes. When done, the cheesecake will rise slightly and be set in the middle. If necessary, continue baking, checking the cake every 10 minutes.

Turn off the oven and prop the door open so that the cake can cool as the oven cools down. After 30 minutes, remove the cake and let it cool to room temperature on a wire rack. This slow cooling process helps prevent the cheesecake from cracking. When cool, refrigerate until chilled, 4 to 6 hours or up to 12 hours.

To serve, unhinge the side of the springform pan. Using a warm knife, separate the cake from the side of the pan. Remove the side of the pan. Cut the cake into pieces and garnish each slice with crushed Amaretti cookies, whipped cream, and candied *pepitas*.

CANDIED PEPITAS

MAKES ABOUT 1 CUP

1 cup *pepitas,* pine nuts, or almonds

¼ cup sugar

2 tablespoons water

¼ teaspoon salt

In a large, dry sauté pan, heat the *pepitas* over medium-high heat, shaking, until they pop open. Remove the *pepitas* from the pan.

Combine the sugar, water, and salt in the pan and heat until boiling. Add the *pepitas* and stir well to coat. Reduce the heat to medium-low and cook, stirring, for 4 to 5 minutes, or until the sugar caramelizes.

Spread the candied *pepitas* on a baking sheet to cool. Once cool, carefully break apart or chop roughly.

SOURCES

HARD-TO-FIND INGREDIENTS AND EQUIPMENT

Following are sources I use in my restaurants for our food and equipment. If there is something you cannot find from local purveyors, one of these merchants may well be able to help you. I have also included website addresses throughout the book where appropriate.

SEAFOOD AND FISH

Browne Trading Company
Merrills Wharf
260 Commercial Street
Portland, ME 04101
Phone: 800-944-7848
Fax: 207-766-2404
www.brownetrading.com
All fish

Honolulu Fish Company
824 Gulick Avenue
Honolulu, HI 96819
Phone: 888-475-6244
Fax: 808-836-1045
www.honolulufish.com
All fish

M. F. Foley Company
24 West Howell Street
Boston, MA 02125
Phone: 800-225-9995
www.foleyfish.com
All fish

Steve Connolly Seafood Company
34 Newmarket Square
Boston, MA 02118
Phone: 800-225-5595
www.steveconnollyseafood.com
All fish

PRIME STEAKS AND MEAT

Allen Brothers Steaks (*my favorite vendor*)
3737 S. Halsted Street
Chicago, IL 60609
Phone: 800-548-7777
www.allenbrothers.com

Jamison Farm
171 Jamison Lane
Latrobe, PA 15650
Phone: 800-237-5262
Fax: 724-837-2287
www.jamisonfarm.com
Lamb

Joseph Baumgartner Company
935 West Randolph Street
Chicago, IL 60607
Phone: 312-829-7762
Fax: 312-829-8791
All meat

Lobel's
1096 Madison Avenue
New York, NY 10028
Phone: 877-783-4512
www.lobels.com

Millbrook Venison Products
499 Verbank Road
Millbrook, NY 12545
Phone: 800-774-3337
Venison

Niman Ranch
1600 Harbor Bay Parkway, Suite 250
Alameda, CA 94502
Phone: 510-808-0330
Fax: 510-808-0339
www.nimanranch.com
All meat

Stock Yards
340 North Oakley Boulevard
Chicago, IL 60612
Phone: 877-785-9273
Fax: 312-733-1746
www.stockyards.com
All meat

PRODUCE

The Chef's Garden
9009 Huron-Avery Road
Huron, OH 44839
Phone: 800-289-4644
www.chefs-garden.com
Vegetables, herbs

Corneille and Sons
Tom Corneille Produce Company
2402 South Wolcott Avenue
Unit 4
Chicago, IL 60608
Phone: 773-847-7631
Fax: 773-847-8402
www.corneilleproduce.com
Specialty produce and foods

Fresh & Wild
P.O. Box 2981
Vancouver, WA 98668
Phone: 800-222-5578
www.freshwild.com
Wild mushrooms, truffles, snails, and other
specialty foods

SPECIALTY PRODUCTS

Anson Mills
1922-C Gervais Street
Columbia, SC 29201
Phone: 803-467-4122
Fax: 803-256-2463
www.ansonmills.com
Stone-ground grits and other grains

The Blue Chip Group
(instant clear gel)
www.bluechipgroup.net

European Imports
2475 North Elston Avenue
Chicago, IL 60647
Phone: 800-323-3464
Fax: 773-227-6775
www.eiltd.com
Specialty foods

Spiceland
6604 West Irving Park Road
Chicago, IL 60634
Phone: 773-736-1000
Fax: 773-736-1271
Spices

Urbani Truffles
1 Selleck Street
Norwalk, CT 06855
Phone: 718-433-1560
Fax: 718-433-1620
www.urbanitrufflesonline.com
Truffle products

For information about me, my products,
and my restaurants, go to:

Tramonto Cuisine
www.tramontocuisine.com

Tru Restaurant
www.trurestaurant.com

METRIC CONVERSIONS AND EQUIVALENTS

METRIC CONVERSION FORMULAS

To Convert	Multiply
Ounces to grams	ounces by 28.35
Pounds to kilograms	pounds by 0.454
Teaspoons to milliliters	teaspoons by 4.93
Tablespoons to milliliters	tablespoons by 14.79
Fluid ounces to milliliters	fluid ounces by 29.57
Cups to milliliters	cups by 236.59
Cups to liters	cups by 0.236
Pints to liters	pints by 0.473
Quarts to liters	quarts by 0.946
Gallons to liters	gallons by 3.785
Inches to centimeters	inches by 2.54

APPROXIMATE METRIC EQUIVALENTS

VOLUME

¼ teaspoon	1 milliliter
½ teaspoon	2.5 milliliters
¾ teaspoon	4 milliliters
1 teaspoon	5 milliliters
1¼ teaspoons	6 milliliters
1½ teaspoons	7.5 milliliters
1¾ teaspoons	8.5 milliliters
2 teaspoons	10 milliliters
1 tablespoon (½ fluid ounce)	15 milliliters
2 tablespoons (1 fluid ounce)	30 milliliters
¼ cup	60 milliliters
⅓ cup	80 milliliters
½ cup (4 fluid ounces)	120 milliliters
⅔ cup	160 milliliters
¾ cup	180 milliliters
1 cup (8 fluid ounces)	240 milliliters
1¼ cups	300 milliliters
1½ cups (12 fluid ounces)	360 milliliters
1⅔ cups	400 milliliters
2 cups (1 pint)	460 milliliters
3 cups	700 milliliters
4 cups (1 quart)	0.95 liter
1 quart plus ¼ cup	1 liter
4 quarts (1 gallon)	3.8 liters

WEIGHT

¼ ounce	7 grams
½ ounce	14 grams
¾ ounce	21 grams
1 ounce	28 grams
1¼ ounces	35 grams
1½ ounces	42.5 grams
1⅔ ounces	45 grams
2 ounces	57 grams
3 ounces	85 grams
4 ounces (¼ pound)	113 grams
5 ounces	142 grams
6 ounces	170 grams
7 ounces	198 grams
8 ounces (½ pound)	227 grams
16 ounces (1 pound)	454 grams
35.25 ounces (2.2 pounds)	1 kilogram

LENGTH

⅛ inch	3 millimeters
¼ inch	6 millimeters
½ inch	1¼ centimeters
1 inch	2½ centimeters
2 inches	5 centimeters
2½ inches	6 centimeters
4 inches	10 centimeters
5 inches	13 centimeters
6 inches	15¼ centimeters
12 inches (1 foot)	30 centimeters

OVEN TEMPERATURES

To convert Fahrenheit to Celsius, subtract 32 from Fahrenheit, multiply the result by 5, then divide by 9.

Description	Fahrenheit	Celsius	British Gas Mark
Very cool	200°	95°	0
Very cool	225°	110°	¼
Very cool	250°	120°	½
Cool	275°	135°	1
Cool	300°	150°	2
Warm	325°	165°	3
Moderate	350°	175°	4
Moderately hot	375°	190°	5
Fairly hot	400°	200°	6
Hot	425°	220°	7
Very hot	450°	230°	8
Very hot	475°	245°	9

COMMON INGREDIENTS AND THEIR APPROXIMATE EQUIVALENTS

1 cup uncooked white rice = 185 grams

1 cup all-purpose flour = 140 grams

1 stick butter (4 ounces or ½ cup or 8 tablespoons) = 110 grams

1 cup butter (8 ounces or 2 sticks or 16 tablespoons) = 220 grams

1 cup brown sugar, firmly packed = 225 grams

1 cup granulated sugar = 200 grams

Information compiled from a variety of sources, including *Recipes into Type* by Joan Whitman and Dolores Simon, *The New Food Lover's Companion* by Sharon Tyler Herbst, and *Rosemary Brown's Big Kitchen Instruction Book* by Rosemary Brown.

INDEX